# THE FINER THINGS

# THE FINER THINGS

## TIMELESS FURNITURE, TEXTILES, AND DETAILS

———

**CHRISTIANE LEMIEUX**

FOREWORD BY MILES REDD

POTTER
NEW YORK

Published in the United States by Clarkson Potter/Publishers,
an imprint of the Crown Publishing Group, a division of
Penguin Random House LLC, New York.
crownpublishing.com
clarksonpotter.com

CLARKSON POTTER is a trademark and POTTER
with colophon is a registered trademark of
Penguin Random House LLC.

Photography credits appear on page 406.

Library of Congress Cataloging-in-Publication Data
Names: Lemieux, Christiane, author.
Title: The finer things : timeless furniture, textiles, and
details / Christiane Lemieux.
Description: First Edition. | New York : Potter Style, 2016.
Identifiers: LCCN 2013047267| ISBN 9780770434298 | ISBN
9780770434304
Subjects: LCSH: Interior decoration. | House furnishings.
Classification: LCC NK2115 .L4335 2016 | DDC 747--dc23 LC
record available at http://lccn.loc.gov/2013047267

ISBN 978-0-7704-3429-8

Printed in China

Book design by Rita Sowins / Sowins Design
Cover design by Ian Dingman
Cover photograph courtesy of New Ravenna
With special thanks to OTTO
Endpapers mural by Matt Austin, mattaustinstudio.com;
photograph by Carl Whelahan

10 9 8 7 6 5 4 3 2 1

First Edition

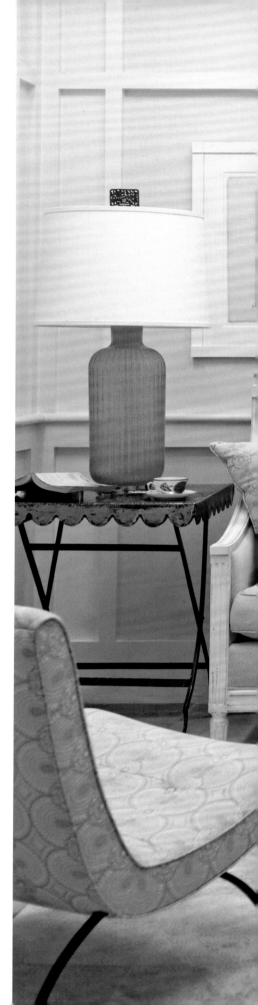

FOR ISABELLE
&
WILLIAM

# contents

# *foreword*

EVER SINCE I WAS A LITTLE BOY, I HAVE BEEN ATTRACTED TO THE FINER THINGS IN life. Even at age five I was hungry for luxury. My letter to Santa included requests for a few items to spruce up my bedroom: a marble mantelpiece (so nice to fall asleep to the dying embers), a rock-crystal chandelier, and a mink bed jacket. As I recall, I—rather disappointingly—received a train set that year, while my sister was given a Georgian-style dollhouse. Let's just say it was a sullen holiday for me until my sister grew tired of her toy and I took it over, decorating the tiny rooms floor to ceiling.

But what does this have to do with the *finer things*? I suppose it helps to have an appetite for them, and exposure to them, because while many of us crave luxury, we might not truly understand what that is until we have encountered it firsthand or stumbled across it in a book like this.

I remember, a few years later, visiting a friend of my parents who lived in a small rural town in Georgia. The drive was long and dusty and riddled with mosquitoes. My expectations were low, but then we came upon the house . . . a nineteenth-century Queen Anne Box filled with the most dizzying array of objects: beige silk banquettes; leggy beechwood fauteuils with a touch of ocelot silk velvet; a pale apricot Oushak underfoot; and Old Master drawings hung next to a Rothko.

I, age fourteen, was dumbstruck. It was like finding a tiny black pearl in a snowdrift. As it turns out, my parents' friend had lived a very worldly and extravagant life (as Coca-Cola heiresses sometimes do) and in her later years had chosen this refuge to get *far from the madding crowd*. The trip was a seminal point for me because, while I longed for the finer things, it was my first time truly being exposed to them, being exposed to someone with a real eye, who had accumulated and edited a refined collection.

Soon after, I moved to New York City to attend college—but mainly because I knew that if I really wanted to taste the good life, New York City had all there was to offer. Alas, it would be a while before I saw any glimmer of glamour. But that in itself was an important lesson: one cannot know the truly good, if one has not seen the truly god-awful. A fabulous penthouse apartment is so much better after you've lived in a derelict tenement cold-water flat (which I did). The point is, the eye must travel everywhere, high and low, to know the difference.

In this love letter to decorating, Christiane Lemieux opens your eyes to a world full of luxuries. *The Finer Things* deftly examines every element that makes for a compelling space. With the help of experts and tastemakers, Christiane sorts through the increasingly dense pile of junk being offered up and uncovers the well designed and the well crafted. I like to picture a five-year-old future decorator somewhere in this world picking up this book and getting a jump start on his or her journey into a world full of The Finer Things.

—MILES REDD

# introduction

THE BEST WAY TO LEARN IS BY ASKING QUESTIONS.

But, with respect to making design decisions about your home in this do-it-yourself culture, whom do you ask? You're lucky if you happen upon a well-informed salesperson or work closely with an interior designer. Most of the time you're on your own, tearing pages from magazines, studying product details on packages, scanning websites, and trying to figure out things for yourself.

One central question matters most when it comes to the things in our home—the question of quality. "Quality is really all that's important in decorating and design," says the interior designer David Netto. "You have to have quality of taste. And something has to be well made."

That's a statement few would disagree with—but what does "quality" mean? How do you develop quality of taste, and how do you judge if something is well made? Interior designers develop a sense of taste and an expertise in judging well-made things over the course of years, with both a formal education and a lot of on-the-job training. "I would say to develop taste, begin to educate yourself," says Netto. "There's never been a better time, because of the Internet. There are so many blogs that are presenting curated bodies of imagery and good rooms, of great designers and people who have influenced taste over the years."

While it is indeed true that the Internet has revolutionized the way we shop and the way we learn, such an education takes a long time. I wanted to create a book that could be a

real resource for people who care about quality and want to know how to define it, in every aspect of their homes. So I asked questions.

I talked to curators and historians, craftsmen and manufacturers, industrial and interior designers. And I got answers—about why we use paint, about what makes a piece of ceramic good, about how a sofa should be constructed, and so much more.

Every expert I spoke to is passionate about quality, a believer in the idea that it's something worth pursuing, something worth investing in. They're very persuasive, and very well informed, so I'll let them speak for themselves.

So many different experts, so many distinct points of view—and yet, pretty quickly, an argument takes shape: That quality matters. Quality in what we live with affects the quality of our lives. And we all deserve to live beautifully.

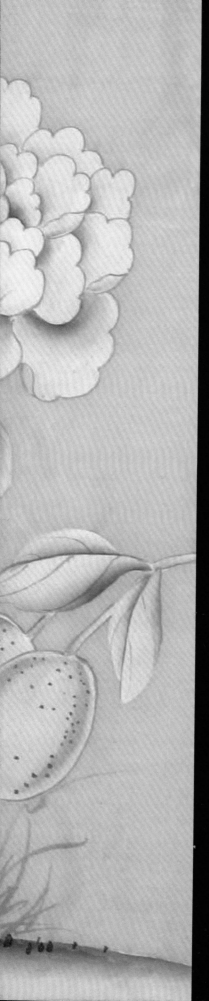

# walls

There are a lot of components in the home. It only makes sense to start with one of the biggest, where even a simple change can have a significant effect on the entire experience of a room. Our walls literally define our spaces, and they are where transforming or personalizing a room begins, whether via paint (both washes of color and decorative techniques like murals), wallpaper, or even the art we frame to adorn our homes.

# *wallpaper*

Wallpaper is descended from tapestries, which, along with other textiles, once adorned drafty castle walls to keep the chill out. But wallpaper's primary function has always been decorative, its ease and comparative affordability part of its appeal. In the fifteenth century, when Louis XI of France packed for a weekend getaway, he took along rolls of painted paper that were hung wherever he and his retinue stopped. Wallpaper as we know it now emerged during the seventeenth century and, aside from the evolution of aesthetics, remains essentially the same.

It's the aesthetics that are of most interest when you're choosing a wallpaper, naturally, but when you're browsing patterns, it's worthwhile to consider how a printer executed a pattern and whether it was printed the old-fashioned way, by hand, as many wallpapers in the market still are, or using more modern technology. It's also worth thinking about how wallpaper interacts with your walls, and the challenges unique to installing it.

Wallpaper not only can dictate the overall mood of a room, but—when chosen wisely—can transform the very spirit of the furnishings around it. Here, a midcentury seating arrangement comes off as wholly modern when set against a bold Graham & Brown wallpaper.

# The Unique History of Wallpaper

### 2500 BC

**EGYPT:** The earliest paper scroll found to date is made of papyrus-reed stems. In the centuries that followed, early wallpapers made of bark and linen were applied to funerary tomb walls.

### 1720

**ENGLAND:** Designer William Kent used wallpapers in the Saloon at London's Kensington Palace instead of heavy wall hangings, making it the first time wallpaper is used in a royal European palace.

### EARLY 19TH CENTURY

**EUROPE:** The word *panorama* is adopted by European wallpaper experts to describe the murals of landscapes and historical scenes painted on papers intended to fill an entire wall space. Shipments of panoramic wallpaper from France to America follow, and in 1817 James Foster of Boston opens a shop selling French papers.

### 15TH CENTURY AD

**PARIS:** Paper merchants who specialize in wood-block–printed papers begin to set up businesses; however, only the *marchand-mercier*, the "ancestor" of the interior decorator, can legally deal in decorated papers. It isn't until the 17th century that *dominotiers* began producing *papier de tapisserie*, inexpensive imitations of materials such as brocade, leather, tapestries, and architectural details that are sold directly to the rising bourgeoisie class.

### 1723

**FRANCE:** Jean-Michel Papillon, "the inventor of wallpaper," registers in the *Graveur et Bourgeois de Paris* as the first professional *tapissier* (wallpaper producer); he later contributes to Diderot's *Encyclopédie* by illustrating the process of paper hanging.

### 1839

**ENGLAND:** Calico printing firm Potters of Darwen, England, patents a printing machine for wallpaper, rendering it more affordable to the masses. Five years later, the first printing machine is imported to Philadelphia.

## MID 19TH CENTURY

Wallpaper becomes so widespread that it is "stigmatized" as a commonplace stand-in for luxury decoration. As a reaction against the mass production of domestic furnishings and materials, "design reformers," such as William Morris, Owen Jones, and Henry Cole, return to medieval traditions of production. At the turn of the 20th century, American tastemakers such as Edith Wharton and Frank Lloyd Wright claim wallpapers get in the way of the architectural integrity of a space.

### 1966

Andy Warhol produces his famed *Cow* wallpaper.

## TODAY

With the capabilities of digital printing and computer production, wallpaper has taken on an entirely unprecedented aesthetic. Designers are using new technologies for interactive wallpapers. For example, Dutch designer Simon Heijdens uses temperature-reacting thermochromic inks that make patterns change, disappear, and reappear. Many contemporary companies continue to employ traditional hand-block and silk-screening techniques, illustrating the importance of craftsmanship in design.

### 1930s

Developments are made in modern screen printing and silk-screening. The first truly "washable" papers are invented.

### 1940s

**AMERICA:** Manufacturers could not print new designs as the War Production Board deemed wallpaper "frivolous."

## POST–WORLD WAR II

Hand-block-printing techniques virtually disappear and are replaced by industrial techniques such as rotary screen printing, rotogravure, flexography, and ink embossing. After the war, the wallpaper industry rebounds and more than 4 million rolls of paper are sold between 1945 and 1947, a level of wallpaper sales that to this day has not been topped.

### 1974

**AMERICA:** The National Guild of Professional Paperhangers is established in the United States.

# How It's Made

WALLPAPER IS SIMPLY PAPER, IN ROLLS, PRINTED USING A VARIETY OF techniques. As with fabric, when the wallpaper is patterned, the motif is uniform, and designed to line up and interact between rolls, in what's called the "repeat."

There's a close relationship between the wallpaper manufacturer, the process, and the finished product's aesthetic. For example, block printing and roller printing are traditional methods (examples of the former date to the third century) that remain in use.

In block printing, a pattern is carved into a block (of wood, rubber, or metal), pigment is applied, and the block is stamped onto the paper. Roller printing is not dissimilar; the motif is carved onto a cylinder, and ink is applied as you might use a roller to paint a wall. They're simple, even primitive, techniques that actually involve quite complex processes.

"I think many people have no idea how wallpapers are made or the amount of time that goes into producing them," says Gregory Herringshaw, an assistant curator at the Cooper Hewitt, Smithsonian Design Museum, who has considered it part of his curatorial mission to educate people on this subject. "For wood-block prints, you need a different block to print each color, and you have to hang the paper up to dry before you can print the next color because all the colors are printed one on top of the other. There's all this hanging, and drying, and laying the paper back on the bed. And you have to carve your wood blocks, which is a skill in itself. It's very labor-intensive."

Wallpaper is also sometimes made by screen printing, in which ink is forced through a mesh that contains the negative image of the desired motif. This process historically involved the hands of a trained artisan, though technology has given us ink-jet printing—imagine an office machine, scaled to accommodate large expanses of paper.

Raw materials don't vary too widely when it comes to wallpaper. It's mostly paper and ink, so the process by which a given design is created often best explains its price tag. "There are really wonderful papers in all different price points," says Herringshaw. "One of the things that affects the price the most is the technology or technique that is used to print it." When buying an elaborate block-printed wallpaper, you're paying for the services of the craftsmen who carried out all the steps listed above.

To create a single roll of Farrow & Ball's signature *Lotus* design, a hand-engraved block is coated with paint and carefully pressed onto a section of the paper, like a stamp. A skilled craftsman repeats this process through the entirety of the wallpaper's eleven yards, ensuring that each stamp lines up perfectly with the previous one.

 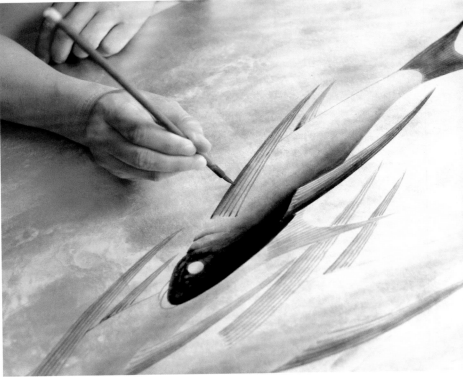

Investing in a quality paper can yield a wonderful return aesthetically. "For me, wallpaper is part of the whole scheme of decorating," says New York designer Alex Papachristidis. "I like a variety of treatments—paneled, mirrored, upholstered, and painted rooms. Wallpaper gives so much dimension to a room. It gives it depth, a sense of interest. There is something about the effect of paper on a wall that never dates."

Papachristidis points out that wallpaper offers you a lot of bang for your buck. "You can put up very little art," he says. "You actually save by putting up incredible scenic wallpaper. It creates this unique world that just totally encompasses you, and it's romantic, beautiful, and magical."

**ABOVE LEFT ›** Crafting a single panel of de Gournay's *Fishes* design starts with gilding the paper, a process in which metal leaf is applied, the panel is glazed, and then antiquing is added by hand.

**ABOVE RIGHT ›** Each of the dozens of fish swimming across these panels is drawn out, then hand painted.

**OPPOSITE ›** Nearly forty hours later (twenty spent preparing the background, twenty spent painting), the finished panel— as much a work of art as it is wallpaper—is ready to be professionally installed.

# The Market Today

WALLPAPER IS STILL MADE THE OLD-FASHIONED WAY—BY HAND—IN many studios, including at Cole & Son, which has been in the business for more than a hundred years. These days, the blocks are cut from rubber, not wood, but beyond that, the process hasn't changed much in a century. While Cole & Son's approach might be historical, their aesthetic is not. "We are a company that has always been led by design," says creative director Shauna Dennison. She emphasizes the connection between aesthetics and process: "The designers liaise with our printers. The customer might not see what goes into the making of the wallpaper, but the process is there, in the slight imperfections in the pattern, in the way the colors interact."

Dennison does not equate quality with perfection. Processes based on handwork and human judgment inevitably also involve error and imperfection. The human eye will never be able to align a block print with the efficiency of a machine—but maybe that's something to value instead of lament. Whether it's in a roll of wallpaper or an article of clothing, that trace of the hand can lend a finished product depth, a sense of interest.

Paul Simmons, of the Glasgow-based design house Timorous Beasties, feels this human touch is essential to his work. "I think that people actually recognize handcraft, even though they don't realize it," he says. "It stands out, it appeals, it has a sort of feel to it. And that's another thing about hand prints—you can actually feel the physical ink on the paper, so they have a kind of tactile quality."

Simmons and partner Alistair McAuley launched their firm in 1990, and initially set out to focus on textiles. "But we couldn't afford to pay for the fabric," Simmons says, recalling the duo's attempt to produce their inaugural textile collection. "We went down to the factory where I'd served my apprenticeship and they gave us old bales of paper." The paper was damaged, but the two cut around the imperfections and hand-printed the remnants using the same technique they'd have used for textiles.

Timorous Beasties launched at a time when few contemporary designers were exploring the possibilities of wallpaper, which for many connoted tradition, even fustiness. "At the time, wallpaper had sort of got itself a bad name," Simmons says. Even today, wallpaper is sometimes unfairly dismissed as staid and grandmotherly. But many smaller designers are investigating the rich potential of this very traditional medium. Wallpaper is in fashion once more.

**OPPOSITE** › Through the decades, powder rooms have served as the ideal spot for big prints, allowing homeowners to explore their bolder side without overpowering a space.

**ABOVE** › Timorous Beasties's *Grand Thistle* print is a signature pattern for the Scottish design house, known for its dark, surreal approach. Perhaps the design's true genius, though, is its exaggerated vertical repeats, which can make low ceilings seem as if they're soaring.

Take the work of Kit Kemp, who with her husband, Tim, operates Firmdale Hotels. Hotels have long been a reliable barometer of trends in interior design. Andrée Putman created the much-imitated, luxuriously minimal Morgans Hotel in the 1980s; Philippe Starck stripped away even more to create the look of the '90s boutique hotel, and those ideas eventually trickled into domestic interiors. In the new millennium, hoteliers are rediscovering the charm and appeal of old-fashioned ornament.

The look of Firmdale's properties was devised by Kit, a self-trained designer, and her rooms feature romantic touches such as canopies, bed skirts, and boldly patterned walls. "I think there should be a little bit of fun in an interior," says Kemp. "Just put a wallpaper in the reveal of a window—it adds something intriguing." Her judicious application of patterns helps create spaces that are eccentric but still inviting. Instead of anonymous hotel rooms, hers feel like rooms in which real people live, thanks in large part to a thoughtful treatment of the walls, the rooms' foundation.

1 › **Ham Yard Hotel.** Tiny rooms leave large impressions thanks to Kit Kemp's unexpected multilayered pattern clashes. 2 › **Crosby Street Hotel.** An effervescent bubble print perfectly offsets an inlaid Moroccan chest. 3 › **Ham Yard Hotel.** Electric-hued fabric climbs the walls and drapes the floor-to-ceiling windows, leaving guests cocooned in a den of color. 4 › **Ham Yard Hotel.** Subdued stripes create a softly defined backdrop, brilliantly setting off the plucky fabric. 5 › **Ham Yard Hotel.** A perfect lesson in scale: the extra-large wallpaper pattern is balanced by an extra-large—and extra-bold—dotted fabric. 6 › **Ham Yard Hotel.** Kemp often uses fabric in lieu of wallpaper, as seen in this library, where walls are covered in bold patterns from her Christopher Farr fabric collection.

Interior designer Lynne Scalo
transformed the small reading nook
of a historical Ridgefield, Connecticut,
home with statement wallpaper and
feminine finishings—a tufted sofa
and a low-hanging chandelier. With
the somewhat wild pattern framed
by formal crown moldings and
baseboards, the overall mood skews
to the glamorous side of traditional.

**ABOVE** › Exquisite de Gournay wallpaper completes the layered look of a luxe, velvet-covered daybed.

**OPPOSITE** › Often referenced as an early inspiration for de Gournay's chinoiserie collection, the Parisian bedroom of Pauline de Rothschild—photographed for a 1969 issue of *Vogue* by Horst P. Horst—was wrapped, door and all, in eighteenth-century Chinese wallpaper.

# The Aesthetics

WALLPAPERS CAN VARY WIDELY. THE RELATIONSHIP BETWEEN process and finished look has been noted, but because it's paper, it can look almost any way an artist could imagine. Among historical examples and modern styles, there are wallpapers that rely on sleight of hand, those that are printed with a moiré technique to replicate the look of silk-clad walls, and those designed to seem at first glance like richly veined marble or even wainscoted walls. Wallpaper can be narrative, with chinoiserie motifs bringing the East to the West in an era that predates photography, or adapting the familiar pictorial storytelling technique of toile.

And modern technology like digital printing now allows artisans a way around the old constraints of the form. "With digital printing, you can do some great things that would just be impossible as a hand print," says Timorous Beasties's Paul Simmons. "So you can have three-meter repeats, and you can have a repeat that has different details, or that changes in color. It's quite amazing." Technology can be harnessed to create custom wallpaper using a one-off design or photograph, or to print massively scaled wallpapers that go up in one panel instead of multiple rolls; the impact of technological liberation on this centuries-old form remains to be fully explored.

Not all young brands look forward, though; de Gournay is a mere twenty-five years old, but the company does things strictly the traditional way, relying primarily on handwork.

"Our highly skilled artists employ the traditional eighteenth-century style of painting, from the characteristic brushstrokes to the traditional bamboo paintbrushes," says Hannah Cecil Gurney, the founder's daughter. "We have not modernized. Every single thing we do is totally done by hand." De Gournay eschews the possibilities of the machine-made in favor of something altogether different. "In the grand palaces in Europe, if you study the chinoiserie, you'll be able to pick out the pencil marks. You'll be able to see each individual brushstroke," says Gurney. The same is true of the designs the company executes today—the artist's hand is very present, and the resulting paper is wholly custom.

A sweeping example of the sheer magnificence of de Gournay wallpaper, its *Early Views of India* design provides all the impact of a hand-painted mural in the sitting room of this San Francisco row house.

**OPPOSITE ›** Blue-and-white rooms tend to skew to the traditional; however, this bright den (designed by Gideon Mendelson) manages to flip those expectations on their head with a thorny floral print that tosses off any connotations of convention.

**ABOVE ›** There are no hard-and-fast rules when selecting wallpaper. Case in point: most designers would recommend avoiding small prints in living rooms. But here, a tight chain-link pattern only accentuates the defined lines and modern furniture arrangement.

# Installing Wallpaper

WALLPAPER IS NOT MEANT TO COVER WALLS; IT'S MEANT TO BOND with them, to take on the wall's shape. Wallpaper is a way to celebrate a room's architecture, its very essence.

Mitchell Ehrlich has been working with wallpaper for three decades, and that hands-on experience counts for more than any quick online tutorial ever could.

The first step in any wallpaper project is, counterintuitively, a fresh coat of paint. "You hang wallpaper on walls that have been primed specifically for wallpaper," Ehrlich says, "so the wallpaper will adhere to a good base." Though there are prep paints designated specifically as an undercoating for wallpaper, Ehrlich recommends a standard-issue primer instead—with a caveat. "Years ago, the average paints used in people's homes were stronger and more durable. Primers today are not as strong, so it's very important that you really know how to prime a wall."

Next, the freshly painted wall is treated with wallpaper adhesive. It's typically a matter of choosing between two generic types, one clay-based and one clear, and which you should use depends on what sort of paper you're installing. If it's a thin paper or a fabric, the latter is the better option so it won't show through, while stronger papers do well with a clay-based backing. These first two steps are critical, even if they'll ultimately be invisible. "A lot of what wallpaper installers do, you don't see," Ehrlich says. "But can you see all the things that BMW does?"

Planning a wallpaper project entails a bit of math. Though priced in units of single rolls, wallpaper is often sold in double rolls. That is to say, you're paying for a paper in units of sixteen and a half feet, but getting it in rolls that are thirty-three feet long—which makes it ultimately easier to work with, in terms of covering a room, but which can feel a bit like navigating a complex math word problem.

When you're purchasing wallpaper, most retailers will give you their own rough calculations of how much you need for a specific project, but wallpapering a room involves quite a bit of waste. Installing around a room's architecture (the columns and doors, the spaces between windows, and in odd corners) can sometimes necessitate a large amount of paper to avoid interruptions in a pattern. "When I buy wallpaper for my own house, I always buy more than I need," says Ehrlich. "With paint, you can go back

**OPPOSITE** › When considering whether to hire a wallpapering professional or attempt the job yourself, take into account the size and complexity of the print. Something like this grass cloth by Phillip Jeffries would be a simple enough first project for the enthusiastic novice.

**ABOVE** › At the very tip-top of the complicated-to-hang scale, you'll find striped wallpaper—specifically, horizontal stripes. Though the results are well worth the effort, working with such an exact pattern is best left to the experts.

to the paint store, but sometimes it takes weeks or months to get more of a specific wallpaper, and the original dye lot may no longer be available."

Ehrlich, who has worked on every manner of project, from small rooms in New York City to the Obama White House, concedes that it's possible to visit a hardware superstore, stock up on supplies, and attempt wallpaper installation yourself. "If you're really interested in fine work," says Ehrlich, however, "don't do it yourself."

**LEFT ›** One of the most revolutionary inventions in wallpaper manufacturing is the somewhat recent creation of temporary wallpaper. These birch tree silhouettes are printed on peel-and-stick fabric that adheres directly to the wall, no paste required, and pulls off just as easily.

**OPPOSITE ›** Similar to temporary wallpaper, wall decals are another short-term wallpaper substitution. The silhouettes stick to the wall while allowing the designer freedom to play around with placement.

# Vintage Wallpaper

WHEN STORED PROPERLY, PAPER IS AN IMPRESSIVELY RESILIENT material. Think of rare books or historical documents: pure, nonacidic paper, in the right conditions, can survive for centuries. Thus there's a small trade in vintage wallpapers, and the preeminent resource for these is the New York–based Secondhand Rose.

The fact that wallpaper is sold in rolls is a factor in its longevity. "This is the miracle of wallpaper," owner Suzanne Lipschutz says. "Even if it has marks from the sunlight on the first few feet, when you unroll it, it's perfect. What's inside the roll is usually safe." Further, old papers have a selvage, a bit of border that doesn't include the paper's print; so even if the ends of the rolls have been knocked about over the years, the patterned part of the paper is usually well preserved.

"It's instant decorating," Lipschutz says. "The impact of wallpaper is so incredible. Out of one double roll, you get a five-foot-wide, eight-foot-high area—that's a huge impact."

Many of her vintage papers predate modern machine printing, and many contemporary papers are still made the same way, by hand, which means that any wallpaper is best installed by a specialist. "It is paper," Lipschutz says. "It doesn't go up with vinyl glue. It gets wet, and it becomes the wall, which is what's so remarkable about it. It looks almost like a fresco when it's up. It doesn't look like a surface." No wall is truly plumb, and no surface is truly flat. Wallpaper doesn't aim to hide a surface's imperfections; in fact, it's a wall's sense of movement that helps bring the paper on its surface to life.

Lipschutz points out the details that set apart vintage papers. There are papers dating to the Depression that are printed on newsprint, and the quality of printing allows the texture of this inexpensive paper to shine through. Hand markings along the selvage of some old papers instruct how to hang the paper so the pattern repeats cleanly. You can find high-end papers on which the application of the ink feels downright painterly.

Lipschutz adds that vintage paper is an excellent option for the decorator who's concerned about being green, and a comparatively inexpensive way to get something truly custom. "Most of my customers know that they're going to have something no one else has," she says, "which is wonderful."

Mention wallpaper and most people's minds go directly to the printed variety, but it would be a mistake to discount its textural counterparts, with their vast talent for creating depth in a space. The Manhattan living room of Jackie Astier is a seductively dark example. The walls are papered in black grass cloth by Nobilis. Had the designer simply painted the room black, the mood would be far more stark and cold. But here, the finely grained material softens the effect, adding an interesting dimensional layer.

# DESIGN CHAMPION: *David Hicks*

THE ENGLISH DESIGNER DAVID HICKS had a unique point of view, a flair for bold, dramatic rooms that made him a favorite of the society set and fashionable types. His projects feel carefully constructed from top to bottom. Hicks strove for a sense of perfection, creating rooms that are more fantasy than real life.

Designers consider Hicks's use of unexpected color and larger-than-life patterns particularly revolutionary. Colors that should be garish feel elegant; patterns that should be overwhelming feel harmonious. Wallpaper played an important role in several of Hicks's projects.

In this master bedroom (left), a bold green floral dominates every surface—the bed drapery, the headboard, the window treatments, the armchair, and even the walls. Hicks upholstered the walls in a printed cotton that he used everywhere else. (One could achieve a similar effect by layering coordinating upholstery and wallpaper into a room.) "This is something very typical of grand decoration of 1650 to 1820, I'd say, especially French," says Ashley Hicks, the designer's son. "Whole rooms done in one fabric, especially bedrooms. You see it at Versailles and Compiègne. My father loved this idea, which he saw in paintings. I think it appealed to his urge for a bold statement."

In this New York apartment (below), the foundation of the room is a startling wallpaper in a geometric motif that's a testament to Hicks's interest in designs and patterns from the Arab world. It's evident from the architecture that this is a run-of-the-mill postwar apartment, but "this ugly concrete box was transformed into a giant Moroccan marquetry box," says Ashley. "The pattern is quite overwhelming in the space, but it's exciting and fun. At the same time he did this, my father did room sets at Bloomingdale's in shocking primary colors and told a newspaper that 'mousy colors are for mousy people.'" The décor is actually quite spare—the room is minimally furnished —but the effect is surely not, a reminder that simply hanging wallpaper is one of the most economical ways to reconfigure a room.

LEFT › Ramdane Touhami and his wife, Victoire de Taillac, used wallpaper to clearly separate the rooms of their former Brooklyn home, covering its walls in several different designs by Cole & Son. The master bedroom featured a fantastical cityscape from the company's Fornasetti collection, a print so elaborate that adding art (or even anything more than just basic furnishings) was almost unnecessary.

FOLLOWING PAGES › In the children's bedrooms, the couple selected motifs (flamingos and gondolas) that were kidlike yet still sophisticated. These patterns served as the jumping-off point for the playful color palettes in both spaces, with paint for the furnishings matched to shades found in the paper.

# RECOGNIZING THE MAJOR PLAYERS
# *Wallpaper Design*

### 1 > ZUBER & CIE

Examples of the extraordinary panoramic wallpaper created by this French company can be seen in the Diplomatic Reception Room of the White House. Founded in 1797 by Jean Zuber, the storied *manufacture de papier et tissus* (painted wallpaper and fabrics) creates each panel using handmade antique printing blocks, and now also offers wall and furniture paints.

### 2 > SECONDHAND ROSE

Based in Manhattan since 1965, Secondhand Rose offers a selection of more than 50,000 rolls of a few thousand patterns of vintage wallpaper and linoleum. There are countless styles, from the expected to the unconventional, dating from the mid-nineteenth to late twentieth centuries.

### 3 > COLE & SON

Cole & Son, founded in 1875, boasts 1,800 block-print designs, 350 screen-print designs, and many original drawings and wallpapers featuring styles from the eighteenth century onward. The British company has supplied wallpapers to Buckingham Palace and other historic houses.

### 4 > TIMOROUS BEASTIES

Design studio Timorous Beasties, founded in Glasgow in 1990 by recent textile design graduates, offers surreal and provocative wallcoverings. Insects, butterflies, birds, flora, and twists on Napoleonic Toile de Jouy fabrics that feature cities from around the globe comprise many of their designs.

### 5 > DE GOURNAY

Luxury firm de Gournay, purveyor of hand-painted wallpaper, fabrics, porcelain, and handcrafted furniture, was founded in 1986 by Claud Cecil Gurney, who was searching for artists to restore his family home's antique wallpapers. De Gournay artisans' strengths include historic reproduction prints, particularly eighteenth-century chinoiserie, Japanese and Korean prints with elaborate gilding, and nineteenth-century French panoramics.

### 6 > PORTER TELEO

Artist Kelly Porter and interior designer Bridgett Cochran's handcrafted wallcoverings and fabrics feature bold colors, refined aesthetics, and high-quality materials. Each panel, made by fine artists at the Kansas City–based studio, is unique, created through wood-block printing, *chine-collé,* Japanese wash-painting, or other historic techniques.

**1** › A de Gournay chinoiserie pattern calls attention to the magnificent architectural details in a Park Avenue duplex. **2** › Tone-on-tone wallpaper sets off the dark wood trim in designer Timothy Corrigan's French château. **3** › Timorous Beasties's hand-painted *Euro Damask* paper livens up an entry hall. **4** › Designer Bunny Williams uses bold stripes to accentuate the curving hallway of a Connecticut estate.

5 › Damask wallpaper frames the fireplace in a Miles Redd–designed space.
6 › A trompe l'oeil library print from Cole & Son's Fornasetti collection brings new life to a living room nook in the home of Ramdane Touhami and Victoire de Taillac. 7 › Designer Benjamin Dhong uses a paper that combines subtle texture with a faded print to create dimension behind a simple, elegant vignette.
8 › Kelly Wearstler surrounds panels of de Gournay's *Askew* design with walls of mirrors, ensuring that wherever you sit in Bergdorf Goodman's BG Restaurant, you're cocooned in the lovely print.

# *paint*

In most homes, paint is not just a finishing touch; it's a key component of every room. Paint has become much more than a decorative flourish, a burst of color—that layer of paint on our walls completes them.

When picking a paint, the first question most people grapple with is, of course, the color, but there are other important factors to weigh as well, including its durability, its ability to go up on the walls cleanly and hide what's underneath thoroughly, and its finish and texture—how well it serves its primary function, to protect the  wall.

Perhaps nothing takes as much confidence as making the decision to paint a wall red. But the brilliant work of interior designer Miles Redd proves that big color risks offer even bigger design rewards.

# FROM THE PAST TO THE PRESENT
# *The Unique History of Paint*

### 15,000 BC

Red and yellow ocher is used in the wall paintings of the caves of Altamira, Spain, and Lascaux, France, and the caves of Grotte du Pech Merle in France's Lot region.

### 1437

In Florence, Cennino d'Andrea Cennini writes a treatise on painting called *Il libro dell'arte* or *Il trattato della pittura*, which includes every recipe for paint during his time.

### 1704

Prussian blue, the first purely synthetic pigment, is discovered in Berlin.

### 7,000–5,500 BC

Archaeological excavations during the 1950s in Turkey uncover evidence of fresco, one of the earliest mural techniques from the period.

### 8TH CENTURY AD

An Arabian chemist named Jābir ibn Hayyān discovers a way to produce cinnabar synthetically; however, it is not mass-produced until around 1785.

### 1480

The discovery of Nero's Domus Aurea (Golden House) in Rome inspires a 16th-century passion for grotesques and fantastical and fanciful forms of vegetal and figurative elements that Giorgio Vasari describes as "a kind of free and humorous picture produced by the ancients."

### 19TH CENTURY

Chemically obtained cobalt and cerulean blue are first sold, and an artificial ultramarine blue is produced to imitate semiprecious mineral lapis lazuli.

### 1850

Because of industrialization, by the mid-19th century, virtually all dyes and pigments are synthetically made.

## 1883

American paint powerhouse Benjamin Moore opens shop, producing "Moore's Prepared Calsom Finish" in Brooklyn, New York.

## 1930s

British paint company Farrow & Ball is founded by John Farrow and Richard Ball in Dorset, England, with a commitment to traditional formulations and natural ingredients, unlike the majority of paint companies at the time, which utilized acrylic and large amounts of plastic in their batches.

## 1970s AND '80s

With the advent of postmodern style, leading Italian design firm Memphis uses paint in completely new ways, favoring bright and over-the-top applications, leading the way to the 1980s passion for neon.

## 1960s

Anthropologist Brent Berlin and linguist Paul Kay conduct an international study of color naming in ninety-eight different languages, and find that English has the largest number of basic color terms.

## TODAY

With color-matching technology, virtually any color can be produced, making the possibilities in paint infinite.

## 1920s

At the famous Bauhaus school in Germany, teacher Johannes Itten studies and teaches the connections between colors and emotions and writes his seminal book, *The Art of Color.*

# On Color

COLOR IS A POWERFUL TOOL. AS THE DESIGN WRITER ALBERT HALSE says: "Color is a very important part of our lives. We are surrounded by it; we select our clothes, automobiles, houses, paintings, and even food packages by it. It is used to make us happy, to make us hungry, to promote serenity, and to encourage piety. It invites us into one architectural space and drives us out of another."

The way paint is created, acquired, and applied has evolved over time, but what has remained the same is our fundamental desire to live with color. The Egyptians did it; the Greeks did it—but of course much of that paint is lost to time, which is why the Greeks are known for stark white ruins, not the reds and blues they used to emphasize various aspects of their buildings' architecture.

For most of us, color is key. It's the determining factor in the paint we choose; it's the thing we fall in love with.

Though choosing a color for a room can be fun, it can also be daunting, as anyone who's ever attempted to navigate the process (and collected magazine tear sheets, fan decks, swatches, and sample pots) can attest. "Color is one of the most difficult aspects to get right," says David Oliver, creative director of the London-based Paint & Paper Library, "because it has as much to do with the light as the pigment, and the light is never constant. A color can look perfect on one surface, next to one color, and then you put it on another wall, with a different rug next to it, and it can pulsate like you didn't expect."

It's a big decision, with important ramifications. "In design, color is probably the best return on investment that anyone can make," says Jill Pilaroscia, the principal of San Francisco–based consultancy Colour Studio. "The ability that paint gives you to transform a space is unlimited."

There's a whole marketplace devoted to color, from firms like Pantone that develop and provide standardized colors to consultants like Pilaroscia who'll help you choose one. There are color trend organizations and trade shows that evaluate what's current (drawing on fashion, architecture, and art) and dictate what will be popular (like Pantone's color of the year).

It might seem counterintuitive to enlist a third party to help you choose something as personal as a color for your bedroom. It's not as simple, though, as if you like blue, pick blue. "The do-it-yourself approach doesn't take into consideration the quality of light in the environment," says Pilaroscia. "That

Though many people's first inclination when considering the palette of a room may be to select one bold color and surround it with softer, complementary shades, layering one rich hue on top of another— in this case, warm brown and cerulean blue—can yield far more striking results.

influences the behavior of color in a room, as do the given elements like the ceiling height, and the pieces that are already there." Pilaroscia notes that you need to understand your space—beginning with the geography, for example (the light in the Pacific Northwest is different from that in the desert Southwest), and the room's actual orientation (whether it has northern or eastern exposures), because those can affect how a color actually looks in a space.

And, in truth, a well-designed room isn't about one color—it's about a color scheme. Color experts and interior designers help their clients decide on an entire family of colors that will bring a space to life; and if you find yourself fussing with sample chips and fan decks, remember to pick enough colors to build a whole scheme, even if you incorporate the complementary hues in accessories or textiles instead of paint.

"People are always asking, 'How do you come up with these palettes?'" says interior designer Miles Redd. "Often, I'll be inspired by a great painter. If you take a walk through the Wrightsman Galleries"—the decorative arts salons at New York's Metropolitan Museum of Art—"you'll realize people have been doing it for quite some time. Any color combination has probably already been used—you just have to look at nature. And if I see it in nature or if I see it in a painting, I know instinctively that it'll work."

David Oliver has a system he prefers over fussing with chips or even painting a color on a test wall. "I use a sample tint or a small quantity of the actual color in a shadow box. You can use a shoebox, if you like. When you view it from above, you see where the color gets darker, or hangs in the corners, because you're looking at it in 3-D, like a room, not on a 2-D object. People often just paint a flat piece of a wall, but they don't really see how the paint is going to look from different angles."

When you're talking about quality, you're not necessarily talking about price. After all, as Pilaroscia points out, "colors behave differently depending upon the orientations and characteristics of the light, of the foliage adjacent, the tall buildings that shadow it. It will always be about the site and the light." An expensive paint might simply not look right in a certain kind of light, so don't just invest dollars; invest time: discuss, deliberate, hire an expert, or try David Oliver's method. Give the decision the consideration it deserves.

**OPPOSITE ›** According to designer Gideon Mendelson, one of the best places to find color inspiration is right outside your own window. When creating his home in Sagaponack, New York, he let its seaside location dictate the soft blues and sandy neutrals.

**ABOVE ›** Color specialist David Oliver's paint test technique uses mounted shadow boxes to give his clients a better gauge of how light will interact with a specific shade or finish.

In this elegant lounge, Miles Redd further proves his mastery of the unexpected color blend by setting a tufted chartreuse sofa against tomato red walls.

# How It's Made

PAINT'S FUNCTION IS TO PROTECT YOUR WALLS AS MUCH AS IT IS TO add color. When it comes to fulfilling this task, the important component of paint is what's called the "vehicle"—the component of the overall mixture that makes paint adhere, dry, and remain on the wall.

The vehicle determines the surface's physical texture and how it responds to light, so it has a lot to do with how a painted space looks and feels. Take oil paint as an example: oil is the key component in the vehicle, which informs the rich sheen and soft texture we associate with oil paint. Most interior paint is what's called "latex" (which has nothing to do with the latex of laboratory gloves).

Once upon a time, paint was mixed in batches on-site, using organic materials such as lime or eggs as a base, and shells, stones, or plant products for color. Today, paint producers like Benjamin Moore are chemists first and foremost, focused on developing formulas that yield the best possible paint. "We have complete control of that value chain," says Carl Minchew of Benjamin Moore. "We make our own polymer, which is the resin that holds the paint together. If you're familiar with the process of buying paint, most of the paint in the store is white and needs to be tinted by the retailer. We make the colorant that goes into the paint."

Consumers today expect a lot from their paint, chiefly durability and consistency. If you paint a room one color, you want every wall to be exactly the same, and further, you probably want to know you can buy a new pot to touch it up a couple years down the road and be confident that the color will be a spot-on match. "We purchase the finest color pigments and make sure they are colorfast, lightfast, will stand up to cleaning and household chemicals, and will react with light consistently," says Minchew. Additionally, should a job require a touch-up after a time, the formulas Benjamin Moore uses assure consistency. "The paint you bought three years ago?" says Minchew. "You can get the same authentic appearance and performance today."

In terms of a paint's durability, consider what your walls go through: They are knocked by feet, smudged by hands, battered by whatever you're carrying in hallways. "When we're formulating these paints," says Minchew, "we want them to perform consistently. So we consider how well the paint can be cleaned and washed and scrubbed. If it's exterior paint, can it stand up to weather? If it's interior, does it stand up to scuffs and scratches?"

OPPOSITE › The paint experts at Farrow & Ball still mix each and every shade by hand, slowly adding rich pigments (a process that takes a minimum of ten minutes) to a base before handing off the batch to quality control to test for color accuracy.

FOLLOWING PAGES › Famed New York designer Steven Gambrel's dramatic tone-on-tone living room schemes come alive with both color and texture.

# Paint & Performance

ABOVE › Matte black walls are both moody and dramatic (though they scuff easily and are best reserved for low-traffic rooms). Here, the light-absorbing shade brings out the antique bureau's gorgeous wood grain.

OPPOSITE › Steven Gambrel eschews the generally recommended eggshell finish for doors and trim, and instead uses high-gloss red paint to modernize traditional woodwork.

THERE'S ANOTHER IMPORTANT CONSIDERATION FOR PAINT MAKERS, which is what the paint is like before it has dried. "How paint applies is an area that we pay a lot of attention to, even though once the paint's on the wall, it's often forgotten," explains Carl Minchew. "A high-quality paint is much easier to apply, and it will often take fewer coats to give a satisfactory job."

Ease of application is important only when you're actually engaged in painting, of course. After the job is done, your primary concern is how the paint performs its task of covering your wall. "The apparent opacity of the paint is one dimension of this property we call 'hiding,'" says Minchew. Hiding is one of paint's most important characteristics—as anyone who's ever used a low-quality paint can attest. It is maddening when, coat after coat, the wall beneath still peeks through.

Minchew says that a paint's characteristics when it is wet can be related to its performance when it is dry. "So, another dimension of good hiding is that the paint goes on smoothly and then flows to a very uniform finish before it dries," he says. "When you apply a paint, it's not uncommon to see brush marks. With a premium paint, those brush marks should completely disappear by the time the paint is dry."

Compared to Benjamin Moore, Paint & Paper Library is a boutique operation, one with roots in the old-school artisan model. "In the beginning, we had each tin of paint hand-mixed, using traditional methods," says David Oliver. "But at the moment, we have two hundred stores in the UK selling the paint, and so we changed over to a more consistent form of colorant." Few customers are willing to roll the dice and see what color a hand-mixed pigment will yield. "As much as I adore those traditional methods like lime wash, where everything was mixed on-site, the colors bloom and change according to how much water is added, how much solvent is added," says Oliver. "That idea, of paint being a handcrafted, artisan color product, is disappearing."

Oliver says, "The paint industry is driven by price rather than quality, with huge department stores rolling out quite inexpensive materials to make it affordable. So the compromise is that you end up with cheap fillers, inexpensive chalk rather than titanium white, which is a really expensive pigment that gives you opacity and lightfastness, qualities that would make the product last longer." The average customer who shops by price may not fully understand what's being sacrificed when he chooses a less expensive paint.

# Paint Finishes
# & Textures

PAINT IS AN INTEGRAL PART OF EVERY DESIGNER'S TOOLBOX, BUT Miles Redd, who's known for exuberant, confident interiors with big color and lots of shine, is a particular expert on the subject. "The one thing that I have learned is that the best paints have more pigment in them. You do notice, when all is said and done, a different kind of luster, sheen, richness, and depth to the quality of the paint." You don't need to have as trained an eye as Redd's to perceive the difference in a paint with more pigments. "You can see it by comparison," says Redd. "Not to say there isn't great quality in lower-priced things, but in terms of paint, I think the difference is super obvious." A paint that derives its hue through a mixture of a half-dozen pigments will have a more complex color than one with three component pigments.

Pigment informs a paint's visual texture, but there's also its physical texture to consider—its finish. There are simple rules to determine whether to opt for a flat, eggshell, semigloss, or gloss finish.

"For interior walls and ceilings, you should use a flat emulsion," says David Oliver. "And then, for anything like trim or woodwork, window frames, or doors, you should use either an eggshell or a gloss for durability." Eggshell and gloss paints dry in a way that makes them softer to the touch but firmer overall, and therefore more resistant to wear and tear.

"The higher the sheen level, the more protection that paint offers," Oliver explains. "People want protection from finger marks, from children with crayons, from suitcases going up and down the hall." Oliver notes that eggshell or gloss finishes are also suitable for ceilings (where they have the added advantage of reflecting light) as well as for walls made of wood or metal.

Another option is the slick, mirrored look of a very glossy paint. This look is increasingly in vogue thanks in large part to Redd—it's one of his signatures. "I've always sort of been a magpie," he says. "I love reflective surfaces and anything shiny. A lacquer finish is ultimately a reflective surface, a mirrored finish. So you have a blue mirror, a green mirror, a red mirror. I love that feeling of reflection and the added layer of rich color."

Achieving this look is labor-intensive. "Basically, the walls need to be like glass," says Redd. "To achieve that takes layers of plaster and lots of sanding. A really high-quality paint job is all in the prep. And I think if you're going to have that kind of paint finish, it's essential to have a great painter who appreciates and understands that finish, that sort of skill."

Lacquer paint creates an almost glasslike finish in an opulent formal hallway designed by Miles Redd. Consider using this high-shine paint in small spaces, since its reflective nature has expansive qualities much like a mirror.

# The Paint Job

**ABOVE ›** Arguably the most popular choice for those experimenting with color is one of the many soothing shades of Mediterranean blue—thanks in large part to its versatile nature. In the Santa Barbara home of photographer Birgitte Aarestrup, it takes on the soft qualities of a French country estate.

**OPPOSITE ›** In a Brooklyn brownstone, this same hue becomes a nod to warm midcentury design.

PAINTING IS ONE OF THOSE TASKS THAT ELICIT A CASUAL SHRUG AND a "How hard could it be?" until one finds oneself in stained clothes, attempting to navigate that awkward inch between the molding and the ceiling while paint drips onto the parquet below. It's usually at moments like these that one concedes the value in hiring an expert.

In the estimation of John Baric, a partner in the New York City firm Simonson & Baric, what makes a quality paint job is easy to explain. "The quality is in the preparation," says Baric. "You can prepare a wall so beautifully that the paint can last twenty, twenty-five years. You can change the colors anytime you want." Baric explains that these first steps, before you even apply paint, are key to the finished job. We might think of a paint job as a superficial application, but a good surface needs to have a good foundation.

Explaining what that looks like, Baric says, "You take either sand or plaster and you level on top of the Sheetrock. Once you've primed that, then you take your cement, and you put an additional four or five coats of primer on top of that. So you're actually making a plaster wall." That level of detail, that commitment to creating a surface that's perfectly level, goes well beyond the cursory sanding, patching, and taping that most do-it-yourselfers consider the boring prep work. High-end designers and painters consider this sort of preparation standard—indeed, imperative. It's a bit of a contradiction that one of a painter's most important tasks has nothing to do with actually applying paint, which could explain the misperception that doing it yourself is as simple as grabbing a brush and getting to it. "Most of the paint job is all intense labor," says Baric. Given that the technical characteristics of a paint inform how and where it should be used, he adds, "You have to have quality workers, who know what they're doing; that's the way a quality job gets done."

Pink walls and a panther print by artist Leslie Hearn define the quirky, cozy, glamorous Manhattan living room of Miles Redd.

# Decorative Painting

THE PHRASE "DECORATIVE PAINTING" MAY SEEM REDUNDANT. IN fact, decorative painting describes a number of highly specialized techniques that trained artisans can execute in lieu of a simple color on the wall (or door, column, floor, or ceiling).

Approaches to the form vary by geography, and the traditions that endure today are associated with either Northern or Southern Europe (France and Italy respectively). The Northern European school emphasizes realism, using shadow, light, detail, and sleight of hand to convincingly replicate something (usually motifs from the natural world). The Southern European school is more theatrical and consciously artificial; a tendril of ivy or the visage of an angel might appear, but it wouldn't be mistaken for a real plant or an actual piece of sculpted marble.

Effects that remain popular today include *faux bois,* in which a surface is painted to mimic wood grain; marbleizing, in which the artist imitates the look of marble; gilding, in which actual sheets of gold leaf (or another metal) are applied to a surface wet with paint; Venetian plaster, in which plaster and paint create a richly textured surface; trompe l'oeil, which replicates architectural features like arches, columns, or wainscoting; and murals, which vary widely aesthetically.

New York–based painter Dina Ivanova, owner of Decorative Painting Industries, didn't learn the craft in an institution; rather, she learned the way generations of artisans have learned—as an apprentice. "My boss basically started us from scratch. For gilding, we had to make sure the wall was a perfect, glasslike surface," says Ivanova. "So we'd plaster the walls, then we would prime and paint, sanding every coat, and on the final coat we would do several passes with different grades of sandpaper to make sure it was absolutely mirrorlike. The last two steps, actually executing the final thing that you'd see, were the job of the boss."

Painter and designer Idarica Gazzoni trained at Belgium's Van Der Kelen Institute, a venerable school that's been instructing painters in the Northern European tradition for more than a century. But her Italian heritage and point of view most certainly show through in her work. The distinction is technical. "In the north, they use a lot of oil paints," says Gazzoni. "Down here in Italy, we use water-based colors, even chalk." It's also an aesthetic choice: "I like the accident of the hand. I don't want it perfect.

Muralist Idarica Gazzoni frames an antique fireplace with decorative columns, drawing well-deserved attention to the beautiful but subtle architectural detail.

In the dining room of designer William Monaghan's cottage in the Hamptons, a wraparound wall mural, painted by Robert Van Nutt, depicts an Atlantic whaling ship setting sail from Sag Harbor.

ABOVE › In the stunning Greenwich Village library of Marc Jacobs president Robert Duffy, a gilt wall mural by Matt Austin covers the room in shimmering fairy-tale silhouettes.

OPPOSITE › With Manuel Canovas's floral fabric as inspiration, a Florida bedroom is transformed into an elegant jungle with murals of fantastical plants ornamenting all four walls.

Because if you make something perfect, it looks like a horrible digital print. I love accidents and errors and colors that bleed a little bit. I like it when it's not perfectly done, even though I'm a perfectionist."

Decorative painting is a time-consuming process, and time is, of course, money. The expense associated with these techniques may in part explain why there's less and less demand for them—save among the set for whom money is no object. But tastes have changed as well. "I think interiors are becoming a lot more modern, so people prefer either straight paint or maybe a decorative plaster," says Ivanova, referring to the technique in which lime or marble dust is mixed with primer and affixed to the wall, resulting in a lushly textured surface that can look either modern or traditional, depending on the color. "It's a little bit easier to live with. But there are still some people who prefer period-style interiors."

It's true that when planning a space, most people can envision a color on their walls, but few can imagine a scene or a decorative motif. As with wallpaper, though, "it can change a house completely and radically," says Gazzoni. "What I always think is that you can spend on a decoratively painted wall—and then need very little afterward."

Obviously, choosing a decorative painter requires even more discernment and thought than choosing a housepainter. You should approach this decision as you would when buying a painting. Few would spend thousands on an oil on canvas without learning more about the artist and studying her portfolio; the same steps are useful when evaluating a decorative painter. Quality is hard to discern when you're making aesthetic judgments, but with a bit of study, your eye will likely be able to distinguish between the acceptable artist and the truly skilled hand.

Regarding this distinction between the fine artist and the craftsman, Ivanova has a clear point of view. "If you were to compare decorative art to very traditional fine art, where it's just your easel, your canvas, your brushes, and your paint, I would say it's very similar in some ways," she says. "But in a decorative painting world, you absolutely have to know that this is going to last. You're not experimenting with materials. This is something that's been tested and tried for years."

That's not to say that the current crop of decorative painters haven't adapted the form for modern life. "I try to stay as traditional as possible, but

you can't spend months and months on the job—they'll kick you out," says Ivanova. "To speed up a mural, you would project it, make an outline, perhaps stencil a design—not do it freehand. You use modern technology like a projector, special tools like Mylar paper and the hot knife stencil cutter, a little tool that has a very sharp tip that heats up." Gazzoni echoes this sentiment; she'll use computers to scan and refine her hand-drawn designs, or place rough sketches over photographs so she and her clients can more clearly envision how a finished mural might look.

Technology has streamlined the process for the modern consumer, but it hasn't appreciably affected the artfulness of these decorative techniques. And a deep study of some of the better interior designers working right now reveals that it is possible to design a modern room around something as traditional as a marbleized wall. Decorative painting is a big investment, but it's also a strong statement—and one that could last for decades.

# The Mural

MURALS DRAW SO MUCH ATTENTION, IT'S NO WONDER THEY'VE historically been used in public spaces, whether depicting sacred scenes inside churches or functioning as political or social metaphors inside great museums or other public buildings. The mural as kitsch (an amateurishly rendered Leaning Tower of Pisa in some third-rate Italian restaurant, for example) endures, but a great mural can make a room or, indeed, a home.

"Most people think of murals as old-fashioned," says Matt Austin, an industrial designer and painter who has done many commissioned murals. "They imagine a landscape of the Amalfi Coast or something, but murals can be really current, exciting. I keep the traditions of mural painting that are relevant, irresistible—and I tweak the rest so there's energy in the work." Austin's murals don't fit tidily within any one particular aesthetic; that is to say, it's not that he specializes in nature scenes, or photorealistic murals, or abstract designs. Instead, he creates a scene tailored to a client's specifications, and, in his words, "each mural takes into consideration so many things—not just how a room is furnished, but whether the residents read in that room or eat dinner there, even the direction of the sun."

"Decoration is an entirely personal perspective, you know," says Hutton Wilkinson, the Los Angeles–based interior decorator and jewelry designer who has a vision as bold and exuberant as that of his mentor, Tony Duquette. "Every interior and every house is individual." This isn't an uncommon sentiment among designers—hence their emphasis on custom furniture and finishes. But Wilkinson's take is as idiosyncratic as Duquette's, in that he doesn't believe that spending more money is always an absolute necessity. Furthermore, he's willing to embrace murals and other old-school decorative techniques many modern designers eschew.

There's a large mural over the staircase in Wilkinson's Beverly Hills home that illustrates the form's potential. "I'm on the board of Save Venice," says Wilkinson. "Venice is my absolute passion city. I would live there if I could, but I can't. I had this set of eighteenth-century Venetian paintings

In keeping with Hutton Wilkinson's more-is-more approach to decorating, the mural he commissioned for the entryway of his Beverly Hills home wraps the entire foyer, extending the full two-story height.

from Palazzo Morosini. . . . I saw that kind of blue sky in these Venetian paintings and I wanted that blue." A mural is a way to pay homage to something near and dear to your heart (Venice, in this instance) and achieve a particular decorative effect (such as adding a specific color). Additionally, Wilkinson points out, "a mural will give you depth as well, not just depth of color. Without knocking out a wall or creating dust or anything like that, you can have a vista by painting a surface to look like the sky."

The element of creative risk involved might sound off-putting, but you may treasure the results as much as you would a piece of art on canvas. The distinction between decorative and fine art collapses entirely if you have something you really love. By the time Matt Austin begins the work of actually painting on the wall, he's already shared sketches with his client, but the element of chance always plays a role in a work of art. Austin will sometimes transfer paper drawings directly onto a wall using a projector, allowing him to trace the rough outlines on the wall's surface. Also, Austin is working with a team of painters who follow his lead—more hands and more opportunities for a chance to intervene. "A lot of freehand work goes into the process," says Austin. "There are all these different techniques: stenciling, casein painting, gold-leafing, layering, gridding—whatever a mural calls for. It comes together and makes for a unique product for each client, and for me working on it. The best projects excite me and the client both."

"I don't think rooms need to be soothing or Zenlike," says Wilkinson. "I think that rooms actually need to be invigorating, and make you feel more alive."

**1 ›** The walls and ceiling in the main sitting room of a country estate were hand painted by Idarica Gazzoni to resemble the inside of a luxurious medieval tent. **2 ›** Two shadowy portraits of Marie Antoinette (by Natasha Zupan) frame the grand mantel of fashion designer Zang Toi's former Manhattan apartment. **3 ›** These hand-painted, twisting birch branches, done in 22-karat-gold leaf, are the work of decorative painter Matt Austin and appear in the foyer of photographer Kate Cordsen's home. **4 ›** A series of botanical studies—painted in the 1920s by a pupil of Piero Portaluppi—surround the fantastical entryway of Italian architect and fabric designer Piero Castellini Baldissera.

# DESIGN CHAMPION: *Billy Baldwin*

FOR FOUR DECADES, BILLY BALDWIN created homes for millionaires. His rooms were stunning but never self-important, tailored but never fussily perfect. Inherent in interior design is a sense of transience, impermanence—the truly innovative residential projects tend to be the homes of wealthy people, and wealthy people change their homes fairly often. So pictures are typically all we have left. Experts and designers continue to study photographs of Baldwin's rooms three decades after his death, elevating many of those projects to iconic status.

These photographs show us the easy glamour of uptown apartments, the inviting color of country bedrooms, the confidence with which Baldwin always worked. It's impossible to pick one project to represent Baldwin's sensibility; he designed by instinct to create homes tailored to his clients' needs and personalities. It's probably most instructive, therefore, to look at Baldwin's own home (seen here).

"He didn't even have a one-bedroom apartment," says Adam Lewis, an interior decorator and writer whose book *Billy Baldwin: The Great American Decorator* is the definitive monograph on the man. "He lived in an efficiency, with a sort of Pullman kitchen to the side. And the way you make a place like that look bigger is to paint it all one color. The dark chocolate brown that he used became a signature color for him. He was for bold statements."

There's a current vogue for moody-colored walls in homes, possibly related to their prevalence in boutique hotels and smart restaurants. Baldwin's home is still one of the best examples of how it's done.

The slick finish on the walls picks up the gleam of the brass étagères (Baldwin used the same shelves in the considerably more opulent home of Cole Porter), so though the color is rich, the room is not dark. "He was an extraordinary decorator and certainly the dean of American designers," says designer Harry Hinson, who knew Baldwin. "Even when he was using very elaborate furnishings and furniture and all that sort of business, he often had cotton fabrics and linen rugs to make things quite simple."

Though Baldwin's home creates an impact, as you examine it, you realize how simple it is. "It's a gift. The ability to create a room is something that you're born with," says Lewis. It's a gift Baldwin used memorably in mansions and just as impressively within the confines of a humdrum New York City apartment.

## RECOGNIZING THE MAJOR PLAYERS
# *Paint*

### 1 > COLOUR STUDIO

Colour Studio founder Jill Pilaroscia has more than thirty years' experience writing, lecturing, and consulting on color. She looks at color from a neurobiological standpoint, aiming to find the color, or harmonious blend of colors, that works best in each individual space to make the people in it feel their best.

### 2 > FARROW & BALL

John Farrow and Richard Ball founded the renowned paint company in Dorset, England, where their paints are still hand-crafted from original recipes using fine ingredients and rich pigments. The company's limited roster of paint colors provide customers with an edited selection of only the richest hues.

### 3 > SHERWIN-WILLIAMS

Sherwin-Williams, the largest specialty retailer of paint and painting supplies in the United States, has nearly four thousand stores across North America. Established in 1866, Sherwin-Williams has remained cutting-edge in the industry with digital tools for selecting the right color from the company's more than 1,500 choices.

### 4 > PAINT & PAPER LIBRARY

Paint & Paper Library creative director David Oliver is an authority on color. His Architectural Colors collection is a color-by-number system that prescribes the optimal way, based on tonal weights, to combine off-white and neutral hues on ceilings, cornices, walls, and detailing. The Original Colors collection offers more options and bold contrasts.

### 5 > COLORHOUSE

Colorhouse is a self-declared "indie" paint company founded in Portland, Oregon, in 2005 to create "paint for the people and the planet." Paints are free of hazardous toxins, air pollutants, formaldehyde, VOCs, and other harmful ingredients that can be found even in water-based paints, but are still filled with rich, beautiful color.

### 6 > BENJAMIN MOORE

In 1883, Benjamin Moore and his brother Robert opened Moore Brothers Paint Company in Brooklyn with just $2,000 and one product, Moore's Prepared Calsom Finish. Today, the company, now located in Montvale, New Jersey, offers thousands of interior and exterior paints and stains—including its award-winning eco-friendly Aura collection—and is sold at more than 4,000 independent retailers nationwide.

**1 ›** Formal furnishings take a
lighthearted spin when contrasted
with pale floors and minty walls.
**2 ›** Bright white paint is used to
draw attention to all the decorative
built-in flourishes: the mantel, the
moldings, the intricate fireplace.
**3 ›** Silk-screened walls mimic
the hedges growing outside the
windows of artist Doug Aitken's
Venice Beach home.

1

3 ›

**4** › Intense magenta walls and luxuriously draped curtains wrap the entrance hall in the storied Upper East Side apartment of Gloria Vanderbilt. **5** › WIth a focus on amplifying light, famed designer Axel Vervoordt used a dusty blue-gray hue in one of the many stairwells in his twelfth-century Belgian castle. **6** › In a room layered with black-and-white patterns, Miles Redd injects subtle warmth by painting the walls pale yellow.

# framing

Besides covering them with paint or wallpaper, there's another important way we change the look of our walls: by filling them with art. With the artwork itself, beauty is in the eye of the beholder. With frames, though, it's important to understand how they're built, and how that affects their performance.

The way we choose to mount a frame, whether a single piece or part of a collection, has just as much impact as the art we display. So though hanging a single picture on the wall may seem like a simple enough task, there are important details to consider and many options to weigh—including whether a particular job could benefit from the help of a professional art installer.

The salon-style art assemblage in menswear designer Michael Bastian's West Village living room was not meticulously measured and hung, but eyeballed and adjusted, proving that gut instinct is often the most accurate design tool.

# FROM THE PAST TO THE PRESENT
## *The Unique History of Framing*

### 2ND CENTURY AD

Egyptian tombs include primitive wood frames for mummy portraits.

### 15TH CENTURY

The *studiolo* becomes a prominent space in the Renaissance Italian palazzo to display personal art collections and antiquities.

### 1737

The Salon Carré begins in Paris, where the French Royal Academy of Painting and Sculpture opens its exhibition of recent graduates' work to the public. The works are hung one on top of another or side by side so all can fit; the Salon soon becomes known for its wall-to-wall display.

### 12TH CENTURY

The first carved frames are crafted out of one piece of wood for small devotional panel paintings in Europe. The area that will be painted is first carved and then painted, while the raised border is painted, gessoed, and gilded.

### 19TH CENTURY

Aristocratic homes favor the picture rail, which provides an easy way to rotate and change artworks without ruining wall coverings.

### 17TH CENTURY

Paintings are hung on top of tapestries in ornate gilded frames or are incorporated into the interior's architectural framework, such as above a mantel or door. The Dutch become known for their deliberate display of framed art over furniture pieces.

## 1893

A. Wayland from Middlesborough, Kentucky, patents the first picture-frame clamp. The next year, the first mat-cutting machine is invented.

## 1925

At the *Exposition des Arts Décoratifs et Industriels Modernes* in Paris, Le Corbusier shocks the public with his modern architecture and new ways of displaying art throughout the interior.

## 1913

The first Armory Show in New York City takes place. Initially called the International Exhibition of Modern Art, the show aims not only to educate people on contemporary art but also to show how art can be displayed.

## 1957

Roger Larson starts his frame-manufacturing company in Braham, Minnesota, and Tom Juhl opens a frame shop in Minneapolis. In 1988, the two merge companies to form Larson-Juhl, the global leader in custom framing.

## 1996

London's National Portrait Gallery hosts the exhibition *The Art of the Picture Frame,* exploring the history of British frame making.

# The Evolution of the Frame

DEPICTIONS OF ART-FILLED INTERIORS ARE A MAINSTAY OF WESTERN art. They document the central role of art in various societies, yielding clues about how previous generations lived with sculptures, objects, and, most of all, paintings.

Take, for example, Frans Francken the Younger's painting of a wealthy Belgian collector's seventeenth-century home, *Banquet in the House of Nicolaas Rockox*. We're able to see the spoils accumulated by the subject. But more compelling, we're able to see how the elite of that period decorated with their artwork. A painting and some busts are displayed in front of a tapestry. Canvases fill every part of the wall, even well above the sight line, crowded together without regard for their subject matter. A large painting aligns with the fireplace below, creating almost a single plane. A bust is nestled comfortably in a niche above a door. The scene captures something intriguing about the evolution of interior design—depicting the way the modern picture frame came to be.

"Frames actually originated from architecture," explains Greg Perkins, of Atlanta-based Larson-Juhl, the world's largest manufacturer and distributor of picture frames. "Niches, window frames, and other molded parts of a building were the inspiration for stand-alone frames."

Of course, for the modern consumer, the principal job of a frame is to protect art, and to fulfill this function, a frame needs to be made of the right materials, and installed properly. The interior depicted in Francken's painting has a clear relationship to the homes of today, where pictures are still framed, for the most part, within structures that replicate the appearance of architecture. Despite their genesis in architectural detail, however, modern frames need not mimic old forms.

Though frames can add architectural interest to a room, their main purpose is to show off what's within. The simple plastic box or minimal metal style takes the very idea of a frame and distills it to the bare minimum, so that the frame recedes and does not distract from the impact of its contents.

The details we associate with the frames around Old Masters works in important museums—ornate moldings, gilding, curlicues, and decorative flourishes—are, though, still in demand. Indeed, a traditional frame can contrast beautifully with a work of modern art. There's no reason such a frame can't look as natural in a modern loft as in the Louvre.

**OPPOSITE ›** At the center of this art assemblage is Louis Bouché's *View of Engineer's Gate.* While a gilt frame draws attention to the prized work, the surrounding art has a far simpler treatment, allowing it to blend with the mahogany wood paneling.

**ABOVE ›** Frans Francken the Younger's *Banquet in the House of Nicolaas Rockox* (c. 1630) is one in a series of paintings by the artist depicting the impressive art and curio collections of the period's aristocracy.

# How It's Made

LARSON-JUHL CATERS TO CUSTOMERS INTERESTED IN A MINIMAL, modern presentation as well as those who want a frame with a sense of heritage. At their Senelar factory, located in northern France, artisans have been constructing water-gilded frames for more than a century. "They still do gold leafing the same way it was done hundreds of years ago, by the Egyptians," says Greg Perkins. "It's a craft that has been passed down from father to son, and in some cases at our Senelar atelier, there are different generations of the same family working there."

Conservation and preservation of the art within a frame are relevant no matter which style of frame you're drawn to—indeed, it's not the visible components, but the frame's innards that determine how the art will weather the decades. The paper in the mat and backing within should be acid-free, and the frame should be sealed tightly to guard against moisture. "If you look at a mat that's maybe thirty years old, at a yard sale or something, the bevels look kind of gold or brown," says Perkins. "That's from the acid." Then of course there's the glass or Plexiglas of the frame's front: Here again, the quality that informs preservation—a surface treatment to filter ultraviolet light—is invisible but worth investing in, especially if you're framing something precious.

These considerations render it a challenge to judge what makes a great frame. Natural materials like wood and acid-free paper are ideal, but so, too, are high-tech treatments on the glass or plastic. Though a vintage frame might be made of natural materials, those are also subject to degrading or contamination depending on the conditions in which the piece is stored. And a piece of glass might be treated, but if it's a frame designed for home assembly, you might not achieve a tight seal, and the art might still degrade.

And of course, a store-bought frame is only going to be available in a handful of standard sizes. For anything truly valuable or meant to last, the best route is probably custom.

Silver leaf is hand-brushed onto an ornate frame from Larson-Juhl's Nouveau collection; the skilled artisan ensures that the thin metal sheet bonds to the surface's every dip, curve, and crevice.

In a cozy English living room, smart homeowners installed a narrow, almost imperceptible chair rail across the top of the wall—roughly two feet below the ceiling. It acts as a physical barrier, helping to visually wrangle the disparate assortment of art clinging to the walls, while giving the collection, as a whole, room to "breathe."

# Custom Framing

CUSTOM FRAMES WILL ALWAYS BE MORE EXPENSIVE THAN SOME-thing bought off the shelf. But a custom job is built to last decades, so it's an investment you'll make only once. Additionally, quality framers prioritize conservation—a painting by Gerhard Richter and a doodle by your kinder-gartener are both irreplaceable in their own way.

Robert Benrimon established Skyframe in 1983. Based in Chelsea, the hub of New York City's gallery scene, Skyframe caters to a number of its neighbors, for whom preservation is a vital concern. "If you bring me a baseball glove, I'll tell you to put it in a shadow box. If you bring me a silk screen, I'll tell you to put it in a floating box frame. If you bring me a photograph, I'll tell you to mat it. The most important thing is to protect the artwork," says Benrimon.

Beyond the demands of the piece itself, there are several factors Benrimon recommends thinking about when working with a custom framer. There's the question of environment—where you live and where the finished product will end up. A photograph destined for a sunny wall in an oceanside home may require something more protective than a photo to be hung on an interior wall in a city apartment.

He also recommends understanding every component of the frame, so you know what you're paying for—and why. From the outside, both glass and Plexiglas can be coated to protect against ultraviolet light. From the inside, a quality framer can use pocket corners to secure the piece, as opposed to an adhesive that might harm the artwork. Additionally, there are interior mats and backings, ideally made of acid-free paper, and finally, the factor of how the frame is sealed—a tight closure protects against moisture.

Objects are often more powerfully displayed when framed in shadow boxes rather than organized on a flat surface. Case in point: in his former Manhattan townhouse, designer Steven Sclaroff hung his collection of framed nineteenth-century chrome splints above the dining table.

# The Art of Hanging

ONCE YOUR ARTWORK IS FRAMED, THE ONLY THING THAT REMAINS is to mount it on the wall. It may seem as simple as grabbing a nail, a hammer, and, if you're feeling precise, a pencil. To be sure, hanging a picture is one of those tasks that even the inveterate outsourcer might feel confident about tackling herself, but for those who fear mangling walls or want to get that painting hung just right, an art installer's expertise can be valuable.

Galleries, interior designers, and non-DIY types rely on installers like New York's ILevel Art Placement + Installation. ILevel's David Kassel explains why a homeowner might seek out his services: "People subscribe to the cliché of the painting over the sofa without thinking creatively about what they have, or what might look unexpected, or more provocative, and cause others to actually look at what's on their walls." Kassel and his team are happy to hang your painting above the sofa, but when you hire an art installer, you're hiring a fresh set of eyes—and an expert one at that. Kassel takes the task of hanging family photos in a hallway as seriously as he would hanging Cindy Shermans in a gallery. "Many people call us and say, 'We don't have anything important,'" says Kassel. "But their things are important—they're important to them."

An expert installer can't offer any real takeaway tips, because the job is always done within the specific parameters of the art and the room in which it's to be hung. Furthermore, though he certainly relies on his experience, Kassel reckons a big part of the installer's task is instinct. "How do you know when you've added too much salt to a hamburger?" says Kassel. "You just feel your way through it. We have to take color into consideration—how people have painted their walls, hung their wallpaper. We have an intuitive design sense of proportion and spacing." Kassel concedes that might sound simple. "If homeowners have a strong sense of space and design, they could do this on their own if they wanted to," he says. "There's nothing technically impossible about hanging pictures on the wall if you have a tape measure and a ruler."

In this London entryway, black-and-white prints are hung with less than an inch of space between each work, an effect that enhances the dramatic gridding seen on the painted floor and antique glass doors.

Manhattan shopkeeper and noted antiques collector Federico de Vera's living room wall is an ode to his love of portraiture—both old and new. Nineteenth-century works are hung in gilded frames, while modern paintings are left frameless.

# The Salon Wall

HANGING ONE PICTURE ON A WALL IS A SIMPLE ENOUGH FEAT, BUT mounting multiple pieces on a single surface—achieving successful spacing and proportion between elements, and coherence as a whole collage—is a more complex endeavor. This collage technique is called a "salon wall," and it's a popular and powerful motif.

The notion of the salon wall can be traced back to the Renaissance form of the cabinet of curiosities (or *Kunstkammer* or *Wunderkammer* in German), a specific means of displaying collections in a dedicated room (in this sense, the collection filled a whole room, so "cabinet" refers to a space, not a piece of furniture). The walls and often ceilings of a room were used to show off paintings, relics, natural history oddities, all manner of treasures—and the "cabinet," in turn, reflected its owner's greatness, his sophistication, his worldliness, his power. Within these rooms, works were displayed haphazardly, sometimes according to when they were acquired. The effect was an assemblage, not an organized structure.

This way of hanging art—loose, casual, deliberately imperfect—has come in and out of fashion over the ensuing centuries. The Salon de Paris was a biannual exhibition showcasing the work of students from France's École des Beaux-Arts that opened to the public in 1737. Installed in the Louvre, the exhibition featured works crammed against one another in a dazzling mishmash. This particular method of hanging art became the Salon's signature (and was in turn documented in many paintings). Centuries later, Gertrude Stein and her brother Leo hung their astonishing collection of modern art in much the same way at their home in Paris.

This style of displaying art evolved into today's take on the salon wall, which can feature a snapshot alongside a flea market paint by number, a vintage rock poster next to a repro Dürer print, an Elizabeth Peyton portrait next to your grandparents' wedding invitation. "It's very popular right now," says David Kassel. "Salon walls of family photos and knickknacks—just totally mixed-up stuff. You could frame your child's photo and hang it across from a Picasso, and I think that's great. What matters is what it looks like, not whether it's a Louise Bourgeois or your child's drawing."

A common tactic to building a salon wall is to lay all the framed pieces on the floor, arrange and rearrange them, and, once you're happy, trace their outlines onto butcher paper, transfer that map onto the wall, and hang

Amid rows of white frames, adding an occasional black frame keeps the eye moving across the wall, breaking up the collection just enough that each and every piece gets noticed.

them accordingly. David Kassel proceeds differently, though. "We can see a group of pictures lying on the floor and know about how much space they'll cover just by glancing at them, and just get to work, as if it were a game of solitaire."

Designers appreciate the salon wall technique as a way to both showcase a collection and transform a room. "If you have enough art to hang all the way up to the ceiling, it adds verticality but it also creates compositions within a composition," says interior designer Steven Gambrel.

Having a cohesive strategy helps unify the visual. "I like the frames to be different from one another," Gambrel says. "I think the frames should have unique profiles, but in order to work together on the wall, the frames should be finished in a similar color palette or stain." Thus seascapes in a range of blues would complement one another well, even if they're quite distinct stylistically. "Artfully hung groupings may not look planned, but they're extremely planned," he says. "It's important that one hang big-, medium-, and small-sized works with both vertical and horizontal images together. The variety of size and shape is what makes the collection work as a whole."

Gambrel cites a salon arrangement on the wall above a staircase in the Westchester home of Brooke Astor, the famed doyenne of New York society. Astor's wall showcased an impressive collection of dog paintings. "The stylish thing about Brooke Astor's art-hanging technique was that she combined paintings regardless of their value," says Gambrel, relaying an anecdote shared with him by Bunny Williams, who was Astor's decorator. "She would acquire a really important painting and then on the way home from wherever, run into a tag sale and see a painting of a dog, which she'd buy and nail up."

**OPPOSITE** › On the walls of Kate and Andy Spade's Manhattan foyer, dozens of framed pieces—components of a collection that the tastemakers have been building for decades—greet visitors to the home. Kate is the founder of the fashion label that bears her name, and Andy is the founder of Jack Spade and the branding agency Partners & Spade. Their ever-growing assortment is as creatively eccentric as the industries they work in and includes pieces by Andy Warhol, Elizabeth Peyton, and a lot of work by friends—all of which move from room to room and wall to wall at the slightest whim of the homeowners.

**FOLLOWING PAGES** › Andy cites the Barnes Foundation, a Philadelphia-based museum, as inspiration for the way in which his own collection is showcased. The museum eschews the typical curatorial practice of arranging works chronologically, or by geographic origin or style. Rather, everything is positioned in what the institution terms "ensembles"—assemblages that incorporate art and artifacts; mini salon walls, if you will. In the Spades' home, that juxtaposition is seen in the interaction between the hung works and the furnishings and architectural details that surround them.

# RECOGNIZING THE MAJOR PLAYERS
## *Framing*

### 1 > ILEVEL ART PLACEMENT + INSTALLATION

When artist David Kassel launched New York–based ILevel three decades ago, he hoped to improve the beauty of art through installation. ILevel, with a staff of artists and art historians, provide handling, placement, and installation services for corporations, residences, retail venues, and other spaces, focusing on how and where a piece can complement the individual interior.

### 2 > SKYFRAME

Skyframe, manufacturers of picture frames and store displays—with all work done in the United States—was founded in 1983 to provide high-end custom framing to Soho, New York, art galleries and artists. Today Skyframe services not only the art world but also the interior design and fashion industries.

### 3 > ELI WILNER & COMPANY

Eli Wilner & Company specializes in American and European frames from the fifteenth century to the present. CEO Eli Wilner is a dealer, restorer, collector, and leading authority on the art of framing whose résumé includes constructing frames for more than ten thousand paintings for private collectors and museums, including the Metropolitan Museum of Art and the White House.

### 4 > LARSON-JUHL

Century-old custom framers Larson-Juhl offers environmentally friendly, American-made products in a variety of classic and contemporary styles for different price points, as well as high-end water-gilded moldings from its Senelar, France, atelier.

### 5 > GK FRAMING GROUP LTD.

Elizabeth Goldfeder's interest in paper conservation led her firm, Goldfeder/Kahan Framing Group, to become an innovator in archival framing, particularly in its use of cutting-edge conservation technology. The firm expanded to produce period carved and gilded frames, as well as contemporary styles. GK Framing Group prides itself on the superior service it grants to both children's art and museum-quality works.

### 6 > LOWY

Lowy, founded as a small New York shop in 1907 by Julius Lowy, is today a national leader in a range of services, including custom framing and framing retail; painting, paper, and framing conservation; photography; collaborating on architectural and interior design details; and curation. Lowy has an inventory of more than 5,000 antique frames from the sixteenth to twentieth centuries culled from across Europe and the United States, the world's largest such collection.

OPPOSITE › The truest sign of well-executed framing is when the frame itself becomes visually inseparable from the art it surrounds, a treatment that's become a signature of high-end design duo Gilles & Boissier.

THIS PAGE › Above his living room sofa, designer Miles Redd hung an assortment of gilded frames (some ornate, some traditional), creating cohesiveness in his varied art collection.

# *floors*

Most casual decorators think of the floors as a given—something you might cover with a rug, or whitewash if you're feeling adventurous, but otherwise as fixed as the ground beneath our feet. Most professional decorators don't distinguish architecture from design, however. Floors are an aspect of our homes we might take for granted, but they can shape and affect the character of a room.

# *wood*

Our homes provide the fundamental human need for shelter. But retaining a connection to the world around us is important. Natural materials and textures play a vital (if sometimes overlooked) role in creating a home, and incorporating wood floors is one of the most effective ways to bring the elemental into our everyday environments.

The type of wood we choose, the finish we apply, even the way in which we arrange each individual plank on the floor, has an impact on the overall aesthetics of a space—especially in terms of scale and flow. Too dark a stain can visually shrink a room, just as too narrow a plank can create choppiness.

You may not notice them on a regular basis, but strong wood floors are the foundation—in both the literal and figurative sense—of a successful space.

The author installed reclaimed European oak floors from Amsterdam in her Manhattan apartment, choosing a waxed finish—instead of stain—to bring out the natural gray-green color of the wood.

# FROM THE PAST TO THE PRESENT
## *The Unique History of Wood*

### 17TH CENTURY

Wide wood planks have become the quotidian material for floors in European and American homes. However, by the late 1600s, some extremely elaborate wood floors are installed in the closets of French royal palaces.

### EARLY 20TH CENTURY

Tongue-and-groove floorboards become the most popular material for European and American homes. In grand homes, wood parquetry is used as borders around carpets. The herringbone pattern becomes one of the most sought after parquetry applications of this time.

### 1880s

With the introduction of steam-powered machinery, factories begin to mill dense hardwoods, like oak and maple, in large quantities. Construction innovations, such as tongue-and-groove joints and blind nailing, provide for a more sophisticated appearance and durable surface. Varnishes made from tung oil are also introduced from China.

### 18TH CENTURY

Polished parquet floors become the most fashionable floor treatment for the Parisian elite.

### 1950s

Carpeting replaces wood as the flooring application of choice. Many wood flooring companies begin to produce carpet in order to stay in business or lower production standards. As a result, wood flooring, especially basic parquet square installations, is cheapened and devalued.

### 1980s

Innovations in prefinished techniques cause a resurgence of wood flooring in the home. By the 1990s, wood becomes the most favored floor material once again.

### 2000s

Reclaimed wood flooring becomes fashionable as a design trend, as well as part of the green design movement.

### 1920s AND '30s

Wood floors come into competition with linoleum and cork materials that require less maintenance. However, with innovations in varnishes and polyurethane, wood floors become increasingly easier to clean.

# The History of Wood Floors

WOOD HAS ALWAYS BEEN A PLENTIFUL RESOURCE IN THIS COUNTRY—never more so than when the nation was in its infancy. That meant even rudimentary Colonial-era homes could have wooden instead of earthen floors. Culturally, Americans for generations thereafter associated wood with floors, until the postwar era, when linoleum and wall-to-wall carpeting became the height of fashion. For a time, carpeting was installed directly atop finished wood flooring—as many a happy renovator has discovered—but eventually inexpensive plywood covered by carpeting supplanted hardwood.

Now, hardwood flooring is again in demand. Technologically speaking, our floors could be made of anything these days, but somehow floors made of wood planks just feel right. They ground our homes, quite literally, in the natural world, and bring a warmth and character to a space that we respond to almost on a subconscious level.

"A wood floor is going to be there for the life of a home," says Milton Goodwin of Armstrong, one of the nation's largest flooring manufacturers. Goodwin points out that the typical home-building process focuses on costly necessities. Décor is a lower priority, and thinking about that sometimes doesn't even begin until late in a project, when budgets and patience are exhausted. This explains why so many new homes or renovation projects involve some compromise when it comes to floors.

"The quality of a wood floor starts with the grade of the wood you're buying. A lower grade of wood will have more knots, more checks, more cracks," says Goodwin. There's a parallel between wood and marble; the industry makes a quality distinction that might not be in line with your personal taste. Flawlessness isn't for everyone, and the natural character of a wood with lots of knots doesn't necessarily mean the floor is of lower quality. "What nature gives me when I cut a tree down and turn it into a wood floor," says Goodwin, "you may think is the most beautiful floor ever made."

Finding the floor that's the most beautiful is a question of considering the wood species and its natural markings, as well as the wood lot and its inherent imperfections, the length and width of the boards, and the finished floor's color. Weighing its quality—its durability as well as its aesthetic value—comes from understanding all of the above.

When architect Steven Harris and interior designer Lucien Rees Roberts restored a fifteenth-century vacation home in Croatia, maximizing flow within the existing floor plan took top priority. To that end, they installed rustic planks in a continuous wall-to-wall length.

# How It's Made

A GREAT WOOD FLOOR BEGINS, OF COURSE, WITH GREAT WOOD. Stephen Estrin, of the New York City floor builder I. J. Peiser's Sons, is so concerned about using the best wood that he largely ignores the industry standards. "We do not abide by the national grading system for oak, walnut, maple, or any species," he says. "A select grade of oak allows for a certain amount of mineral streaks, sapwood, and knots within a given square footage of flooring. That is unacceptable to us as well as our clients."

This natural variation is only the starting point; a floor's look is informed by the wood's color, its grains and knots, the length of the boards. This has a lot to do with Mother Nature, but not exclusively. "Many components go into beautiful flooring," says Estrin. "Milling, color grain, length of the planks, etc. Although sometimes you don't really have to break it down like that. You can simply look at it and see it is beautiful."

But raw wood would not work on our floors, of course; the wood is treated to ensure its longevity and achieve a certain look. This task is one Estrin's firm handles in-house, though the flooring components at most retailers come already treated. "We generally do not use prefinished floors," says Estrin. "The finishes that are typically used often have an 'industrial strength' quality to them. They may never scratch, but they are hideous. Depending on the project, the species of wood we're working with, and the client, we'll use an array of finishes, such as alcohol- and aniline-based dyes and tung oils. The dyes will allow you to do special, deeply rich colors, and the oil gives the finish a less plastic feel."

"To be really good at making hardwood flooring, you have to be really good at drying wood," says Armstrong's Milton Goodwin. At his company, the process takes sixteen weeks, but it's a vital step. "If you don't dry wood properly, you'll have all types of issues—bowed, crooked, and cracked wood. And if the finish is put on before it's dried properly, you'll get defects—moisture will show up as white spots on the wood. A lot of bad things can happen if the wood is not dried."

1 › When a tree is cut down, it's typically transported to a sawmill where the preparation for shipment to a flooring manufacturer differs. Some major mills leave a tree's bark on to allow individual flooring manufacturers greater flexibility in determining a plank's final width. 2 › In contrast, other sawmills will strip the bark before slicing a tree into planks, as seen here. 3 › Once cut, flooring planks are sorted by wood grade and size, then shipped to their final destination via highly organized pallets.

1

2

3

Exotic panga-panga wood flooring is used throughout a renovated 1960s London bungalow, echoing the richly restored paneled walls and ceilings.

# The Aesthetics of Wood Floors

AESTHETICALLY, THE PRIMARY VARIABLE, AND IN ALL LIKELIHOOD the trait that makes you opt for one wood over another, is obvious: "Ultimately, color is king," says Howard Montgomery, Armstrong's creative design director. And not simply the color of the floor; the color of the rest of the space. "It's about the composition—how this color works with my cabinetry, my countertops, my furniture." With wood floors as with any other industrial product, consistency is a concern: You want a subtle spectrum of color across a floor, but not a kaleidoscope effect. As nature contains a variety of hues, this requires some intervention by the manufacturer. "The color gets put onto the surface of the wood," says Montgomery. "Then it gets treated and coated on top of that to seal the color, and to layer and coat the actual wood itself." Montgomery advises taking home as many samples as possible, looking at different finishes and distinct colors, and living with those options much as you might a test coat of paint on a wall.

Beyond color, you'll also want to consider how a given wood will perform in the climate in which you live, and whether it's tough enough for a certain kind of room. "Your choice of species has dramatically increased," says Montgomery. "It's no longer just oak. You're seeing now more hickory, a lot of maple, cherry." Again, standards and grades are assigned to the wood available to the consumer to help navigate these factors—just remember that those are the salient questions to ask a retailer.

A final consideration is the plank size itself; widths can vary from two to seven inches and beyond, and a similar spectrum of lengths is available. Consider that a manufacturer can cut around flaws and still yield a two-inch-wide plank; when the width is greater, it's less forgiving of imperfection. Thus, wider planks will almost always be made of a more flawless wood. Cutting a very long floorboard also requires a large piece of source wood; you're using more material so that's going to be more expensive. And again, a long cut of wood with no flaws will be harder to find, and priced commensurately.

**OPPOSITE AND ABOVE ›** Like paint, floor finishes come in multiple sheens—matte, satin, semigloss, and glossy—and have just as much decorative sway as the stain selection itself. Take these two spaces, both with identical dark wood stains: the room above has a satin finish and feels very low-key and contemporary, while the room opposite has a glossy sheen that's far more grand.

Caroline Legrand's London apartment had not been touched for nearly forty years when she stumbled upon it. The large, lateral space got little light but was resplendent with period architecture, specifically the refined herringbone floors, which she stained an inky hue. Rather than detract from the dark elegance of the apartment, the interior designer amplified it by painting the walls black and taking a glamorous approach to the furnishings and art she carefully (and lovingly) chose to fill her home.

# Engineered Wood

THOUGH ARMSTRONG AND OTHER SUPPLIERS STILL PRODUCE BASIC planks of wood, technology has yielded entirely new forms, like engineered wood. This is not to be confused with the much-maligned laminate—the cheap stuff you can buy off the rack at most home retailers, which doesn't bear much of a resemblance to real wood. "Engineered wood is solid wood veneer on top of a substrate, typically plywood," says Milton Goodwin. "Laminate is high-density fiberboard, with a picture on top of it, and a melamine wear layer on top of that. Engineered wood is a natural product; every piece will be uniquely different. The width and length will vary, because it's cut just like real wood. Laminate will have a repeat in the design, and it is not wood; it is a photographic image applied to HDF."

Goodwin points out that most bamboo flooring is engineered wood. Bamboo (which is a grass) is usually a veneer affixed to a plywood base. "Engineered wood is made by taking oak, maple, cherry, whatever species," says Goodwin, "and then rotary peeling that tree, like a roll of paper towels. You have a top layer that is real wood, and then the substrate is plywood, and the bottom layer is usually the same as the top layer, because you want a stable structure."

With engineered wood floors, like this Brushed Oak Kalispell by Kentwood, the lower the gloss level of the finish, the more closely it resembles solid wood.

# The Look of Wood

WOOD FLOORS CAN BE ELABORATE CONSTRUCTIONS OR SIMPLE STATEments. Parquetry has its roots in France, and involves the creation of pattern by interlocking and overlaying pieces of wood, almost like a jigsaw puzzle. On the opposite end of the spectrum is the understated, natural look that's closely associated with the interior design of Scandinavia and Northern Europe, which celebrates the simplicity of the unadorned wood.

"With the Scandinavian look," says Belgian interior designer Gert Voorjans, known for his eclectic flair in blending European antiques and global influences, "the bareness, the knots, come more into focus, because we treat the floor like a furnishing." Voorjans notes that the form has particularly deep roots in his hometown of Antwerp, a port city where wood was always plentiful. "Before, floors were purely practical," Voorjans says. "Today's wooden floors you appreciate as a decorative element. Before, there were carpets, sofas, and lots of chairs, and floors were just a practical building element. I think now we appreciate more of the beauty."

What Voorjans is talking about isn't minimalism; it's a reinterpretation. Floors that once seemed rustic or rough-hewn now seem the height of sophistication. "We see the trend of washing and cleaning floors to make them more blond. It feels younger than classical parquetry, which was more traditional, often a chestnut or walnut color," explains Voorjans. Perhaps this reevaluation of floors reflects a larger cultural embrace of the authentic, the humble. "Twenty years ago there was a lot of wall-to-wall carpet," he says. "Now we prefer more simplicity, more roughness. People do not want any more of those cheap, look-alike woods. We want things to have much more character."

The conundrum is that achieving this understated look can be a significant investment, demanding the very best wood. Voorjans points out the question of cost per use. If you love to cook, he says, buy an expensive stove, but don't worry about your cabinets—those can always be upgraded later. Using this equation, of course, you shouldn't be troubled if your floor is the most expensive thing in your home, because you'll use it every single day.

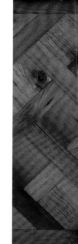

The artisans at I. J. Peiser's Sons, a New York flooring institution for more than a century, are especially gifted at restoring detailed antique parquetry work, as showcased by this impressive display of their projects.

# Reclaimed Wood

IT'S A TESTAMENT TO WOOD'S INHERENT DURABILITY THAT THERE'S an entire industry—albeit a young and fairly small one—dedicated to harvesting and rehabilitating wood from abandoned buildings. "Reclaimed" wood, as it's called, has in recent years seen a boom in popularity that supports Gert Voorjans's assertion: "Modern consumers are interested in floors that celebrate the material's very essence."

These days, dealers who exclusively handle reclaimed wood have a niche but steady market. Jim Stafford runs San Francisco–based Restoration Timber, which transforms old beams into raw material for a new generation of floors. "'Reclaimed' used to mean someone taking down their old barn and using it as paneling in their living room," says Stafford. "It has been around a long time, but I think the aesthetic really took off with the computer age, because people wanted more texture, something that is more real in their homes. You spend your day in a cubicle, and it is so cold and so harsh, and you want to go home to something that is a little bit more human and soft."

The bulk of the wood that Restoration Timber deals in comes from barns across the Midwest and Northeast. It's typically beams—pieces large enough that they can be chopped into floorboards. Transforming this wood into planks requires some refinement, including reshaping them to include tongues and grooves, the structures on the planks' sides. One plank's tongue snaps into its neighbor's groove; this is what holds the floor together. "We will take the beams, re-mill them into flooring planks, and kiln-dry them, and then we'll get them into the hands of a flooring installer. They customize it, hand-scrape it, stain it," says Stafford.

The entire process is analogous to recycling, but Stafford and other fine dealers aren't simply selling everything they find in the field. "Reclaimed white oak is our number one product," he says. "We identify only one type of reclaimed oak that we're willing to work with: Northern reclaimed white oak. The Northern climate makes a much denser growth tree. It also preserves the wood better, because the cold kills the bugs every winter."

Restoration Timber has no use for the smaller wood elements in an old building from which it might be harvesting. "We concentrate on the length of a floor," says Stafford. "The longer the boards, the more old-world and luxurious a floor feels."

**OPPOSITE** › The original blond pine floors of Gert Voorjans's own parlor in Antwerp are left bare in the Scandinavian style, a look that suits his eccentric (and colorful) collection of antiques.

**ABOVE** › Instead of dismantling an old barn and repurposing its wood, this family moved the *entire* nineteenth-century structure from Canada to Connecticut, turning it into a sprawling weekend home with all the original, rustic floors intact and beautifully refinished.

Though the wood is treated before it becomes your floor, it would still fail to pass muster if subjected to the standards applied to new manufactured wood flooring. "We think of reclaimed wood as perfectly imperfect," says Stafford. "You feel the history through the use marks, through the nail holes with their ancient oxidation, the fact that the wood is so much older, with a super-tight grain and the different colors that come through from time and use. All of that stuff is rejected in the new-wood world."

In addition to its attractiveness, reclaimed wood is a smart investment because of its durability. "With reclaimed wood, your performance is going to be better than with any new wood," says Stafford. "It is older growth and it is much more dense. The wood has been dry and has done all of its movement for the last hundred years, so the wood is oxidized in a way that actually makes it harder."

For the renovator who still believes that the newest always equals the best, Stafford points to a recent development: engineered reclaimed wood, in which the central structure of wood pulp is overlaid with a thin layer of reclaimed lumber. It delivers the worn look with the solidity and durability of a brand-new product.

"My experience is that the floor is one of the first things that you feel, as a welcome mat to a home," says Stafford. The idea of barns may conjure images of centuries-old homesteads, but in fact, high-quality reclaimed wood wouldn't feel out of place in the most modern of homes. It's a means of honoring the past.

In Gert Voorjans's office, which is tucked away below his main living quarters, the well-worn finish on the narrow pitch-pine planks symbolizes a high-traffic space and lends rustic charm.

# DESIGN CHAMPION: *The Palace of Versailles*

VERSAILLES PARQUET, so called because of the groundbreaking use of the technique there, features geometric patterns that so charmed the tastemakers among the European elite that they were replicated in fine homes across the Continent. The term refers to a familiar pattern: large squares inset with smaller squares at an angle, which creates an effect that looks almost woven. It was originally called *parquet à la française* but was so closely associated with its use in Versailles, it eventually assumed the name. Of all the kinds of parquets, Versailles parquet remains, even centuries later, the best example of the overall form.

"Parquetry is a plain oak floor with a square pattern," says Anne Marie Quette, an academic who specializes in French design. "It's a square pattern element, but it makes a kind of jagged line, which gave a very nice proportion to very large rooms." It's hard to appreciate unless seen firsthand, but the way the lines of parquet panels interconnect across a room—whether a palatial one (like the Palace of Versailles, at left) or a smaller space (such as the sitting room in the Belgian castle below)—helps unify the space.

Historically, trends were disseminated a bit differently than in today's wired world. "From the mid-seventeenth century to the French Revolution, all of Europe found inspiration in Versailles," says Quette. "Versailles was open to the public, so a visitor from England or Germany could easily see the space." All that foot traffic took its toll, naturally, but an advantage of parquet flooring's tongue-and-groove construction was the replaceable dowels that held together the individual pieces on each panel; the floor could be touched up without being wholly thrown out. "Oak is very strong, but it can't last forever when you have a million visitors," says Quette. The original floors endure in some parts of the building, but mostly what today's visitors find is a twentieth-century reproduction created in the same manner as the original.

## RECOGNIZING THE MAJOR PLAYERS
# *Wood Floors*

### 1 > BRUCE

The century-old brand, which sources most of its products from the Appalachian Mountains, focuses on producing and selling high-quality, meticulously inspected hardwoods with few streaks or knots, clear grain, and consistent color in a variety of shades and wood species at affordable prices.

### 2 > MIRAGE FLOORS

Based in Quebec, Canada, Mirage Floors is often voted by industry professionals and trade magazines as one of North America's top hardwood flooring brands. Unlike other manufacturers, Mirage uses a dry saw cutting method for its engineered floors, showcasing natural grains while providing uniformity and durability.

### 3 > ARMSTRONG

This time-tested, nationally recognized company began manufacturing hardwood floors in 1946, specializing in an original parquet style. Today Armstrong prides itself on parquet, strip, and plank floors created with various woods, grains, patterns, colors, and finishes.

### 4 > SOMERSET FLOORS

Somerset Floors offers more than 150 styles of residential prefinished solid and engineered flooring, which the company manufactures from forest to floorboard. With lumber sourced from the Appalachian Mountains, Somerset's Made-in-the-USA flooring is known for its high grade and commitment to sustainable forestry practices.

### 5 > PID FLOORS

Family-owned PID Floors, based in New York and Connecticut, was established in 1989. The full-service hardwood flooring company is devoted both to high-quality products, offering traditional and contemporary styles, and high-quality service.

### 6 > LV WOOD

The brother-and-sister team behind this New York–based flooring atelier inherited the family business from their parents and quickly repositioned it as a leader in the sustainable flooring field. LV Wood goes above and beyond to ensure that its selection of high-quality hardwoods comes exclusively from the United States and the Netherlands, never from a rain forest.

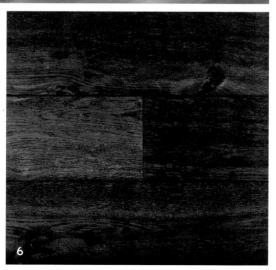

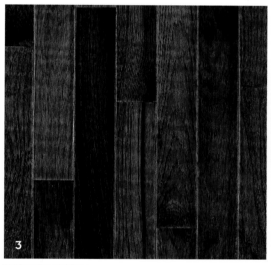

**1** › Narrow-plank bleached wood floors are a nod to Old Hollywood in the Los Angeles home of stylist-turned–interior designer Estee Stanley. **2** › To save the exotic panga-panga wood from eventual fading, the flooring in this modern indoor-outdoor living space received an extra, durable layer that helps reflect the sun. **3** › A Brooklyn triplex marries sleek contemporary architecture with matte dusty-gray floors for a striking cross between modern and organic designs. **4** › Floors by the experts at I. J. Peiser's Sons complete a Richard Meier–designed spiral staircase in a Manhattan penthouse.

**5** › Ebony floors have an almost glasslike finish in the elegant old-world entry of Tessa Neleman-Pimontel and Hans Neleman. **6** › Painted inlaid "boxes" accentuate and elevate the dark detailed parquetry in designer Miles Redd's living room.
**7** › In a kitchen designed by Katie Ridder, pale wood planks alternate with dark wood planks, emphasizing the room's luxurious length. **8** › In such a texturally layered living room—like the Neleman-Pimontels'—glossy, light-reflecting floors create a sense of airiness.

# *stone*

Consider the unlikely fact that the Taj Mahal—one of humankind's most graceful accomplishments—is made of the same material found in high-end kitchens and bathrooms. Marble, once prized by artists, is now prized by artisans as the gold standard for kitchen countertops and bathroom floors.

Choosing a marble or other stone for the home requires knowing the material's natural properties—its strength, its resistance to water—as well as learning the many aesthetic variations that nature provides, and understanding the ways in which skill and technology can improve on this raw material.

An all-purpose entryway with grand details, this soaring room blends a honeycomb-patterned marble floor with speckled travertine walls, so the homeowners need very few furnishings to complete the space.

# The Unique History of Stone

### 2584 BC

Construction begins on the Great Pyramids and Great Sphinx of Giza, for which limestone is transported across the Nile by boat to the desert.

### 1163–1250 AD

Notre Dame Cathédral, the finest example of French Gothic architecture, is built out of cut stone on an island in the Seine River in Paris.

### 15TH AND 16TH CENTURIES

Marble becomes the prominent building material for the grand rooms of Italian and French palaces, most impressively at Louis XV's Versailles.

### 500 BC

Greek and Roman civilizations build large structures, primarily to house images of the gods, using limestone and other local stone varieties. Perhaps the most famous stone building, the Parthenon, is constructed out of Pentelic marble and limestone.

### 17TH AND 18TH CENTURIES

British trading ships carry sandstone to America, where the material is exchanged for cotton and becomes the prominent material used for constructing buildings and roads.

## 1850

A massive storm in Scotland results in the unexpected excavation of Skara Brae, a prehistoric village located near the white beach of the Bay of Skaill. Because the village had been covered for nearly 5,000 years, it is considered one of the best-preserved groups of prehistoric stone houses in Western Europe.

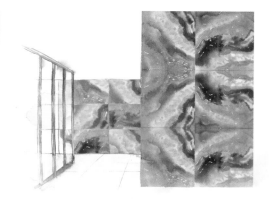

## 1925

Art Deco designers such as Émile-Jacques Ruhlmann showcase exotic stones in their furnishings at the Exposition Internationale des Arts Décoratifs et Industriels Modernes in Paris. Four years later, Ludwig Mies van der Rohe designs the Barcelona Pavilion for the 1929 International Exposition in Barcelona where his building becomes known for its awe-inspiring use of marble, red onyx, and travertine.

## 1980s

Japanese-inspired interiors become popular in America, and designers incorporate stones and pebbles to evoke a Zenlike quality.

## 19TH CENTURY

Industrial methods allow for new techniques in stone fabrication, such as veneering, which renders stone more available as a building material.

## 1958

Vowing to clean up the "slum of legs" that traditional furniture had, Eero Saarinen debuts his Pedestal Collection featuring a streamlined marble-top table that is now a design icon.

## TODAY

Designers continue to use stone as a building material, specifically for bathrooms, kitchens, and fireplace mantels, while employing newer technologies like LED lighting to enhance stone's natural beauty.

Old wood paneling was removed to unveil original, almost two-foot-thick limestone walls in Steven Harris and Lucien Rees Roberts's restored fifteenth-century Croatian villa.

# The Look of Marble

STONE IS A VERY BIG CATEGORY, INTO WHICH FALL SO MANY FORMS that are popular in interior design. Even marble, perhaps the most beloved of stones, encompasses many different types of stone harvested at points across the planet, each with its own signature characteristics. Marble is no longer strictly the province of quarries—you can buy it at almost every big-box retailer—though specialists and retailers affiliated closely with actual quarries tend to have a greater expertise in the form.

"If I'm looking at marble, I'm looking for beauty and for soundness," says Vermont Quarries Corporation's Todd Robertson. "There are no cracks or fissures in the material." Buying from a quarry, which will understand and enforce its own standards before sending the results into the market, is safer than buying at retail, where the stone might have passed through the hands of a couple of middlemen before ending up on the shelf.

"Stone was formed over millions of years," says Nancy Epstein, founder of the New York–based Artistic Tile. "There are ranges of color, but there is no one authority that deems what is acceptable and what is not acceptable. It is an aesthetic judgment call." A luxury brand like Artistic Tile enforces a strict standard on your behalf—what you're paying for isn't just the product, it's the work of ensuring that you are sold only the best. "We very carefully vet our suppliers," says Epstein. "Before they ship anything, they have to take photographs of the shipments, we all have to approve of those photographs before we'll release for shipping. When it gets here, a guy in the warehouse doesn't check it in. A senior executive of this company must do the physical inspection."

The process is painstaking, and involves unpacking about seven thousand square feet of tile and examining each piece under color-corrected lighting to ensure uniformity of color and pattern and suss out subtle imperfections. "You can get bad finishing, where you see wheel marks, the edges aren't polished well, things are actually out of square," says Epstein, meaning there might be damage to the tile during the cutting process, or the occasional specimen that's not the shape it should be. Not all dealers apply such a rigorous litmus test. Pieces of stone that would be rejected as unacceptable by luxury dealers because of their coloration or other physical flaws still find their way to the market.

Though distinctions in quality determine what ends up on the shelves

Hand-cut and -laid rainbow, honey onyx, cappuccino, and Calacatta marble segments were utilized in this decadent Kelly Wearstler–designed Bel Air foyer.

at a home-improvement store and what's destined for the luxury dealer's showroom, it is all still marble. If you have to shop at the retail level, Epstein advises taking a hands-on approach: "Open up boxes and see if what's in one box has anything to do with something in another box," she says. "Move the tile around to see if the polishing is decent. Check to see if there's a finely beveled edge." If you can't pay the premium for an expert eye, at least try to understand the material enough to use your own best judgment.

Though its properties make stone an ideal surface in utilitarian rooms like the kitchen or the bath, by no means should it be strictly limited to these hardworking spaces. "So many people use faux stones, synthetic stones, and I just do not," says interior designer Kelly Wearstler. Wearstler employed stone to great effect in her own Beverly Hills home; elaborately veined stones are set in the walls of the master suite. "Mother Nature is the best designer. Real stone installed on the walls just has richness and importance."

Epstein concurs. "You can get a sapphire or you can get a piece of blue glass," she says. "The difference is in the emotion. And stone has emotion." It's important to weigh cost against use in any expenditure, and with stone it's especially salient. "You don't want somebody to say in twenty years, 'Hmm, time for that to go.' You want somebody to love it forever," says Epstein. "Stone will last forever. It has been man's building material since antiquity. The pyramids are still there."

Completely ahead of its time, this T. H. Robsjohn-Gibbings-designed living room from 1953 utilized full, uncut slabs of marble across the floor and up one statement wall.

# The Properties of Marble

STONE AND MARBLE QUALITY DEPENDS ON MORE THAN PRESENTA-tion, of course; performance is key. "I'm also looking beyond the visible," says Vermont Quarries's Todd Robertson, discussing his selection process. "Knowing the physical characteristics of a stone is important. Stone is a very precarious material."

We think of stone as having permanence, strength—so it's odd to hear it described as precarious. But there are ways to measure a stone's quality, and these aren't subjective distinctions. Stone is rated on an internationally accepted scale set by the American Society for Testing and Materials International (ASTM). If you're shopping a mass retailer, look for the ASTM rating, which will explain how the material performs according to various measures like porosity and flexibility. Based on those measures, this rating will indicate what uses the stone is suitable for.

Always look for specific details, whether in the ASTM measurements or other product information. "Every stone on the market is measured for compressive strength, which is hardness; flexural strength, which tells you if the material bends; scratch resistance; and absorption, which is one of the most important characteristics, aside from aesthetics," says Robertson. To help put the abstract compressive strength measurement into context, marbles typically score between eight thousand and fifteen thousand pounds per square inch (psi), telling you how much force it can withstand before shattering. The pressure of a high-heeled shoe is seven thousand to eight thousand psi; a hammer generates about fifteen thousand psi.

The stone's absorption rate tells you how the stone interacts with liquids, obviously significant if you're dealing with a kitchen or bath. "A marble counter that has a high absorption rate can work," says Robertson. "But you have to treat it and seal it more often than you would other materials. No matter what you do, you're probably going to get stains. Now, if you can live with a used, patinated look—and some people can—then you have no problems. But it is best to utilize a material that starts with a low absorption, much like building a house with a strong foundation."

To further complicate the task of choosing a stone, there are several different types of marble. What seem like brand names—from Danby, Vermont, alone there are eight types, including Imperial, Eureka, Royal, and Montclair—actually refer to specific categories, differentiated usually

In addition to the physical characteristics Todd Robertson suggests noting, veteran installers recommend researching where a stone is obtained—especially if you're eager to have marble in a bathroom. Typically, the closer to Italy and Greece a stone is sourced, the better it holds up in a wet environment.

**OPPOSITE ›** Fashion designer Zang Toi used full slabs of Carrara marble—instead of cut tiles—along the floors and walls of his Manhattan bath for an effect that's both formal and elegant.

**LEFT ›** Designer Steven Gambrel employed a similar treatment in this Hamptons guest bathroom, blending beautifully veined marble slabs with modern chrome fixtures, which gives the space a far more traditional finish.

by color and the amount of veining in the stone. Find the look you love, but be sure to pay attention to all the ASTM numbers as well.

Another consideration is whether you're buying stone that has been treated. Marble is typically either honed (leaving it with a matte finish) or polished (resulting in a slick, glossy finish). "But some materials have been treated with dyes or epoxy resin," Robertson says, noting that these can pose challenges in terms of upkeep. "A marble or granite distributor is going to know if their materials have any kind of topical solution or dyes within, and that's something to be aware of, because it affects the care and maintenance."

Stone and marble seem like a simple fix—after all, you can't improve on nature. Still, Robertson adds, "customers think, 'I've got stone; it's going to last forever.' But marble can scratch and etch much easier than granite. The care and maintenance is a little bit more involved—but minimal; maybe resealing once a year, which is like polishing a piece of furniture."

# DESIGN CHAMPION: *Ludwig Mies van der Rohe*

IT'S THE RARE ARCHITECT whose name becomes an adjective; however, that's been the fate of the modernist titan Ludwig Mies van der Rohe, often referred to as Mies for simplicity, but with affection. Van der Rohe played a significant role in shaping the modern American city—ersatz imitations of his storied 860–880 Lake Shore Drive apartment complex in Chicago sprang up from coast to coast, and many buildings decades later still reference the clean, unadorned look of glass and steel that was his signature.

Van der Rohe also profoundly affected the way we design our interiors. Not merely as a designer of furniture—his Barcelona chair and couch are ubiquitous—but also in his approach to architecture and material, in particular the way he used stone.

The project that best demonstrates his unique approach is the Barcelona Pavilion (shown here), a structure truly deserving of the overused term "iconic." "I think it is accurate to say that Mies invented a new kind of use for natural stone," says Edward Windhorst, co-author, with Franz Schulze, of *Mies van der Rohe: A Critical Biography.* "He doesn't use stone in the traditional way, as masonry."

We read the architecture of the midcentury, often, as minimal, but that's not quite accurate. Van der Rohe distilled design to its essence, and celebrated structure as beautiful in and of itself. But his buildings were ornamented. "The onyx wall at the center of the Barcelona Pavilion," says Windhorst, "is just slabs of beautiful stone that are attached to a steel frame. The joints are actually open. And you can see the wall on both sides; you can see the thickness of the material. It's not really minimalism; it's more abstraction." The building was disassembled shortly after construction, and then rebuilt in the 1980s, according to the same plans. Archival photographs support Windhorst's assertion—the space doesn't feel minimal; the stone has a beauty that's almost extravagant.

This use of stone as ornament feels as fresh today as it did decades ago; that same celebration of the material's beauty happens in Kelly Wearstler's California home. Van der Rohe valued the honesty of material.

# RECOGNIZING THE MAJOR PLAYERS
# *Stone*

### 1 > ABC STONE

Brooklyn-based ABC Stone offers a wide variety of stones—marble, onyx, limestone, granite, travertine, quartzite, semiprecious, and more. Styles include standard flat stone for tiling, mosaics, and cubic elements that can form bath fixtures. Additionally, ABC helps support sculptors, showcasing their art in its showroom.

### 2 > ASN NATURAL STONE, INC.

ASN Natural Stone was founded in San Francisco in 1992 as Alex Stone Network after owner Alex Sajkovic. The company specializes in custom, large-format architectural stonework for interiors and exteriors using marble, limestone, sandstone, basalt, gray quartzitic sandstone, and more.

### 3 > STONE SOURCE

Stone Source has exclusive relationships with quarries around the world and provides more than 150 material options in the categories of natural stone; porcelain, ceramic, and glass tile; engineered stone; and reclaimed wood. Founded in 1986, Stone Source is committed to keeping up with the times, and now offers twenty sustainable product lines.

### 4 > VERMONT QUARRIES CORPORATION

The Danby Marble quarry already had a century-old history of high-end production when Vermont Quarries Corporation took over in 1992. The company says the stone is "the most prestigious white marble produced in North America," and produces and distributes it for a range of needs, from kitchen counters to public monuments.

### 5 > STONEYARD

Stoneyard produces its specialty natural stone building material, a LEED-certified reclaimed New England fieldstone, as a thin veneer in five shapes—Round, Ledgestone, Ashlar, Square/Rectangular, and Mosaic—to be used on fireplaces, chimneys, and columns, as well as on exterior architecture.

### 6 > WALKER ZANGER

For more than sixty years, Walker Zanger has offered clients high-end marble and stone from specialty quarries around the world, each selected and evaluated by the company's award-winning stone masters. With a strong belief in hands-on production, from start to finish, the company offers everything from Moroccan ceramics to Italian stone mosaics to rare French marbles.

1 › Marble tiles line the floor and wrap a small ledge circling the Miami living room of artist Michele Oka Doner, serving as an elegant but minimal backdrop for her impressive collections. 2 › Streamlined modern fixtures in the bathroom of Steven Harris and Lucien Rees Roberts set off hand-scuffed terra-cotta floors and fifteenth-century limestone walls. 3 › Inspired by Dorothy Draper, designers Hillary Thomas and Jeff Lincoln contrasted a black-and-white marble floor by Ann Sacks with a traditional striped wallpaper from Farrow & Ball. 4 › Channeling her Parisian roots, designer Olatz Schnabel installed checked marble tiles on the floor and walls of her New York City master bathroom.

**5** › Combining the elegance of a French parlor with the ease of seaside living, Tracy Rochestie used unpolished black-and-white marble tiles throughout her Santa Barbara home. **6** › In a sprawling New Delhi estate, French designer Jean-Louis Deniot contrasts seductive, curving furniture with a graphic custom marble floor. **7** › Perforated marble "jali" screens, commissioned by Doris Duke in India in 1935, surround the Taj Mahal–inspired master bedroom of her remarkable Shangri La estate in Hawaii. **8** › Alexa Hampton designed a striking patterned marble floor in the formal hallway of a grand New Orleans estate.

# *tile*

"Tile" is a broad umbrella term that we use to refer to a bewildering number of things: colorful mosaics on the floors of Roman villas, ceramic ornaments unearthed in the deserts of Egypt and dating back millennia, the clean white surfaces of most bathrooms and kitchens.

Centuries ago, clay tiles were hand-formed and dried by the sun, ensuring that no two were ever perfectly alike—and therefore their use, in most cases, was purely decorative. Modern technology has given us factory-made tile: so easy, so reliable, so inexpensive, so uniform that tile is the material found in most institutional spaces today. It's often used in the same contexts as stone, and when shopping for tile, it's best to master the same information, to understand how it was created and how it will perform.

Casa Mollino in Turin, Italy, is the storied apartment of noted architect and designer Carlo Mollino, though he never actually lived in it. Every lavish detail, right down to the glazed Italian majolica floor tiles, was designed to be an extravagant backdrop for photo shoots.

# FROM THE PAST TO THE PRESENT
## *The Unique History of Tile*

### 5TH CENTURY BC

Assyrian tiles depicting the lion, the symbol of the goddess Ishtar, are used in architectural design.

### 1ST CENTURY BC

One of the most important architectural elements the Roman Empire produces is the mosaic tile floor, used in both domestic and public buildings.

### 12TH CENTURY

Persian buildings include elaborate tile brickwork that forms geometric patterns or Kufic inscriptions.

### 13TH CENTURY

Lashan, a city about 120 miles south of Tehran, becomes an extremely important tile-making center. Lashan's tiles are exported throughout Persia.

### 4000 BC

The Egyptians produce tiles with a turquoise-blue surface glaze that are used to decorate the doorjambs in the Step Pyramid at Saqqara, south of Cairo.

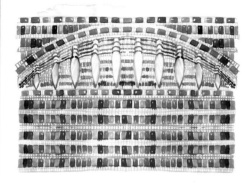

### 622 AD–712 AD

The prophet Muhammad migrates from Mecca to Medina, and the Islamic faith spreads across Syria, Palestine, Mesopotamia, Persia, Egypt, North Africa, and Spain. Ceramic tiling is used in Islamic architecture as an important decorative element more than anywhere else in the world.

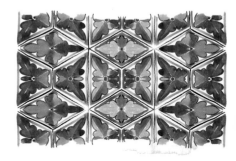

### 15TH CENTURY

Valencian tiles, known as *maiolica*, are exported to Italy for Pope Alexander VI's Vatican apartment.

### 16TH CENTURY

In Istanbul, tiles with under-glazed painting, a method originally derived from Chinese blue-and-white porcelain, reach their height of popularity.

## 17TH CENTURY

The campaign for Dutch independence causes many artists and craftsmen to flee north to Holland, where they take their ceramic skills, resulting in the Dutch tile-making centers of Rotterdam, Delft, Haarlem, and Utrecht. Around 1620 to 1640, Dutch tile decoration becomes predominantly blue and white, drawing inspiration from exported Chinese porcelain.

## 1842 AND 1845

British designer Owen Jones records in detail the geometric ornamentation of the tiles of the Spanish Alhambra and publishes *Plans, Elevations, Sections, and Details of the Alhambra* in two volumes.

## 1915

Britain's Design and Industries Association is set up to establish partnerships between manufacturers and designers. One of the most successful partnerships is Carters of Poole, which produced ceramic tiles.

## 1939

The May issue of *Architectural Review* features an eight-page supplement on tiles.

## 1756

John Sadler and Guy Green make history with the most important innovation in English tile-making when they successfully transfer an image from a printing plate (at first a wood block but later engraved copper plate) to a tile.

## 18TH CENTURY

Tiles produced in Europe are exported to America, where the well-to-do use them in fireplace surrounds.

## 19TH CENTURY

The Industrial Revolution introduces new techniques for preparing and forming clay into tiles. In 1840, Richard Prosser takes out a British patent for pressing ceramic buttons from clay dust, and Herbert Minton quickly adapts Prosser's method to the manufacture of wall tiles. Minton's process of mass production spreads throughout Europe and in 1846 the German firm Villeroy & Boch installs presses at their factory.

## 1980s

Handcrafted tiles have a revival in Britain and become a popular decorating trend.

## 2000s

The ubiquitous white subway tile becomes a popular wall application in modern kitchens and bathrooms.

THIS PAGE › Hotelier Sean MacPherson installed decorative Portuguese tiles as a backsplash in his ninteenth-century West Village apartment, filling the kitchen with old-world charm.

OPPOSITE › Subway tiles are placed in a basket-weave design, achieving the high-end look of the traditional pattern done on an exaggerated scale.

# How It's Made

THE MAJORITY OF TILE SHARES A COMMON DENOMINATOR: IT IS made from clay—earth, really, mixed with water, subjected to fire, and transformed into a hard, useful material. That's an oversimplification, of course; an artist can use one of many variations on this recipe to create the blue and white porcelain we associate with Northern European tile or the elaborate geometrically printed tiles prevalent in Islamic architecture . . . the list goes on.

Because tile is tough and accessible, it's prevalent in cultures across the globe. Today it's mostly prized for its practicality; we tile our kitchens and bathrooms, foyers and outdoor spaces. That wasn't always the case; a century ago in this country, tile was used as a decorative flourish wherever one was needed: around window frames, inlaid into doors—and it was a very popular finishing touch around the fireplace. Tile can be both utilitarian and exceptional. The question is how to tell the average tiles—the mass-produced materials you find at the local hardware store—from the very best.

Possibly the smartest method is to let someone do this heavy lifting for you. Ann Sacks is a boutique tile retailer that applies a fairly rigorous standard, paying attention to the aspects that define a quality tile, like glaze, color, and edging. "When you go into our stores, you know you're going to find something that's been really well edited," says Ann Sacks's John Hart. "There are so many choices out there. Part of what we try to do, regardless of the price point or the material—it might be porcelain tile, it might be glass, it might be something in stoneware—is to bring the best of what we think looks great and functions in the right way."

Looks are an important part of the equation, of course, when you want to train your eye to spot the differences between the good and the so-so. The glaze on a tile, even a simple white tile, adds a layer of depth, a visual texture. Hart argues that another advantage of smaller-batch tile is that this glaze is applied more thoughtfully, more carefully, yielding a product that simply looks better when you do a side-by-side comparison with mass-produced tile.

Unlike its clay counterparts, cutting stone into tile is an exacting practice. It requires the use of a water jet machine, which pumps water at up to 60,000 psi (pounds per square inch) through a small orifice while a Garnet tip slices clean edges.

# The Properties of Tile

IN TERMS OF PERFORMANCE, NOT ALL TILES ARE CREATED EQUAL, so it's worth thinking about the end use. A tile installed on the wall doesn't have to be incredibly durable, whereas something destined for the floor should be. Again, retailers provide this information for the consumer—tiles should be labeled with an indicated use, and those are rules you'd be wise to follow. If you fall in love with something at your local big-box store and there's no information provided about its intended use, be wary.

"When we're selecting a subway tile, for instance," John Hart says, "we'll ask ourselves questions like, 'What does the tile look like once it's installed? Does it have a lug on the side?' If it's self-spacing," he says, referring to tiles with protrusions on their border that ensure a uniform look when they're laid down, "what kind of space is there for the joint? Does it have a soft edge or a sharp edge?" Again, as with stone, when you're shopping, it's worthwhile to work with a specialist, because they simply understand the material better.

A boutique retailer is likely the only place you'll encounter true handmade tile—a very different animal from factory tile, even the special, smallbatch stuff. "Making ceramic tile by hand is one of the most laborious processes out there," says Artistic Tile's Nancy Epstein. "To get from wet clay to finished ceramic tile, there are a multitude of processes and the touching of many hands." Again, it's important here to understand the value of the middleman; a handmade tile has to meet certain standards before Artistic Tile will accept that it's good enough to pass on to their customers.

Handmade tile—like most anything handmade—is probably going to cost more and take longer to acquire. Mass-produced ceramic tiles are precisely uniform in cut and character; handmade tiles have less-than-perfect lines and variations in glaze, imperfections that are evidence of the artisan.

Regardless of how much you're investing in the tile itself, experts agree you should not skimp on the installation. "Being a tile installer is not easy," says Epstein. "They have to be crafty and mathematically bright. No matter how many times you measure the wall and how many times you verify the pattern, our walls are rarely completely plumb. If you choose an installer whose best qualification is that he is the cheapest, then you can take the most beautiful materials in the world and have a disaster on your hands."

Expert tile installation comes down to attention to detail. In this spectacular London bathroom, a single, slightly crooked tile would have thrown off the larger, repeating scheme.

# DESIGN CHAMPION: *Doris Duke*

THE HOMES OF THE MEGA-RICH are generally show-stoppers, and part of what is so striking about the Hawaiian estate of socialite Doris Duke is its almost humble profile. "It's the opposite of Hearst Castle," says Deborah Pope, executive director of Shangri La (seen here), once the heiress's vacation getaway and now the home of the Doris Duke Foundation for Islamic Art. "It's not the thing on the hill that you build for everyone to see and admire. It's a very personal statement."

Islamic art was one of Duke's many interests, and she dedicated part of her considerable fortune to its support and preservation. Islamic art encompasses a massive range, from painting to calligraphy to the decorative arts—mosaics, textiles, ceramics.

In her collecting, Duke cast a wide net: furniture inlaid with mother-of-pearl, stained-glass windows and other architectural details, glass bottles and vessels and decorative objects. She wasn't building a museum, not at first—she was making a home.

Tile is well represented in the collection at Shangri La. "The majority of our tilework, which we've had extensively surveyed by our conservators who specialize in that medium, is quite stable," says Pope. "Even though it was clearly not made for a damp climate, it has acclimated well." What problems have arisen have

less to do with the tile and more to do with the way it was installed. That is worth noting—the tiles Duke collected are not displayed behind glass; they're actually mounted.

Architecturally, Shangri La has a simple profile that's within the midcentury modern vernacular. "The house, especially if you look at the construction photos and you are able to see it before all that ornament goes on, is a very modern, spare, low-slung concrete building," says Pope. "It's almost like Duke created the blank palette on which to hang all the applied ornament: the cornices, the columns, the capitals, the mirrored column shafts that are in the patio, all of the tilework, and the Moroccan ceilings."

This mix of modern lines and centuries-old ornamentation is striking and wholly idiosyncratic. Duke wasn't thinking as a curator, she was thinking as a decorator, and so her rooms really showcase these pieces, and how people might actually live with them. "Throughout the house, you see that kind of mix, that interesting blend of things that are really modern, like the wide-wale corduroy sectional sofa that sits in the living room, underneath the carved, painted, and gilt ceiling that she commissioned in Morocco. There's a tension between the two that makes the place live."

# RECOGNIZING THE MAJOR PLAYERS
## *Tile*

### 1 > SONOMA TILEMAKERS

Manufacturing and distributing more than twenty handcrafted luxury product lines, Sonoma Tilemakers mixes ceramics with glass, stone, and other materials to create unexpected visual appeal in a range of classic, contemporary, and innovative styles.

### 2 > NEW RAVENNA

Designer and manufacturer of handcrafted stone and glass mosaic tiles, New Ravenna creates not only decorative effects but artistic works for homes and businesses. The Virginia-based company, founded by artist and designer Sara Baldwin in 1990, specializes in custom projects requiring extraordinary detail.

### 3 > ARTISTIC TILE

Artistic Tile founder Nancy Epstein travels the world seeking unusual tiles to introduce to the North American market, adding to the company's already eclectic stock of tile and natural stone products.

### 4 > CLÉ

Declared "the preferred house for artisanal tiles" by *Vogue,* this Northern California brand was founded by tile enthusiast Deborah Osburn and stocks the basics (including penny rounds and ceramic subway tiles), but is best known for its boldly patterned cement tile selection, as well as its artist collaborations and Moroccan imports.

### 5 > ANN SACKS

Ann Sacks founded her eponymous design company in 1981 to bring fine tile and stone designs to the marketplace, and has since become an industry leader. Part of the Kohler manufacturing company since 1989, Ann Sacks encourages customers to use its products to "discover how home feels."

### 6 > BISAZZA

Bisazza, established in Northern Italy in 1956, produces luxury glass mosaic tiles for interior and exterior use—including mosaics with 24-carat gold and the jewel-like *avventurina,* a seventeenth-century Venetian synthetic stone. The company has worked with leading designers, artists, and architects, including Tord Boontje, Michael Graves, Alessandro Mendini, Andrée Putman, Ettore Sottsass, and Marcel Wanders.

1 › In the Los Feliz home of Commune founder Ramin Shamshiri, hand-stamped concrete tiles from Mexico run between the kitchen and the courtyard. 2 › A custom-designed tile map of Shelter Island, New York, acts as a backdrop in the eat-in kitchen of a light-filled home on the island. 3 › The walkways of Doris Duke's iconic Shangri La are framed in intricate tilework, an ode to the great Middle Eastern palaces that inspired them.

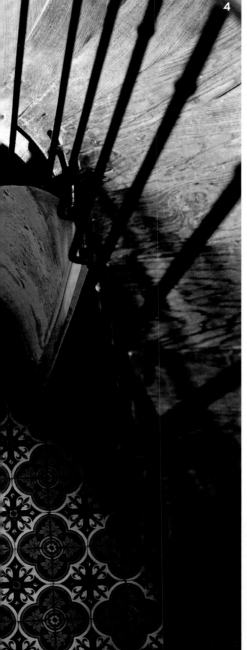

**4** › Imported traditional Turkish tiles draw attention to the period stairwell of a French country home. **5** › Designer Darren Brown used richly hued penny tiles to create textural depth in his tiny Manhattan bathroom. **6** › Almost every inch of floor in Positano, Italy's, famed Le Sirenuse hotel is covered in tile, with varying patterns from the traditional to the more modern. **7** › This stunning formal dining room in Pebble Beach, California, is wrapped in a custom tile mural by Atelier Prométhée.

# furniture

The walls and floors are a home's foundation, but the furniture is what injects life into a space. Furniture enables us to live well in our homes, where we relax, where we rest. But as much as furniture's function matters, the style is key in the way we begin to truly build a home.

# *furniture basics*

Furniture is a form as old as human history—we see nobility upon thrones in ancient Egyptian frescoes—and furniture design and manufacturing, like fashion and painting, reflect their cultural moment. We talk about furniture the way we talk about art, classifying it into styles by the dominant forces in the culture that created it, as Directoire refers to the post-Revolution French government, or Georgian to anything originating during the reign of Britain's four King Georges. Much of this terminology is widely enough used that even non–design historians know what's meant by, say, midcentury modern furniture.

Furniture today is significantly different than it was a century ago, a consequence of mechanized production and evolving tastes. Yet with furniture (as opposed to cars, for example), it's possible, oftentimes preferable, to buy something a century old and live with it in an everyday way—just as it's possible to buy something of our time that has been built precisely as furniture was built a hundred, even two or three hundred, years ago.

Furniture is typically classified as upholstered or case goods. Case goods are anything constructed wholly of hard materials, whether wood or metal. Upholstered furniture describes anything that involves padding and fabric.

The most successfully designed spaces blend upholstered furniture and case goods—essentially, comfort and function—in a way that's unique and personal, a true reflection of the people who live in them.

At its core, Jackie Astier's home library is rather pared-down; it's the furniture's robust details—tufted velvet, polished brass, exotic burl wood—that give the minimalist arrangement its richness.

# *The Unique History of Furniture*

## 7TH–2ND CENTURY BC

The ancient Greeks construct four basic seat forms: the throne chair (*thronos*), side chair (*klismos*), stool (*diphros*), and couch (*kline*).

## 16TH CENTURY

During the height of the Italian Renaissance, carved walnut furniture, including tables, cupboards, and buffets, becomes increasingly refined and intricate, while sumptuous silks and velvet fabrics used for upholstery add a level of unparalleled opulence.

## 18TH CENTURY

French life becomes dominated by social conventions defined by the aristocracy, which furniture design reflects, yielding countless types of chairs for different social standings, such as the bergère, *marquise,* chaise lounge, and *canapé.*

## 30 BC–500 AD

The Romans continue Greek traditions and styles of furniture-making but employ more extravagant materials, such as curly maple, ebony, tortoiseshell, ivory, gold, silver, and bronze inlay. The most notable Roman addition to furniture design is the table (*mensa*); although the Greeks produced tables, the Romans are able to curve the legs and apply intricate decoration. The Romans also use the sideboard (*abacus*), which is introduced from Asia during the 2nd century BC.

## 17TH CENTURY

Trade with Asia, dominated by the Dutch, causes an influx of lacquered furniture in the European marketplace. Soon European furniture workshops offer "japanning," an imitation of Asian lacquer, as a finish option.

## 1725

English furniture makers begin using exotic woods such as mahogany, imported from the British colonies, and by 1850, mahogany replaces local walnut as the most desirable wood.

## 1754

Thomas Chippendale, the British craftsman, publishes *The Gentleman and Cabinet-Maker's Director,* the first pattern-book entirely dedicated to furniture, setting a precedent for other furniture pattern-books, such as George Hepplewhite's *The Cabinet-Maker and Upholsterer's Guide* (1788) and Thomas Sheraton's *Cabinet-Maker and Upholsterer's Drawing-Book* (1791 and 1794).

## 1830s

As machines and industrial methods develop, furniture design becomes increasingly elaborate and romantic. Many historical styles are revived, like the Gothic style, in which chairs and case pieces take on the aesthetic of grand cathedrals.

## 1861

William Morris, the famous design reformer, establishes his firm, Morris & Co., as a reaction to the increasing commercialization of furniture. Chief furniture designer Philip Webb designs simple, everyday furniture with exposed construction details and unassuming materials.

## 1925

French furniture designers such as Émile-Jacques Ruhlmann display their sumptuously extravagant pieces at the Exposition Internationale des Arts Décoratifs et Industriels Modernes in Paris. The show popularizes the Art Moderne style, which in the 1960s becomes known as Art Deco.

## 1960s

By the end of the 1960s, plastic furniture is being developed and produced throughout the world. Verner Panton designs stackable one-piece plastic chairs, and Knoll Associates introduces a new line of injection-molded plastic furniture.

## 1917

Dutch designer and architect Gerrit Rietveld constructs his revolutionary painted wood armchair, which becomes known as the Red Blue Chair and is a symbol of the De Stijl movement.

## 1919

Walter Gropius begins the Bauhaus, a design school in Germany that focuses on uniting the arts and crafts, and ultimately incorporating industry. One of the school's earliest students, Marcel Breuer, creates his innovative cantilevered chairs, which have since become modern design icons.

## 1939

The New York World's Fair of 1939 helps to promote modern design to the American people who respond enthusiastically to Swedish design.

## 1940

The Museum of Modern Art in New York City sponsors a competition for "Organic Design in Home Furnishings." American designers Eero Saarinen and Charles Eames take first prize.

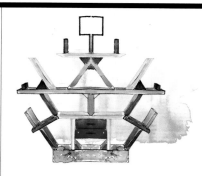

## 1980s

Italian design studio Memphis redefines furniture, claiming that, like fashion, furniture can be trendy, colorful, and fun.

## TODAY

Many designers and craftsmen utilize technology and traditional handcraft methods to create furniture out of sustainably sourced materials.

# case goods

Case goods are designed for practical purposes: they're where we store our things, where we eat. But they're also the things that command attention (and floor space) in our rooms, so we typically approach choosing a table, cabinet, or shelf by thinking about how it looks. That matters, of course.

But with case goods, it's helpful to understand material and construction techniques, and how these relate to durability—to dressers and shelving that can withstand daily use. Decades ago, the primary consideration with furniture was strength; we wanted chairs, beds, and everything else to last as long as possible, and antique furniture usually bears testament to the skill of previous generations of craftsmen. We may now live in an age of constant renovation and disposable commodities, but the hallmark of a great piece of furniture remains its ability to endure.

Well-chosen case goods have the ability to look "built in," as much a part of a room's framework as the walls themselves. This was the goal architect Julie Schaffer had when squeezing a vintage Florence Knoll credenza into the small nook under her stairs.

Quality materials separate case goods that last for decades from those that last for a few years. The designs of these DwellStudio pieces are quite simple, but the materials (Belgian gray wood, French oak) ensure longevity.

# The Question of Craftsmanship

*ARTISAN* IS SOMETHING OF A BUZZWORD THESE DAYS. A GENERATION ago, linoleum flooring and TV dinners encapsulated that era's interest in harnessing science and technology to make life easier. Now, though, there's an interest in craftsmanship and simplicity, an old-fashioned reverence for products that take time and skill to create.

Quality case goods typically reflect the thoughtful choices of a craftsman, but they can also be the product of skilled high-tech manufacture. A quality piece is generally constructed of the finest materials—natural wood, pure metals—but not always. In truth, the defining characteristic of a great case good is that it is built to last, and judging this doesn't require any specialized knowledge: even if you've never bought a dresser before, you can feel the difference between high- and low-quality ones.

Tyler Hays, of New York's BDDW, agrees that longevity is the true measure of quality. The clean lines and elegant forms of BDDW's furniture are clearly inspired by midcentury designs but are updated with a refined, slightly industrial sensibility uniquely their own. This is furniture you can live with and interact with every single day, for decades; your kids can pull on the drawers of BDDW's dressers, and you can eat every meal at their tables, and the pieces will remain essentially unchanged.

We think of design as being a humble craft, but Hays values science as much as art. "I have several people on staff with engineering degrees," he says. "It's about aesthetics, but also material science and physics." We think of man's hand being preferable to the work of machinery, but Hays says, "With machines, I can achieve ten times the quality of when I used to do it all chiseled by hand. We are trying to create the best quality possible, and that is about it lasting for several hundred years. I am equally interested in the well made and well engineered as I am in the handmade."

Hays also has a novel point of view with respect to materials, working with more than traditional cherry, mahogany, and the like. "I use a lot of the throwaway, the garbage wood if you will, and it's twice the amount of work trying to make furniture out of it. We've repopularized some woods that people turned their nose up at. There are hundreds of species of trees in America you can build furniture from."

Quality-crafted old pieces blend seamlessly with the new in Estee Stanley's L.A. dining room, where a custom BDDW table is surrounded by vintage midcentury chairs.

# How It's Made

THE VAST MAJORITY OF FURNITURE AT BOTH LOW-END AND MIDDLE-end retailers has been designed as multipurpose: to fulfill its given function, to travel easily, to sit in warehouses without taking up too much space, and to yield the manufacturer a specific return on investment.

Traditionally, a dresser was produced as a single, solid piece. Today it's not uncommon that the dresser you buy might require assembly, because it was less expensive for the manufacturer to ship in components, and easier to store those components than a finished dresser. Traditionally, that dresser would have been built of a material chosen for its strength and durability. Today it's commonly a mix of materials, often including MDF (medium-density fiberboard, created of a mix of wood bonded to resin), chosen because they're less expensive or lighter weight for easier transport. Traditionally, you'd find actual joints wherever planes meet, and nails or long dowels. Today you'll find furniture held together by glue and short, flimsy dowels. Even furniture that's pretty expensive may rely on these kinds of cost-saving shortcuts; a dresser with a hardwood exterior, for example, might have drawers with fiberboard bottoms.

Fiberboard and dowels are easy to spot, but this kind of shortcut manufacturing can be so well done that the downsides are not immediately apparent—and the price tag is often seductive. The ramifications of these shortcuts may not be apparent for years, when hardware screwed into MDF gives way, or the bottom of a drawer held in by glue collapses. Price should always be weighed against longevity. You might spend more for real wood, but your wood dresser won't collapse in a few years' time.

Custom furniture is essentially the opposite of what you find at retail. Most designers go to a workshop with something particular in mind, but custom furniture builders are often equipped to work with nonprofessionals, even if you don't have a detailed sense of what you're looking for. Jean-Paul Viollet, who descends from a line of woodworkers dating back to 1832, runs a small Brooklyn-based atelier, building furniture to order for designers, architects, and the general public. "I start with the materials," says Viollet, "and I try not to be too ornate. I have utter respect for nature, and natural materials, so I let the materials be the focus. When you design furniture, you know that the piece is going to be touched, to be in contact with a human being."

At the BDDW studio, days are spent mending live wood slabs—chiseling and dry-fitting butterfly joints into the natural grooves found in a piece of wood to prevent further splitting—before they can become gorgeous dining tables.

Viollet acknowledges that custom work is not for everyone. "My mother used to say that chic is always too expensive," he says. "IKEA makes a lot of sense. They're providing mass-market furniture that is easy to assemble and use, and functional. I have nothing against that. And then you have middle market. If you go to Crate & Barrel, and you see a nice sideboard, and you bring it home, it might be three inches longer than you would desire. We design and fabricate a piece of furniture that will fit an environment to a precise dimension, one that will be very well-balanced in this environment."

The biggest difference between custom and mass-produced furniture isn't simply finding a credenza that fits snugly in that niche in your living room—after all, the market is big enough that if you're willing to look, you'll probably eventually find something that works almost perfectly. And it's not hard to find nice hardwood furniture at big retailers, sometimes on sale to boot. With custom furniture, what's valuable may not always be obvious. "We pay a lot of attention to something that is not visible," says Viollet. "The joinery or the construction of a piece that you may not see and not be able to appreciate, because it's covered with some other materials, is very important." The custom-furniture maker is deeply invested in building just what you want, of course, but they'll do so using great materials and smart techniques, so longevity, the best measure of quality, is a given.

When great furniture becomes collectible furniture, that's the truest sign of excellent craftsmanship. Every hard-sought piece in this living room—including Pierre Chapo's L'Oeil coffee table—is a modernist design masterpiece from the 1930s to the 1960s.

## RECOGNIZING THE MAJOR PLAYERS
# *Case Goods*

### 1 > ATELIER VIOLLET

Founded in Seyssel, France, in 1836, Atelier Viollet is currently lead by Jean-Paul Viollet of the family's seventh generation of artisans. The luxury-furniture workshop prides itself on its use of rare or exotic materials—shagreen, straw, shell, parchment, horn—particularly when applied to the ancient art of marquetry.

### 2 > BAKER

Baker, founded in 1890 by Dutch immigrant Siebe Baker, offers styles ranging from ornately carved and gilded to contemporary, and nearly every influence in between. Known for its high-quality materials, Made-in-America furniture, and exquisite detailing, Baker continues to create new collections that demonstrate its keen eye for design.

### 3 > CENTURY FURNITURE

Century Furniture's reputation for high-end, high-quality furniture began when founder Harley Ferguson Shuford built an eighteenth-century-style mahogany dining suite in his new case goods plant in North Carolina, in 1948. Today more than seven hundred pieces of furniture are made in the company's North Carolina factory from predominantly domestic materials.

### 4 > BDDW

Painter, sculptor, ceramicist, and builder Tyler Hays founded BDDW in 1998 as a maker of heirloom-quality wood furniture using traditional joinery, domestic hardwoods, and hand-rubbed finishes. Hays designs all pieces—which have been likened to high-end versions of simple Shaker styles—in his Philadelphia studio.

### 5 > HENRYBUILT

Cabinetmaker Henrybuilt, founded in 2001, offers the ultimate customizable kitchen, bath, and residential storage systems. The Seattle-based company's specialty is no doubt its modern, sleek customizable units, but it would be a mistake to overlook its curated collection of benches, tables, and desks.

### 6 > THEODORE ALEXANDER

Thousands of designs—Renaissance European, early American, Victorian, French Louis, Deco, midcentury modern, and more—comprise the renowned Theodore Alexander collections, made with traditional handcraftsmanship and diverse, high-quality materials.

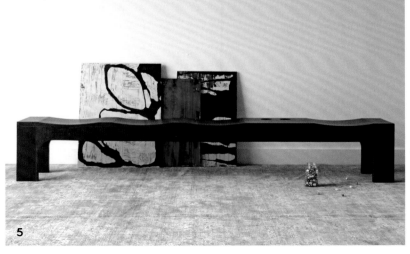

**1 ›** For professional furniture builders such as Aaron Scaturro, the placement of dowels and the intricacies of design become a custom signature, one that's as recognizable as a name written by hand. **2 ›** The remarkable ribbonlike curves of Bodo Sperlein's Contour collection take weeks to create; craftsmen toil for hours to get a solid piece of oak to bend just a few centimeters. **3 ›** Among the clean lines and pale shades that define this Upper East Side living room, an antique secretary desk makes for a grand contrast. **4 ›** Inspired by ancient Japanese techniques, Bill Sofield's collection for Baker features hand-applied finishes and distressed gold-leafing. ●

5 › A bird's-eye view of one of BDDW's custom walnut slab dining tables, with its beautiful live edge and expertly dry-fitted butterfly joints. **6** › A single, statement piece—combining beautiful wood and rich leather—greets you at Commune founder Ramin Shamshiri's front door. **7** › BDDW's Lake Bureau comes in seven finishes; however, for the true wood lover, its oxidized maple is a gorgeous display of the natural knots and streaks created by Mother Nature.

# upholstered furniture

In the words of the legendary designer Bunny Williams, "If you do not have a place to sit, you do not have a room."

The principal point of upholstery is to create a comfortable surface with which the body can interact. And unless you're an ascetic or eccentric, the chances are good that your aim in building a home is to create a sense of comfort, so understanding what differentiates quality upholstered furniture from lesser-quality furniture is important. As with case goods, aesthetics matter, but tastes are specific to every one of us; far more important are materials and construction techniques. Natural materials tend to last longer and provide more comfort, and time-tested construction yields furniture that will fulfill its most important function—to last.

With upholstered furniture, how fabric meets at the seams is a telltale sign of quality; the edge should always be smooth, with no puckering.

The original Knole sofa was designed in the seventeenth century as a throne for traveling royalty; the arms drop down for less formal occasions. This modern-day version by George Smith is slightly larger but was made with the same keen attention to detail.

# How It's Made

"ONE OF THE FIRST THINGS YOU BUY WHEN YOU HAVE A HOUSE IS A sofa," says Bunny Williams. In buying as in love, it begins with looks—and the way we buy these days has everything to do with appearance. Images of overstuffed sofas seduce from the pages of magazines or across the Web. But comfort isn't a question of plump pillows. "The comfort of a sofa really comes from the way the frame is made," says Williams. "A lot of inexpensive-furniture makers make a very cheap frame and put a lot of stuffing on it to try to make it comfortable, but when the stuffing goes, the furniture is not going to be comfortable."

Peter Howlett, director of design at George Smith, agrees that what's inside is more important than what's outside. "I would never dismiss any furniture other people make, because obviously everybody has their own market," says Howlett, "but the average sofa in a department store would be made with foam and plywood and staples." The UK-based George Smith is interested in comfort, but always in service of durability. "We're providing the ultimate in sustainability. It won't end up in the landfill," says Howlett. "The sofa that I have in my house is from 1840 and is made the way we make our furniture today. Our silhouettes and our furniture are able to last generations. Not a couple generations. Many generations."

Obviously, you need some expertise to understand whether a sofa's component parts are of the highest quality or not. Among the details that make George Smith sofas so widely respected is that their frames are joined by wood dowels, creating a bond significantly sturdier than staples, which are widely used in mass manufacture. If this information isn't immediately apparent when shopping in stores or online, ask—it makes a difference.

With custom furniture, you don't need to worry about the details of construction and material; you'll have a relationship with the craftsmen who are building your sofa or chair, and they can walk you through every decision that's being made in bringing it to life. Whether you're shopping retail or buying custom, these details matter for a reason. "I think comfort probably supersedes longevity," says Howlett. "But they really go hand in hand. It's hard to make something comfortable without integrity of craftsmanship."

Almost every sofa contains springs, but not every spring is created equal. Pocket springs are widely used; essentially, several springs are lined up in a row, each clad in a layer of fabric webbing and connected to the spring on

Nailhead trim isn't purely decorative; it also disguises the point where upholstery is tacked into a wood frame—so essentially, the trim is helping to keep the fabric in place.

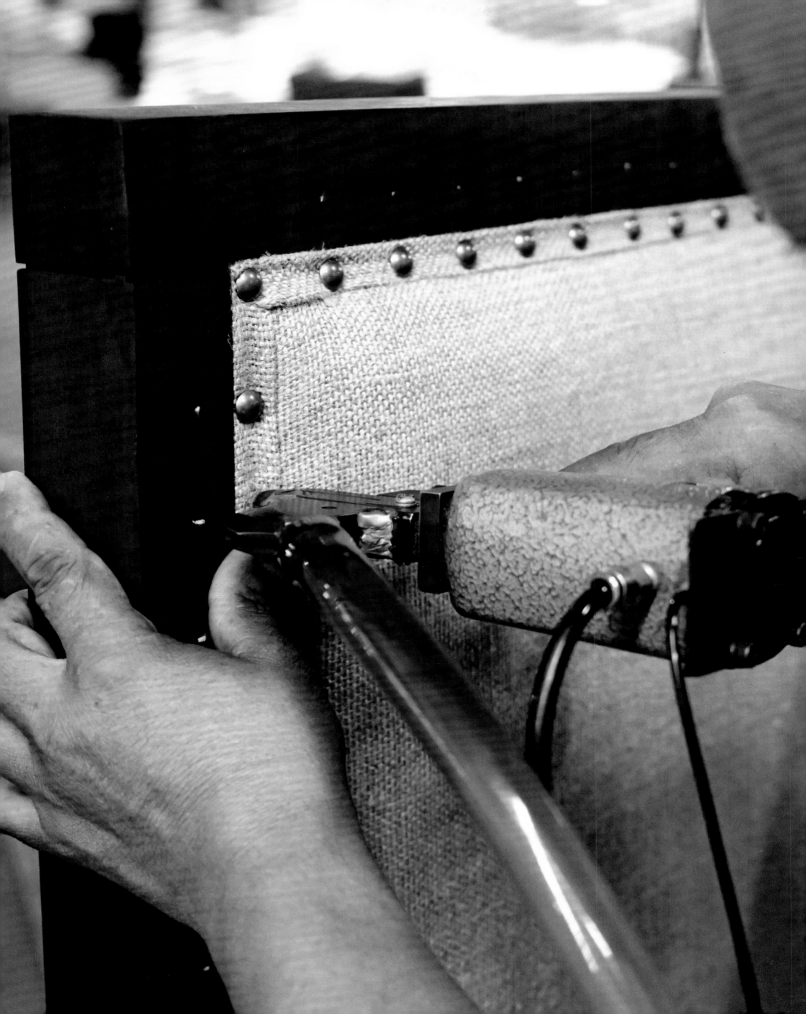

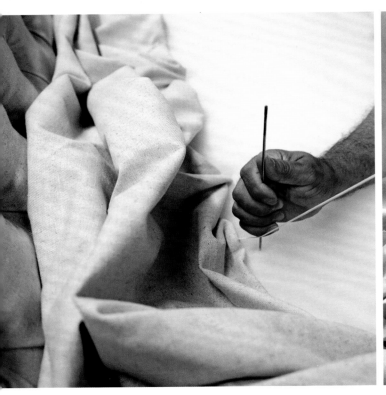

either side of it. As a result of the way they're strung together, the several springs in a pocket construction really function as one spring; when you sit, every spring depresses. George Smith uses steel springs, and each is tethered to its neighbors by eight ties, not two, which is commonplace in mass manufacture. This creates a surface that's more dynamic, and more sensitive to the pressure you're applying to it. "It's a difficult thing to comprehend and explain, but if you sit on one, you'll notice," says Howlett. Underneath the spring structure inside a George Smith sofa is a layer of webbing made of jute, the same material used to link the individual springs; by contrast, the substructure of most sofas is plywood. It's reasonable to assume that most people would rather recline on the former.

The New York custom furniture studio Chelsea Workroom takes a similarly thoughtful approach to construction. "For example, we have coil springs that we hand-tie with Italian twine onto cotton jute webbing," says Chelsea Workroom's David Feldman. "And in the seat, the first three to four rows of springs are tied a little bit firmer, and the last three are a little bit softer. When you sit down, we want you to sink in a bit more at the front edge so it gives you that subtle reclined feeling."

**ABOVE LEFT ›** At George Smith, tufting is still done by hand, a painstaking process that requires extremely strong fingers to work a twelve-inch-long bayonet-pointed needle.

**ABOVE RIGHT ›** To prepare the piece for tufting, holes for each tuft (or button) are made in the chaise's padding and marked on the fabric, so sewing is simply a matter of lining the two up.

**OPPOSITE ›** After twenty hours of tufting (thirty if working with leather), the finished chaise is put to a stringent quality test, one that ensures that the pattern is symmetrical and each tuft is pulled tight.

When you sink into a sofa, it's also what's between those springs that you'll feel. Fine sofas like George Smith's are stuffed with cotton battening; the sofas you see on the curb on trash day almost always have some kind of polyester foam spilling out of their innards. "A lot of furniture that's mass-produced is just foam with Dacron padding," says Feldman. "And a lot of the mass-produced brands that give themselves a higher-end identity approach construction the same way, without much consideration for how the piece should look and feel."

At Chelsea Workroom, the preferred stuffing material is horsehair; most craftsmen agree that when it comes to creating comfort, natural materials are superior to synthetics. Feldman doesn't object to mass production, but he decries the mass manufacturers' methods. "It's what's on the inside and the materials used that determine a perfect sitting experience," he says. "You have to use a kiln-dried hardwood frame, quality coil springs, and premium fills like horsehair and down to get a beautiful and comfortable piece."

# Aesthetics

RETAIL MANUFACTURERS BUILD COLLECTIONS WITH AN EYE TO things like color, pattern, and fabrics, and how those factors relate to the larger trend cycle; workshops build whatever you ask for, and are thinking primarily of details so small you may not notice them. If a retailer's hallmark is the look of its furniture, the workroom's signature is to be found in its quality of construction, because the look is always dependent upon the client.

"Beauty is in the eye of the beholder," says David Feldman. "There are certain fabrics I might not have chosen, or the thickness of an arm or the color of a leg, but the clients chose it, and it's theirs, they're calling it their own, they're putting their own mark on it. It's going to live in their home and so it's going to be beautiful to them."

"There isn't one 'right,'" says Emily Nomer, of New York custom builder Manzanares Furniture Corp. "There's a 'right' that's specific to each person, designer, set of circumstances, use, room that it's in, and type of life it's going to lead. What's right in a teenager's TV room is going to be totally different from what's right in someone's Park Avenue sitting room."

With upholstered furniture, when talking about aesthetics, many people focus on the fabric. "When you choose your fabric for upholstery, you need to do it with its properties and behaviors in mind. Just because a fabric is pretty doesn't mean it's going to make for a successful result on your furniture," says Nomer. "It may be something that's narrow and therefore can't be railroaded, another thing you have to explain to people." "Railroading" refers to lining up the fabric so the pattern on it connects seamlessly; a complex pattern, like a diagonal stripe, needs to be lined up perfectly in order to look right, but depending on the width of the fabric bolt, that could require several seams across the body of a sofa.

Then with fabric there's the question of end use. "Let's say you're using it in a television room," says Nomer. "Will it stand up to that wear and tear? Is it too thin or too thick? If it's too thin, you'll tend to see the things behind it or it might not look good. You have to choose, in context, what you're using it for."

Another important factor in discussing aesthetics is the question of proportion. "One should be very careful when buying a sofa," says Bunny Williams, who recommends studying the whole proportion. "If the sofa is

**OPPOSITE ›** Upholstery has the ability to embolden a minimalist design, a fact that rings true in London-based designer Danielle Moudaber's living room, where a tufted, curving banquette has an almost larger-than-life quality.

**ABOVE ›** Traditionally, leather upholstery is equated with dark, masculine rooms, but here, in an unexpectedly bright blue, the material defies those connotations, punctuating the serene, sunny entry.

very deep, the seat needs to be low, because if you have a high seat and a deep sofa, you cannot get into and out of it. If you have a shallower sofa, the seat height can be a little bit higher."

What Williams is articulating will be evident if you test out a sofa—the pitch needs to be right, the proportion needs to be right; otherwise it won't be comfortable. Pictures just can't impart this kind of information; online shopping is convenient, but it is not helpful when judging quality. You've got to see furniture in person.

Designer Eddie Lee gave an extravagant Hamptons' beach house a sophisticated spin by upholstering ornate antiques with comfortable, casual textiles, including linen, cotton, and chenille.

# Vintage Furniture

BECAUSE QUALITY ENDURES—BECAUSE LONGEVITY IS THE BEST measure of quality—you can find the best furniture without visiting a custom workshop or a high-end retailer. You can buy it used.

"If you go to auctions, house sales, or whatever, you can buy amazing quality for no money," says Bunny Williams. "It is secondhand, it may have belonged to someone else, but it is just amazing what you can find. I think that you can have quality on a budget. It means you need to know something, you need to pay a little attention, and you need to know shopping."

Richard Wright's eponymous Chicago-based auction house has established itself as the destination for connoisseurs of important midcentury design.

"I deal primarily in postwar design," says Wright. "What I love about the period is it was a real time of optimism in the design world. It was one of the heroic moments in American design specifically." Wright deals in the period's iconic names like Eames, van der Rohe, Bertoia, Breuer, and Nelson.

But the very familiarity of those names (and the fact that many of their more iconic designs remain in production to this day) can make judging their quality a vexing task. "The connotation of quality in that era is very mixed, and I would say fairly so," says Wright. It was, he points out, "a time when mass manufacturing was ramping up, and there's a whole history of knockoffs and cheaper, fabricated examples of most of the pedigree pieces of the era. Those are different both in visible quality and in material quality, so understanding material quality is a very good guide to helping people really understand the things they bring into their home."

Obviously, Wright and his team of experts carefully vet whatever lots they're willing to represent, so when you shop at his and most auctions, that dirty work has been done for you. But what to do when you discover what you think is a mint Jacobsen chair at an estate sale, or come across what looks like a Nakashima bench at the thrift store?

"In some cases you need a trained eye, but I think that if you become more aware of the quality of the manufacturer and you start to look at what are hallmarks of quality, certain things become apparent," says Wright. "Like a Barcelona chair by Mies van der Rohe: The originals are solid stainless steel. The straps underneath are leather. The seats are leather. The quality of the leather, the quality of the stitching, is of the highest caliber. At a

There isn't a single Miles Redd–designed room that doesn't incorporate vintage furniture, whether in its original form or reupholstered in modern fabrics.

Designer and antiques dealer Cliff Fong approaches the décor of his own Los Angeles apartment with a true collector's sensibility, filling it with iconic twentieth-century pieces, including a rare Bruno Mathsson chaise covered in sheepskin.

cursory glance, a knockoff Barcelona chair may look very similar, but if you examine it, you'll see the way that it's actually screwed together. It's not one solid piece. The frame is lighter because it's hollow or it's chrome-plated, and the underlying straps might be vinyl or secondary leather."

The goal when buying secondhand is to get well acquainted with the piece—inspect it, learn its details, how its designer intended it to be made, and handle it, see it, and touch it for yourself. "Generally, once you become a collector, your eye becomes sensitized," says Wright. "There is a visual difference between the vintage pieces and the contemporary pieces, even if they've stayed in continuous production. There's just a different sense. There's kind of a brand-new garishness about a lot of the reissue pieces. If you like things with a patina, you're drawn to the vintage world." What he means is that the estate-sanctioned modern manufactured design by some iconic designer might use a different kind of wood than the designer originally intended, and even if every ingredient is the same, the final piece has a showroom newness that you might not care for. And when you're buying vintage, you're buying something used, thus sometimes a decades-old piece is actually cheaper than its modern sibling, in addition to possessing that patina of wear that collectors value.

These days we hear words like *handcraft* and *artisanal* a great deal, but these labels aren't always indicative of quality—and these are concerns specific to our time that don't necessarily relate to midcentury furniture. "The distinction that something is machine-made versus handmade is not always a direct parallel to quality," says Wright. Much of the iconic midcentury design we still covet was developed precisely to be manufactured on a mass scale, and that manufacture in no way diminishes their quality—mass-produced is not, in short, always a bad thing. "Herman Miller makes very high-quality furniture, and they did at the time, so the consistency of their manufacturing process and their quality control is quite good," says Wright. "Many of the better pieces of the fifties were made at manufacturers that had a lot of integrity—Knoll, Herman Miller, Dunmore furniture have incredible quality. There's great handmade furniture. There's also some really crappy handmade furniture. Just because somebody made it doesn't necessarily mean that it's a high-quality item."

Sterling examples of important design such as those in which Wright

traffics are a big investment—but likely a safe one, almost certain to retain their value. "It's amazing to me how modern and contemporary many designs from the fifties and sixties look today," says Wright. "I think if you're trying to design a chair that looks like something that's going to be around in 2075, well, visually, you end up still drawing on this source material from the 1960s and '70s." There's price—and there's value. "If you buy something inexpensive and it doesn't last, is that a good value?" Wright asks. "Quality almost always is more expensive, but in the long run, it can be cheaper."

Wright is careful not to confuse provenance with value, however. He sees the value in buying whatever it is you love. "If you go on eBay and see a chair you love and you buy it, I'm not against that at all," Wright says. "I think you'll typically enjoy that chair more if you've actually learned the backstory, and it has more to give you if you place it in a context, but one thing I love about design, as opposed to fine art: People are very comfortable judging design. They will immediately look at a chair, sit in it, and tell you if they like it or they don't like it. I don't think there's a wrong choice. There could be choices that from my perspective might be better, but I'm not trying to trump anyone's passion about a flea-market chair. I love that side of vintage, too."

Famed early-twentieth-century French designer Madeleine Castaing was as known for her eccentric Left Bank antiques shop, where her reluctance to actually part with any of her treasures is a thing of lore, as she was for her grand decorating schemes, which includes the iconic salon at Maison de Lèves seen here.

# Appraising a Collection

ONCE YOU'VE AMASSED A COLLECTION—WHETHER AN ASSORTMENT of midcentury pottery inherited from a relative, or a cache of early-twentieth-century glass you've cobbled together at flea markets—you'll want to know if your collection or a given piece has any value. If it does, you'll probably be curious about how to convert your collection into cash.

The auction house is an old-school model that remains relevant to today's serious collector. Auctions might conjure visions of impeccably dressed millionaires waving paddles to purchase Old Masters, but they're actually an important and easy way to buy and sell.

"There are affordable ways to buy at auction," says Alexandra Gilbert, a design consultant who has worked closely with both traditional and online auction houses. "Sometimes people are put off, thinking that it's just going to be exorbitant. There are good regional auction houses, and there are great sales that are targeted to lower price points. I always encourage people to at least experience it, even if you've never looked at a catalog or gone to a sale."

Obviously, when an auction house evaluates an object, it's primarily to determine its monetary value. That said, the experts at these houses are highly trained and can help educate you about more than your possessions' dollar value.

You needn't be a serious buyer to browse (catalogs are often complimentary and available digitally, and many major auctions have a preview period during which lots are on display for all comers to inspect). And you don't have to be a dealer or a specialist to use an auction house's services. "Go onto the website, find the appropriate department," says Gilbert. "Take some good photographs of the pieces. Look for manufacturing labels or artist signatures ahead of time. Give the specialist as much information as you have."

When it comes to determining quality, an auction house is interested in various aspects of a given item. The maker or designer is one, but there are others. "The auction record and past comparable sales go into considering the value of the piece," says Gilbert. She also points to aesthetics—is a piece representative of its time, a strong example of a specific movement or derivative thereof? Then there's material; generally gold will be more prized than brass, of course. As for function, does the piece do what it's designed to, and does it do it well?

OPPOSITE › An icon of the Modernist design movement, Knoll's Barcelona chair is just as recognized—and coveted—today as it was when Ludwig Mies van der Rohe first designed it back in 1929.

FOLLOWING PAGE › Antiques dealer Cliff Fong is quick to point out that in both his home and his store, Galerie Half, furniture is rarely refinished; instead it bears its original patina, making it even more of a prized possession.

If you're a novice collector, or simply buying what you love, it can be hard to say whether something is truly original, or know if the design will be worth more when you're ready to part with it. So be it. Gilbert says if it's money you're after, you're better off playing the stock market: "I never recommend someone collect something that they don't appreciate aesthetically and they don't want to live with in their home." It's wiser to buy what you love—if it ends up having monetary value, so much the better.

Of course, when collecting antiques, you're dealing with goods that may have wear and tear that predates life in your home. That doesn't necessarily negatively impact their value. "Condition is more complicated to evaluate," says Gilbert. "An appropriate indication of age and use on the piece of furniture adds to its quality. It's a delicate balance, where you never want the structure or stability of the chair or sofa to have been compromised, but you want to see that it's been used and loved. Sometimes wood looks more beautiful when the oil from someone's hands has smoothed it and mellowed the patina over time." So there's no reason to keep your collection packed away. Use it, live with it, admire it, love it—this may well enhance its value in the end.

Gilbert considers design to be a great field for auction novices, as buying at auction can be on par with buying retail, in terms of price and ease. "People are already spending a fair amount of money on their furnishings," she says. "Just putting a little bit of extra thought into where it comes from, who designed it, why it's special, or why this material is beautiful can be done without that much more work."

While buying at auction might seem vastly different from shopping at a store, in the end, it's not all that dissimilar. You needn't be armed with any specific knowledge, but approach it with common sense. "Don't be afraid to ask to flip an item over and look at a label," Gilbert says. "There's typically a signature, a manufacturing label on older pieces. You can learn a lot about construction by flipping over a new piece."

These questions and details are salient whenever you're considering bringing something into your home. While it's fun to watch people hit the jackpot on *Antiques Roadshow,* the truth is, Grandma's sugar bowl means something to you because it's connected to a fond memory—there is a difference between something that has monetary value and something that is valuable to you.

## RECOGNIZING THE MAJOR PLAYERS
# *Upholstered Furniture*

### 1 > LIGNE ROSET

French design house Ligne Roset, established in 1860, remains a family-run company—now in its fifth generation—committed to providing the best in contemporary design through artistic collaborations that often push the existing boundaries of modern furniture.

### 2 > MITCHELL GOLD + BOB WILLIAMS

Mitchell Gold and Bob Williams founded their eponymous home furnishings company in 1989 in North Carolina, and have since been growing their business with the simple mission "to make the world a more comfortable place." Their upholstered and slip-covered furniture is offered in hundreds of fabrics and frames from retailers nationwide.

### 3 > GEORGE SMITH

George Smith's upholstered furnishings, inspired by the work of the nineteenth-century namesake furniture maker, are made in the company's workshops in Northern England. Offering edited collections and custom services, George Smith has set the standard for beautifully handcrafted, high-end furniture.

### 4 > CISCO BROTHERS

Los Angeles–based designer Cisco Pinedo began crafting custom furniture in the 1990s, and has grown his business into a major market competitor. Cisco Brothers focuses on eco-friendly materials and production, boasting the first-ever collection of 100 percent FSC-certified sustainable upholstered furniture.

### 5 > CHELSEA WORKROOM

This boutique Manhattan studio specializes in custom drapery and upholstery for interior designers. Owner David Feldman was influenced by his Russian immigrant grandfather, who had a downtown New York upholstery shop. Feldman and his wife, Donna Feldman, also run the Dmitriy & Co. design studio and showroom. They emphasize natural materials and time-tested processes to create beautiful, comfortable pieces.

### 6 > POLTRONA FRAU

Founded in Turino in 1912, Poltrona Frau has expanded into a global brand of elegant, top-of-the-line Italian-made goods. It still manufactures some of its earliest, time-honored styles, but now has a focus on contemporary designs and spaces: in addition to furnishing houses and offices, Poltrona Frau has also designed for automobile, airplane, yacht, and helicopter interiors.

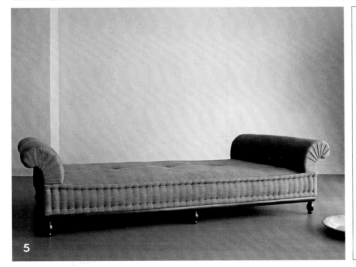

1 › Master of the print mix, designer Fawn Galli covered a pair of chrome-framed Milo Baughman look-alikes in hyper-hot-pink fabric.
2 › In a vibrant Robert Allen fabric, this wood-framed antique tuxedo sofa becomes the showpiece of an already stunning pattern play.
3 › In the Hamptons home of public relations executive Scott Currie, a centuries-old George III armchair goes from formal to beachy with a simple upholstery job.
4 › Chair cushions, inevitably, have a limited lifespan, but a well-made frame like this one has the potential to last for decades, even centuries.

5 › There is no lack of lounging space in Ramin Shamshiri's textile-rich den, where a kilim-upholstered ottoman sits next to a bold George Smith sofa covered in custom pillows. 6 › Jaklitsch/Gardner Architects were tasked with creating "his" and "hers" seating in this SoHo loft, a look they achieved by mixing a plush velvet sofa with a sleek tufted daybed. 7 › Quadrille's Independence Toile pattern (in contrasting backgrounds) covers the walls and the overstuffed daybed in the Maine master bedroom of the company's founder.

# textiles

If our homes are a sensory experience, the textiles within are doubly important—appealing to our eyes, but also to the touch. Fabric is everywhere—shielding our windows, covering our furniture. It's our bedding, our rugs, our carpets . . . one of the principal ways we make our homes places of comfort.

# FROM THE PAST TO THE PRESENT
## *The Unique History of Textiles*

### ANTIQUITY

Textile fibers are made from animal (wool and silk) and vegetable (linen, hemp, and cotton) products, and by 1000 BC selective breeding among sheep to improve the quality of fleece is well under way.

### 3RD CENTURY AD

A woven wall hanging from Egypt depicting goldfish swimming in a translucent green stream shows that the impulse to decorate with fabrics has a long-standing tradition.

### 10TH CENTURY

The cultivation of the silkworm, known as sericulture, is introduced to North Africa and Spain, and by the 12th century, Italy begins its own silk industry.

### 1733

John Kay invents the flying shuttle, a simple device that speeds up weaving and requires weavers to exert less energy.

### 1764

James Hargreaves invents the spinning jenny, a mechanized device that replaces eight hand spinners in one step.

### 552

The silkworm is introduced from Asia to Europe, creating a demand for silk fabrics and yarns imported from China. The trade route becomes known as the Silk Road.

### 16TH CENTURY

Leonardo da Vinci illustrates the complex processes involved in spinning fiber into thread, and invents a single device that performs all actions, but it isn't until two hundred years after his death that people begin to explore his design.

### 1662

Jean-Baptiste Colbert purchases the Faubourg Saint Marcel Gobelins factory as the general upholstery and tapestry manufacturer for Louis XIV. Charles Le Brun serves as the director and head designer from 1663 to1690.

### 1771

Richard Arkwright sets up the first textile factory along the Derwent River in Cromford, England. Inspired by Arkwright, Rhode Islander Samuel Slater opens the first American textile mill in 1792 and Francis Cabot Lowell of Boston sets up his factory shortly after in Waltham, Massachusetts.

### 1830

Richard Roberts invents a "cam mechanism" that revolutionizes the textile industry by finally making it possible for a machine, without the intervention of a human during the process, to spin fiber into thread.

### 1785

Edmund Cartwright patents the first power loom in Doncaster, England. He also invents a wool-combing machine in 1789.

### 1793

Eli Whitney and Hogden Holmes revolutionize the cotton industry by inventing a sawtooth gin that removes the seeds from the cotton lint.

### 1935

American company DuPont produces nylon, the first synthetic fiber.

### 1990s

Globalization allows for inexpensive textile production and companies move manufacturing to wherever the lowest price for labor is.

### 1801

Joseph Jacquard debuts his mechanical loom at a Paris exhibition and demonstrates how patterned textiles could be manufactured by a chain of punched cards connected into a continuous sequence that corresponds to a design. After Jacquard's invention, the textile industry is inundated with machine-made fabrics.

### 1950s

Abstract prints are at their height during the postwar era, when modern art movements heavily influence the textiles industry.

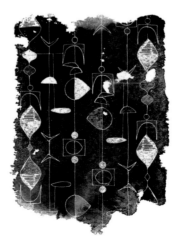

### TODAY

The majority of the textiles currently produced are made on industrial looms; however, many textile designers and craftspeople are reviving traditional methods of weaving and printing for small-scale production.

# *fabric basics*

Textiles are not an afterthought. They're a foundation, as important an aspect of the overall decorative scheme as paint. Fabrics imbue a room with color and with texture, and they're part of the space you'll interact with in a most intimate way: via touch.

When buying textiles—fabrics for upholstery or window treatments, a throw pillow or bedding—the measure of quality is in their component materials, how the textile is made, and the type and weight of fabric suited for the intended use. Before considering these aspects, it's important to master a few terms and concepts that are widely used, if not as widely understood.

Layering fabrics in a space is as much about mixing patterns as it is about mixing textures, a sentiment that Italian fabric designer Idarica Gazzoni always addresses in her collections, insisting that every bold print have a beautifully textured solid counterpart.

# On Material

SUSAN BROWN, AN ASSOCIATE CURATOR AT THE COOPER HEWITT, Smithsonian Design Museum, defines textiles as an agricultural product—a surprising but nevertheless accurate way to think of them. The cotton of your dish towels, the wool of your rug, the cashmere of your throw blanket all began life as a crop, tended as carefully as the crops that end up on our tables as food. The fact that fabrics come from organic material is wholly lost in our experience of buying them. We think they come from store shelves, maybe warehouses before that, but it's fair to say that when choosing a textile, we should use the same care we exercise when it comes to nourishing ourselves.

"People are becoming very sensitive to food quality," says Brown, "and fiber quality is comparable. An organically grown tomato is going to be a lot better than a tomato that you buy in cellophane at the grocery store. They're both tomatoes, but there's a certain level of care and attention to the growing, to the picking, to the post-harvest processing, that seriously impacts the quality of what you get, and people are starting to understand that that quality is worth paying for."

The same forces that have revolutionized the way we eat have affected how we use textiles. The components of our fabrics come from farms, which are industrialized now, so the small organic grower, once the norm, is the exception. And just as you'll find chemicals and synthetic ingredients in a lot of food, you'll find synthetic ingredients (principally derived from petroleum products) in a lot of fabrics.

Today we tend to associate the monetary value of a textile with its component material—cotton being less expensive than silk, cashmere being more expensive than wool—whereas historically, the value of a textile was related to the time it took to create it. "It was a perfectly common thing," says Brown, "that it might take you several years to make all of the furnishings for your bed. It would be a big investment of money, but also of time, working on the embroidery or the sewing yourself, or waiting while they were fabricated by someone else. But then once you had them, you would keep them for years, and pass them on to your children."

What was once a true luxury item has devolved into a disposable commodity. Today you can pop into any discount retailer and buy a set of cotton bedsheets for as little as ten dollars. Of course, you'll never be able to leave ten-dollar bedsheets to your children; they'll disintegrate in a few years.

This isn't necessarily only because the cotton is of a lesser grade; it's because there's less of it. Brown explains, "The staple fibers are very short, and the spinning is not very tight, which leads to pilling."

It's natural to be tempted by the bargain, but important to remember that there's a difference between the thirty-dollar pillow and the three-hundred-dollar pillow, though both tags might say "100 percent cashmere." The difference is in the actual fibers that make up the finished fabric. Some of those fibers—in the case of cashmere, they're harvested from goats—are short, and some are long. Simply put, the longer fibers yield finer cashmere. "It's like trying to braid straight hair," says Brown. "Short hairs stick out, and it's not as smooth, it's not as tight. Wool producers grade the staple fibers—the longest, finest hairs are the most expensive, and shorter or coarser hairs are cheaper." These lower-grade cashmeres are then sometimes spun to create a light feel and the softness we associate with the material.

Industrial classifications are boring, and that information isn't something that's shared with consumers; few would buy a product advertised as containing third-grade cashmere. But if you know what to look for, it's not hard to spot the difference. "If you feel your grandmother's cashmere sweater, it's not so puffy soft," says Brown, "because the staple fibers are very long and the spinning is very tight. The individual yarns are smooth, and so the finished knitting is very smooth. There's not so much surface fuzz, and it's not as airy feeling. It'll be a little bit denser."

Specialists and designers often talk about an almost ineffable characteristic termed "hand." It's used to describe how the fabric feels, but not simply its texture. Hand is also informed by a fabric's weight, its density, its resistance to your touch. Judging hand is a skill you can develop, simply by handling all manner of textiles. Touch a cotton (or linen, or wool, or anything) that's expensive and one that's inexpensive, and try to discern the difference. Feeling is imperative when it comes to textiles. The heft of a fine wool, the delicacy of silk, the luxurious softness of cashmere, even the simple comfort of cotton—all these inform how the room feels, in a very literal way.

When you're picking fabrics, you can't get the whole story from pictures of swatches in a magazine; you'll touch your sofa every day, so it's worth taking the time to touch an actual swatch, to visit a design showroom in person. Start by browsing, and eventually you'll learn what's worth buying.

PREVIOUS PAGE › At the Kelly Wearstler–designed Viceroy hotel in Santa Monica, the guest lounge has a textural explosion that's pure tactile magic: nubby linen and buttery leather, heavy silk and shaggy wool.

OPPOSITE › In his gypsy-den of a guest room, Brazilian editor Fabrizio Rollo layers small repeats with large geometrics and Christian Dior scarves with ikat blankets, throwing out traditional rules in favor of a riotous color mix.

# About Thread Count

TO FURTHER COMPLICATE THE SHOPPING PROCESS, SOME CLASSI-fications that manufacturers use are if not meaningless, then certainly slippery for consumers. Take "thread count," a term widely applied and generally misunderstood, one we encounter most often when buying bedding. A higher thread count is thought to imply higher quality. This is true for textiles with plain-weave construction; when speaking of sateen construction, though, a high thread count has no relationship to quality.

Thread count is a measure of the number of threads used in a square inch. In a plain weave, the threads are interconnected in a crisscross fashion, one thread over another. Percale is a kind of plain weave, one used commonly in bedding, and the word refers only to the technique, not to the component materials. Another common option in bedding is sateen, which does describe a fabric (cotton), but more important, is about a weaving technique in which a supporting thread is woven under a few other threads. Percale yields a tight weave, and a durable fabric. Sateen yields a glossier and softer fabric, but one that's durable.

Thus, thread count matters in a percale, as those threads actually fit together, and the number of them speaks to the fabric's resulting strength. In a sateen, the number of threads being used doesn't indicate the product's quality, if you measure quality as longevity and softness. In fact, a high thread count in a sateen could imply lower quality—to accommodate eight hundred threads within a square inch, they must be quite thin, so they'll abrade more quickly. You can't just go by the numbers: an eight-hundred-thread-count sateen is indeed lower quality than a three-hundred-thread-count percale.

Instead of trusting the number on the package, develop the aforementioned hand. "It's partly finding retailers you trust and partly developing a hand and being able to feel quality," says Susan Brown. "And high-quality things, generally speaking, feel better than low-quality things. If you spend some time touching things, you can usually develop a feeling for what's good and what's not. Even if you can't afford to buy something high-end, you should go look at it, touch it, and that's how you'll recognize quality."

When shopping, look for words like "Egyptian long-staple," "pima," and "Supima," which all denote the use of a specific type of high-quality, long-staple cotton that makes for noticeably softer sheets that won't pill.

# How It's Made

THE VAST MAJORITY OF TEXTILES (USED IN EVERYTHING FROM CLOTH napkins to airplane seats to bedsheets) are woven in mega factories; the fine mills of the world are now but a small part of a very large supply chain.

Before the mechanization of the weaving process, textiles were an investment, a sign of wealth. "Textiles were so valuable that you would leave them to your children in your will," says Susan Brown. It's well documented that often people bequeathed their textiles to the church, where they were then cut and repurposed to dress the altar and the clergy. Accordingly, she adds, "fabrics were very lovingly cared for, through really all of history until the nineteenth century."

The fabrication process is still complex, if less time-consuming. A material like wool must be harvested from the sheep, washed, cleaned, and spun into thread before that thread can be woven to create a textile. This is the work of mills, separate from the actual fabric house whose label appears on the textiles you buy. The house is usually a design team that dreams things up—the perfect stripe, a bright floral, an elaborate toile. The mill is where that design is brought to life.

France's renowned fabric house Pierre Frey controls that process more than some houses, as it has its own mill; nonetheless, outsourcing to specialist mills remains a key part of the business at Pierre Frey and other luxury houses. Patrick Frey, son of the namesake owner, cites India as an example. "The people of India have embroidered for thousands of years," he says. "They have perfected it. We travel there regularly, we give them our designs, we double-check, we triple-check, to be sure that it is produced to our expectations. We know that when it's then shipped to a designer in Los Angeles or San Francisco, the product is going to be perfect. For me, quality is the work of the hand and the eye. When you look at it, when you touch it, you say, 'My God, it's so beautiful.' That makes all the difference. The feeling is as important as the look."

Another consideration when shopping is whether the fabric is woven into a design or printed with one; here, the way the aesthetic effect has been created affects the quality of the end result. T4 by Tillett Textiles specializes in prints, primarily painterly florals and nature motifs based on watercolors by founder D. D. Tillett. The base fabrics Tillett uses are linens, cottons, and silks, sourced from the world's finest mills; they screen their

OPPOSITE › **1** › At DwellStudio in Manhattan, before a pattern ever reaches a fabric mill, designs are hand-sketched right in the studio. **2** › Every textile collection starts with a trip to the company's library, where vintage tomes filled with endless inspiration abound. **3** › Block printing is applied using antique hand-carved wood blocks, which have been collected from all over the world. **4** › The perfect hue is meticulously selected and triple-checked at every stage of production for accuracy.

FOLLOWING PAGE › DwellStudio's popular Indochine print is a nod to the East-Meets-West chinoiserie style of seventeenth-century European décor. Unlike most bedding, it is a full screen print, meaning it's printed in much the same way wallpaper would be, and from ideation to retail took eighteen long months.

designs onto those fabrics by hand. The screening process is labor-intensive. "Certainly all of the fabric that is intended for printing has to be prepared," says Patrick McBride, the founder's grandson. "It has to be washed and shrunk; otherwise you just have all sorts of crazy things going on when you print it. That's a very interesting thing, especially with new patterns: when you start printing them, there are so many little techniques that you have to think about. You have to look at the material and almost listen to it."

Screen-printed textiles are always going to make a different statement from traditional wovens; in Tillett's case, the technique, as well as the painterly quality of their prints, yields fabrics that are almost art more than traditional textile. Even their subdued prints could be framed and hung on the wall. That aspect is due to the original designer's eyes and the current makers' hands. "Our stripes are all done by a human being," says McBride. "As you look at them, there's movement to them. It's almost the difference between candlelight and fluorescent light. Fluorescent light is very flat, and candlelight has life and movement. To me, it's organic."

Tillett's current focus is on what they term "print to order." They stock various fabric options and a handful of premixed pigments; when an order is placed, they need only to pull a screen, print the fabric, and send it off. This model yields customizable fabrics (a given pattern in another color, for example) at a very quick turnaround.

Fabrics can also be woven into a pattern—something as simple as two colors blended together or as elaborate as a realistic floral. The more finely detailed the image, the more colors of thread used, the more complex it is to create. Printed fabrics can be likened to paintings because they involve the application of pigment to a surface. Woven fabrics can be thought of almost like sculpture, then: the individual threads are shaped into the desired form, whether it's polka dots, a scenic toile, or a chevron stripe. With wovens, the pattern and the fabric are one and the same. Weaving a fabric is always a complicated process; weaving a fabric with an intricate pattern on it even more so.

"Just think that you live with your curtains, your cushions, or your sofa 365 days a year," says Frey. "They will be with you throughout everything that happens in your life. The choice of what you put in your home, I think, is much more important than you realize."

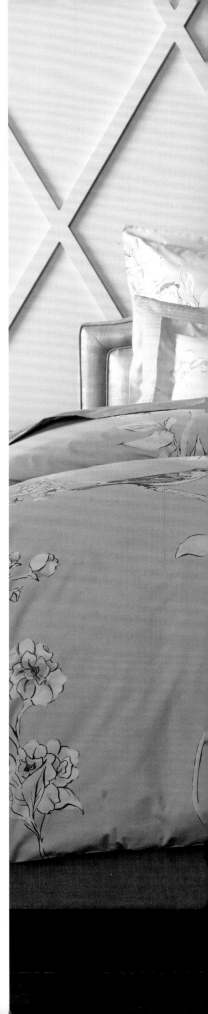

# End Use

JENNIE WILDE, OF THE TEXTILE HOUSE ROBERT ALLEN, POINTS OUT that all of us women have a dress we've never worn hanging in our closet— and if choosing a fabric is like picking a piece of clothing, you don't want it to be the gamble that just didn't work out. "You may be attracted to a fabric for its appealing color," Wilde says, "but you really want to understand that fabric, and the characteristics that relate to its form."

The relationship between the fabric's properties and its intended use— lighter cottons and linens for drapery or a pillow, more durable velvets and jacquards for upholstery—is one of the principal concerns for textile designers. "When we have artwork on paper we think *how* we want to use it," says Christy Almond, a designer at Robert Allen, explaining the journey from sketch to finished product. "Do we want it to be a drape? Do we see it as a bedding fabric? Do we see it as an upholstery fabric?" After Almond determines its potential destinations, she then considers which mill of the several around the world Robert Allen deals with will be best able to bring her design to life.

A fabric's intended use matters for the consumer as well; not every fabric is right for every job. "If you're going to do something for a drape, you should get a sample," says Wilde, "then drape it and put it in front of the window and see how much light comes through. When you think about drapery or bedding, the fabric itself contributes a lot to creating that form. There's no understructure."

Samples and swatches are imperative for any project you have in mind. For upholstery projects, Wilde says, "put the sample on an arm of the sofa, even if it's not the sofa you're going to cover. Just see how it's going to shape to the form." So many variables contribute to a textile's properties that even if you are comparing two upholstery-grade cottons, they can be quite different in the way they hug a curve, the way they'll wear over the years. Samples tell you what online shopping simply cannot: how the fabric handles, and how it feels. "You buy a chair, but what you really interact with is the fabric," says Wilde. "That's what you sit on. That's what your hands go on. Select something you are going to want to live with."

**OPPOSITE ›** With something like a tablecloth or cloth napkins, which are guaranteed to see a spill or two, fabric content is of utmost importance; because of its durability, linen has long been the preferred choice (there's a reason they're called "table linens," after all).

**ABOVE ›** An inspiring look at smart—really beautiful—fabric selections: the canopy, curtains, and headboard are all a heavier, more durable material, while the bedding is a mix of soft cotton and luxurious silk.

A single, gauzy-sheer curtain panel transforms ᵤe canopy bed into a bohemian dream.

In a historic Antebellum home in Madison, a simple linen cushion and rustic throw pillows ᵃᵗe the French provincial mood perfectly.

# Upholstery

MANY OF THE FINER TEXTILE HOUSES DEAL EXCLUSIVELY TO THE trade, typically via showrooms and design centers that are open only to interior design professionals. It's an old-fashioned model, one critics fault for denying interested consumers access to the wares of finer manufacturers. "I think in the world of decoration, it's good to have someone to help you," counters Patrick Frey. "It's not as easy as it seems to do it on your own. If I tell you tomorrow, 'You're going to paint all of the walls of your living room in red,' you might say, 'This guy is crazy.' But if I show you that in red, it's going to be beautiful when mixed with other items, you're going to be more convinced. If you want to make your home spectacular, you have to work with someone who knows what to do."

When you buy furniture, even at a fairly high-end retailer, you typically have only a few fabric finishes to choose from. However, you need not settle for the handful of options the retailer has laid out for you, and it's key to consider all manner of surfaces—the sofa, the armchairs, the dining room chairs, the window treatments, the headboard, even the bedding. Shop a showroom and find a seamstress and you can create a home that truly reflects your taste.

"There is so much sameness in the world today," says Frey. "We all have similar watches, our cars look the same, our clothes look the same. We all look alike in the street. The one place that truly reflects our personality is our home, where we express what we like, what we want, what we find over the weekend in the shop, what our father gave us."

"You can really freshen up a room just by changing the fabric," says Christy Almond. "It's an easy change, a way to bring fashion into the space." Understand the most important characteristics of textiles, develop your sense of hand, and the possibilities are limitless. Design a pillow to fit snugly in the arm of your favorite chair, bring a vintage sofa back to life, take a store-bought piece and put your own spin on it.

For her newly renovated Victorian cottage in Georgia, textile designer and artist Susan Hable Smith shopped for vintage furniture with interesting shapes, and then reupholstered everything in a dreamy mix of fabrics.

In the famed Beverly Hills Greystone mansion, designer Martyn Lawrence Bullard expertly pairs multiple patterns from his own fabric collection.

**ABOVE ›** Exhibition of hand-weaving from Black Mountain College, spring 1942.

**RIGHT ›** Rug by Anni Albers, 1959.

**OPPOSITE ›** Anni Albers card weaving at Black Mountain College.

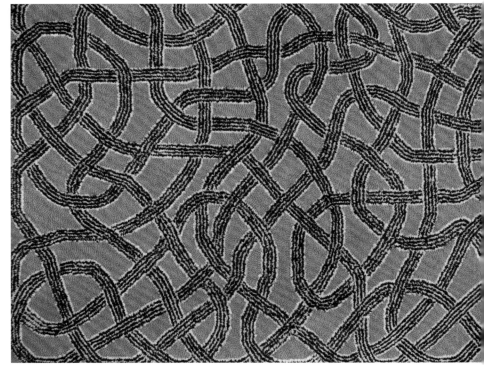

# DESIGN CHAMPION: *Anni Albers*

BORN IN GERMANY, the textile designer and artist Anni Albers was part of the diaspora of artists and intellectuals who came to America during World War II. Albers and her husband, Josef, the celebrated painter and art teacher, were affiliated with both the Bauhaus and North Carolina's Black Mountain College.

Albers was a truly innovative designer, and achieved a level of acclaim rarely afforded to someone who specializes in textiles. She was interested in rhythm, in creating dazzling patterns with a logic that's not immediately evident. Her use of striking color combinations and unusual materials was experimental; the results feel fresh even now, decades after her death.

Albers was celebrated as an artist in her lifetime (the Museum of Modern Art gave her a retrospective), but probably a greater measure of Albers's significance is the role she played at Knoll, where she worked closely with the company's textile division. Knoll helped create and burnish the aesthetic we now term "mid-century modern," and their designs, for institutional and residential use, were incredibly popular—indeed, they still are. Albers was therefore in the unique position of being both celebrated in museums and in demand among the middle class.

## RECOGNIZING THE MAJOR PLAYERS
# *Fabric Basics*

### I > ROBERT ALLEN

Seventy years ago The Robert Allen Group pioneered fabric books and the concept of organizing and designing fabrics by color. Robert Allen offers designs ranging in scope from traditional to contemporary, eco-friendly options, and collaborations with cutting-edge design firms, including DwellStudio.

### 2 > DONGHIA

Interior designer Angelo Donghia focused on aesthetics, quality, and comfort in designing his interiors, and his forty-year-old firm continues that legacy with its collections of furniture, textiles, wallcoverings, lighting, and accessories sold to the trade throughout the world. Textiles range from traditional to modern, in both manufacturing techniques and styles.

### 3 > T4 BY TILLETT TEXTILES

Kathleen Tillett and son Patrick McBride of Tillett Textiles & T4 offer the colorPAD collection, which gives customers an instant way to create their own custom fabrics online— an armchair designer's fantasy. While embracing the digital age, the physical fabrics remain handprinted and hand-striped, losing none of the luxury or sophistication for which they have been renowned for four generations.

### 4 > SCHUMACHER

Founded in 1889, Schumacher, still a family-owned company, has developed a long-standing reputation for high-quality decorative textiles, wallcoverings, and furnishings, sold strictly to the trade. Styles include silks, wovens, modern patterns, and collaborations with well-known interior designers, including Alessandra Branca, Celerie Kemble, and Matthew Patrick Smyth.

### 5 > MAHARAM

Founded by Russian immigrant Louis Maharam in 1902, this company evolved from a source for theatrical textiles in the 1940s to a pioneer of performance-driven commercial fabrics in the '60s. Today it offers an impressive range of styles, including its much-lauded collaborations with well-known designers, from both the past and the present.

### 6 > PIERRE FREY

In the true spirit of the storied French *maison de luxe* (luxury design house), Pierre Frey designs, creates, and manufactures fabrics and wallpapers. This family-owned business was founded in 1935, and today offers no fewer than 7,000 styles in its extensive fabric library.

THIS PAGE › Mixing plush velvets with crisp linens, furry throw pillows with textured wool carpet, Ashley Stark's cozy-dark den is pure decadence.

OPPOSITE › Tucked away in a tiny corner of Carlo Mollino's much-lauded Italian flat sits a vintage daybed swathed in rich silk fabrics and leopard prints.

# *window treatments*

Every home has windows, and almost every homeowner has reason to cover those windows, whether to make a decorative statement, seek respite from the sun, or hide from prying eyes. So when trying to find the right treatment, consider your priorities: is it privacy or prettiness that matters to you most?

It is possible to have both, but how you rank your needs will influence how you approach dressing your windows. If privacy comes first, then the initial layer should include blackout shades or shutters. If, however, prettiness is your biggest concern, then let the desired mood dictate the fabric chosen, from breezy sheers to decadent heavy velvet. In either scenario, look for treatments that enhance the architecture of your windows and rooms, and involve thoughtful work by skilled hands.

At a time when heavy velvet drapery was *toute la rage*, French designer Madeleine Castaing framed the windows of Maison de Lèves, her iconic estate, in gauzy-sheer muslin, an attempt to invite the lush green gardens indoors.

# Then—and Now

ONCE UPON A TIME, WINDOWS WERE DRESSED AS LAVISHLY AS WOMEN. Think of Scarlett O'Hara, recycling Tara's drapes into a dress (and hat to boot). Those elaborate treatments of yore (billowing swags, cascading pelmets, frilly jabots) have long fallen out of fashion, and today's Scarlett would be hard-pressed to upcycle much more than a simple shift dress out of the panels and drapes you'd find in most homes. Once, we dressed our windows in dozens of yards of fabric, the equivalent of a couture gown; today, most windows are clad in ready-to-wear.

Windows are architecture, and architecture is what defines a space. Successfully putting a room together requires understanding and celebrating the space's architecture—the height of its ceilings, the quality of the natural light, and, indeed, its windows. "I always start with backgrounds—the biggest elements of the room," says interior designer Richard Keith Langham. "The floor (including whatever the rug will be), the walls, and certainly the curtains. They establish the whole complexion, the personality of the room. Then the furniture comes in."

Langham is one of those true believers who has never forsworn the graceful look of lavish custom curtains. "Windows are the eyes of a room, and obviously, one of the biggest architectural elements in the space," says Langham. "I like to dress them in an important way. I prefer the traditional or classic English curtains—curtains that have an extravagant silhouette but are often made in a very simple or humble fabric. Great curtains are all about the finesse of making them with dressmaker details like ruching, braids, fringe, tassels."

It's not hard to find something that satisfies functional considerations like keeping out the light or the gaze of neighbors and passersby. Simple cotton panels in a few one-size-fits-all dimensions are widely available, but if you want something special, something that is practical but also pretty, you're not going to find much on the shelves. "If you're after a look that you see in interior design magazines," says Ian Gibbs, creative director at The Shade Store, "those are for the most part custom interiors, and it's pretty hard to get that look with just off-the-rack stuff, because no one's windows are the same."

In small spaces (like this 375-square-foot studio), it's not the quantity of things with which you fill it but the quality of those things that counts; exquisite custom window treatments make all the difference.

OPPOSITE › If decadent volume is the goal, then stiff-but-lightweight silk—sewn with a pocket-rod edge—will have tight, gathered folds on top and beautiful, full volume at the hem.

THIS PAGE › Piped window valances give roman shades all the finished formality of full-length curtains.

# How It's Made

"CURTAINS ARE VERY INVOLVED TO MAKE," SAYS RICHARD KEITH Langham. "Quality curtains should have three layers of fabric: the face, the flannel inner lining, and the outer lining." Langham takes things one step further. "I always like to add another fabric as the final lining," he says, "because I hate to see white curtain lining from the outside of a house. It looks like sheets hanging in the window. I always like to do a small pinstripe, a tiny check, or a solid color."

The window treatments found at retailers—even at the highest end of the market—aren't constructed this thoughtfully; designers like Langham deal directly with experts like David Haag, who runs a workshop specializing in window treatments. After a stint in the fashion business, Haag came to focus on custom window treatments, learning the trade by practice. "I don't know someone who can teach it," says Haag. "When I made clothes, I was intrigued by the bias cut, and I learned how to drape fabric and how to make it do what I wanted. I worked in a costume shop. I watched the best drapers, and saw how they made patterns and how they put things together."

A generation ago, there were several workrooms like Haag's, small shops where dedicated artisans practiced their specific skill. Over time, the landscape has changed, and that old model is increasingly rarer. "Curtain making is a couture thing," says Langham. "There are fewer and fewer workrooms that can make old-world curtains. It's so nice to not have to look at black glass and black windowpanes at night. It is sumptuous and cozy to be able to draw the curtains at six."

The downside of the couture model is the investment required—of both money and time. "Typically a custom window treatment requires anywhere from two to three months' lead time," says Ian Gibbs of The Shade Store. "We're able to cut things down to a matter of days or weeks, without losing sight of our core values, which are based on quality craftsmanship and service."

The Shade Store has revolutionized the very notion of the workroom. Everything they make—utilitarian roller shades, roman shades, blinds, drapery—is still built by hand, to the customer's specifications. But rather than visiting a workroom, customers visit a website. Rather than selecting from limitless options, they choose from a range of available fabrics.

The Shade Store's New York workrooms are equipped with the latest state-of-the-art machinery, but every stage of assembly—from cutting fabric to pressing pleats to sewing hems—is guided, if not wholly done, by hand.

Despite the modern point of entry, The Shade Store remains a very old-school business. "To make one roman shade takes the same amount of time today as it did in 1946," says Gibbs. "The only thing that's changed is the material we're making it from, the textile, and a few more strictly enforced safety laws and mechanisms. But one person is responsible for each shade from start to finish. It's not put on a conveyor belt. It's all cut by one person."

Gibbs is mindful of the fact that even this more streamlined model of custom production isn't for everyone. "There is always going to be a ready-made customer market out there. Let's face it—you can't necessarily take a custom shade with you. You buy a sofa, you can take it with you. Or you can recycle it. With window treatments, it's not so easy." That said, you can look at custom window treatments the same way you would a coat of paint or a roll of wallpaper; you may not take it along to your next home, but it may enhance your current one enough to be worth the investment.

The Shade Store is able to do in mere days what would take months for a boutique atelier to sew—without sacrificing an ounce of the quality you expect from a job done by hand.

# DESIGN CHAMPION: *Stéphane Boudin*

IN 1962, FIRST LADY JACKIE KENNEDY led NBC viewers on a guided tour of the White House, the restoration and redecoration of which had occupied her during the first year of her husband's administration. The Kennedy Library estimates the program's viewership at eighty million—a staggering testament to the Kennedys' influence in the culture, and especially in the worlds of fashion and interior design.

As any blue-blooded wife and mother of the day would have done, Kennedy turned to experts for help: American designer Sister Parish was responsible for the family's private rooms, and Stéphane Boudin, of the French firm Maison Jansen, tackled the White House's ceremonial and public spaces. "Sister Parish's success was in creating livable, comfortable spaces," says James Archer Abbott, author of several studies on interior design. "That's not what the State Floor of the White House is. Boudin was trained as an interior architect. That's what French designers are. It may have been that French discipline that helped to make the Kennedy interior so successful."

And a key part of that successful interior was the window treatments. "Boudin's belief was that often designers can go overboard, and window treatments can become the only focus of a room," says Abbott. "It was his belief that draperies were part of an entire scheme. They were not to be the focus of the room. They were integrated into a whole." Prior to the Kennedy restoration, the State Rooms' windows were perhaps more elaborately dressed, with passementerie, swags, tiebacks, and yards and yards of fabric. Boudin stripped away much of that.

Abbott perceives in Boudin's handiwork a nod to the neoclassicism prevalent at the time. "In architecture, think about Brasilia, think about Lincoln Center, think about the planned cultural center for Washington, D.C., that ironically became the John F. Kennedy Center for the Performing Arts," he says. "Those are all classical compositions that are stripped down, very linear, but all the same, they are born of the Acropolis and great ruins of the ancients." The draperies in the Green Room and Red Room (seen at left) fell straight, in columns, and were relatively unadorned. The effect was surprisingly modern in a building completed in 1800, and appropriately on trend for a project meant to reflect the new president's youth.

Boudin worked with a rigor that's largely been lost. "Boudin would not decorate a room until he had seen the space in the evening, with the client in it," says Abbott. "He then worked on the palette and the lighting so the Kennedys would look their best." Furthermore, he had an interest in even the smallest of details. "If you go through the Jansen order books for elaborate window treatments," says Abbott, "the valance was just one shade darker to keep your eye from going above the window treatment. It's not a major color change. It's just subtle enough to keep your eye from going up, and a beautiful way of framing the overall composition."

THIS PAGE › Semi-sheer café curtains are paired with blackout roman shades to ensure privacy in a window-filled master bath.

OPPOSITE › A small guest room makes a large statement thanks to a wall of voluminous graphic black-and-white drapes.

## RECOGNIZING THE MAJOR PLAYERS
# *Window Treatments*

### 1 > THE SHADE STORE

The Shade Store began in 1946 as a small fabric shop outside of New York City and is now run by the family's third generation of businessmen focusing on quality, style, and value in custom window treatments. The Shade Store handcrafts all products in the USA.

### 2 > CALICO

What started as a little store in Bedford Village, New York, in 1948 has become one of the country's largest fabric retailers. In the beginning, Calico specialized in selling secondhand designer fabrics (at the time, only interior designers had access to that segment of the market). Today the company stocks an extraordinary selection of styles, giving customers firsthand access to a lot of fabrics exclusively available to the trade. It is also equipped to take on custom projects for clients, including hand-sewing window treatments.

### 3 > SMITH & NOBLE

California-based Smith & Noble has offered affordable, DIY-style, custom-fit window treatment solutions since 1987. The selection includes drapery, blinds, shutters, shades, and panels in a range of styles.

### 4 > LUTRON

Lutron was founded in 1961 by Joel and Ruth Spira. Joel, a physicist, invented a solid-state dimmer that allowed people to change light intensity in their homes. Lutron now holds more than 2,700 worldwide patents and offers 15,000 products. The company's high-tech shading solutions help users year-round to conserve energy, protect furnishings, and reduce glare.

### 5 > DAVID HAAG

David Haag is a renowned curtain maker who works with some of the nation's top interior designers to create elegant, elaborate window treatments that have been compared to couture fashion. Haag, whose workroom is based in Manhattan, is known for his skillful cutting, draping, and pleating, perhaps the result of his background in fashion design.

### 6 > KNOLLTEXTILES

Knoll Inc. has been a leading manufacturer of modern furnishings for nearly a century. Knoll Textiles, founded by Florence Knoll in 1947 as a department of the larger company, offers both an archival collection of midcentury styles, as well as new designs to suit contemporary trends.

**1** › Jet-black curtains flow like liquid from the ceiling to the floor, breaking up the bedroom's continuous print. **2** › Oversize tiebacks (embroidered with an urn drawn by the homeowner, designer Kelee Katillac) gather the curtains in the master bedroom, adding a couture-like finish. **3** › Small framed silhouettes dangle from Katillac's dining room shutters (upholstered in a cheery Isaac Mizrahi stripe).

**4 ›** Big, bold florals break up the dark, masculine mood of a formal study surrounded by wood-paneled walls. **5 ›** Striped roman shades act as a graphic design anchor in the lush lounge of fashion designer Tamara Mellon. **6 ›** Elegant decorative valances (created by David Haag) extend to the floor, framing the almost ceiling-high windows while hiding panels of silky-sheer curtains. **7 ›** To complement the neoclassical moldings in her drawing room, Katillac had small, decorative bows sewn along the top of each box-pleat curtain. **8 ›** Whisper-thin sheers underpin gauzy, block-printed curtains in a sun-drenched living room.

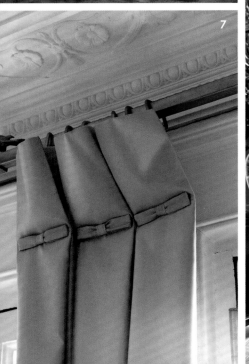

# rugs

In many parts of the world, a room is simply not finished without a rug. Think of the nations we associate with great textile- and rug-making—Turkey, Pakistan, Afghanistan, Morocco; in homes in those countries, rugs are afforded a central place in every room. They are as important in welcoming guests and signifying comfort and hospitality as a sofa is in the United States. In these cultures, all predominantly Islamic, shoes are generally not worn inside the home, where cleanliness is prized; rugs cover the floor but also offer a place to sit.

When in the market for a rug, consider the look (color, pattern, and proportion), but also its texture, both how it feels underfoot and what it adds to the mix of textures within the rest of the room. You'll also want to think about its intended use and whether its materials and construction suit its setting.

Placing a wool rug directly next to the bed has become a modern-day necessity, acting as a soft barrier between bare feet and cold floors.

# FROM THE PAST TO THE PRESENT
## *The Unique History of Rugs*

### ANTIQUITY

Animal-printed Oriental carpets are described in classical Greek literature.

### IITH CENTURY AD

During the Crusades, carpets are brought from the Near East to Europe, and soon European manufacturers begin imitating Oriental carpets.

### I502–I736

The Safavids in Persia become famous for their richly colored carpets with figurative depictions of animals, hunting scenes, and gardens.

### 17TH CENTURY

Europeans import thousands of carpets from India by way of the East India Trading Company.

### 1791

William Sprague establishes the first American woven carpet mill in Philadelphia.

### 15TH CENTURY

Western paintings depict interiors decorated with Oriental carpets featuring repeating geometric patterns and animal motifs. Usually carpets are shown as table coverings.

### 1626

The Savonnerie factory is established in France and becomes known as the most esteemed European manufacturer of knotted-pile carpets. In the beginning, Savonnerie carpets copy Persian designs, but eventually the designs reflect French culture by depicting bouquets of flowers and armorial medallions.

### 1839

Erastus Bigelow invents the power loom for weaving carpets, which immediately doubles production, then triples it by 1850. He issues thirty-five separate patents between 1839 and 1876 for his invention, and introduces the first broadloom carpet in 1877.

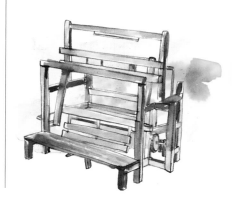

## 19TH CENTURY

With the invention of the Jacquard process and the application of steam-powered looms, patterned carpets become more readily available. During the second half of the 19th century, design reformers such as William Morris react strongly against what they perceive as the degradation of design by returning to hand-produced carpet production.

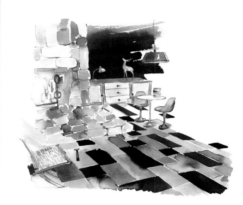

## 1950s

With innovations in synthetic fibers and technical equipment, more carpets are tufted, a less expensive way of producing carpet than weaving. During the post–World War II housing boom, the carpet industry sells about 6 million square yards of tufted carpet for wall-to-wall application, and by the 1960s, that number grows to 400 million.

## 1917–1919

During the United States' involvement in World War I, carpet looms are converted to manufacture Navy blankets and tents.

## 1970s

The industry's ability to produce all types of piles and textures results in a "carpet revolution," during which people are excited to try out anything new, perhaps most famously the shag.

## TODAY

Homeowners incorporate area rugs, more than wall-to-wall carpeting, in a variety of colors, patterns, and textures. Oriental rugs remain a status symbol, as many communities throughout Asia continue to manufacture them by hand as their ancestors did.

# A Room's Foundation

"RUGS CAN BE, DESIGN WISE, QUITE OFTEN THE STARTING POINT OF a room," says designer Martyn Lawrence Bullard. "Because if you find a good rug, it's a great place to pull the colors from, and to decorate your room around."

Clearly, pattern and color are the aspects of a rug's design that will catch your eye. And rugs are an ideal place for the commitment-phobic decorator to experiment. "So many people are scared of color," says Bullard. "If you've got a white room and you're scared to put color up on the walls, an easy way to bring in color, to bring that burst of character to the space, is with a rug. In an all-white room, you can put a red rug on the floor and instantly change the whole vibe." If it doesn't work out, removing a rug is a lot less complicated than repainting your walls.

Beyond the obvious aesthetic factors that make you fall in love with a rug, it's also important to think about proportion. Some designers prefer all the furniture within a room to sit squarely on a rug, while others recommend the rug float under the coffee table but stop short of the sofa and chair legs. The proportion of the rug should relate to your aims for the room: a rug considerably smaller than the overall room will help you delineate a cozy nook or sofa-and-chairs arrangement. Conversely, a rug scaled to the room's proportions can soften the space but recede visually and function almost like a carpet.

The decorative should also appeal to the sense of touch. Rugs bring texture into a room, whether the simplicity of a worn-in antique or the luxurious shag of a lavish woolen flokati. And texture is a vital part of creating a balanced space. "Our feet are one of the erogenous zones of the body," says Bullard, who points out that soft textures are particularly important in places like the bedroom. "And so whatever you're walking on, you want it to feel great. If your feet feel great, it makes the rest of you feel great."

Texture is principally a reflection of the rug's materials, and there is a consensus on which materials are best. "I'm all about natural fabrics," says Bullard. "So when I'm buying a rug, I want to make sure it's wool, or silk, or raffia. Once you start adding synthetic products into a rug, you create static, and quite often it causes a strange sheen on the top of the rugs. Stores like IKEA, Crate & Barrel, Pottery Barn, Restoration Hardware, they have amazing products, made from natural fibers that are really affordable."

**OPPOSITE** › In a bedroom, much of the floor is covered by the bed itself; centering an area rug on the available floor space instead of within the four walls allows for more coverage.

**ABOVE** › Shaggy rugs are luxuriously soft, but they're also susceptible to crushing in high-traffic areas, so careful placement is the key to endurance.

An interest in the very finest materials took Christopher Sharp, who co-founded The Rug Company with his wife, Suzanne, far off the beaten path. "There's only one way to make a really good rug," says Sharp, "and that's going back to the traditional way of making it." The Rug Company's production is based in Nepal, principally due to the quality of the wool available there. As that wool is harvested from animals that live at a very high altitude, it therefore contains more lanolin; the presence of these natural oils yields wool that's incredibly durable. "If you drop some water on one of our rugs, the water will sit there for a while. It won't get absorbed, because there's so much oil in the actual wool that it repels it, and it stops it from getting dirty," says Sharp.

Most important, a rug's component materials tell you whether the rug is up for the job you have in mind. If you're looking for a floor covering for a heavily trafficked, kid-friendly living room, you may want to stick with a sturdy cotton dhurrie, while a sophisticated, adults-only living room can sustain a comparatively more delicate rug of wool and silk.

Patterned rugs can be used to emphasize (or visually alter) the sense of space in a room. Here, Martyn Lawrence Bullard utilizes a subtle stripe, echoed in the assemblage of throw pillows, to highlight an airy living room's gorgeous length.

# How It's Made

TEACH YOURSELF THE BASIC TERMINOLOGY BEFORE YOU MAKE A BIG purchase like a fine rug; the effort is worth it, as this isn't the kind of purchase you'll make many times in your life. That said, what might be most compelling about a quality rug (or a high-quality anything) is not something you need to teach yourself—it's something you need simply to be open to perceiving. "It's almost like poetry," says designer Madeline Weinrib. "A poem that's really beautiful just has a soul to it, and you can't dissect it too much, because then it will lose that poetic feel. If you look at a handmade product and you look at a machine-made product, you can dissect it, but in the end there seems to be a soul attached to a handmade product that just doesn't carry through the machine."

Weinrib designs rugs and textiles. She's based in New York, but her work is executed by weavers the world over: Central Asia, Turkey, Morocco, and Nepal. Weinrib's rugs aren't created in factories; rather her business is, in her words, a "cottage industry." Her network is comprised of artisans who handle every step of a rug's production from start to finish, using their own hands—hands so skilled that Weinrib refers to these specialists, respectfully, as "masters." It's fair to liken Weinrib's role in the actual execution of these designs to that of a conductor, overseeing those who bring her vision to life.

"There's one master who's in charge of the dyeing—he'll mix all the colors," says Weinrib. "Then you have the weavers, so that's two people or two teams of people. Then you have the people who wash the product. The washing is a very important aspect because it helps with the texture. Those are three steps along the way. So you're involved with three different experts, and they're not necessarily all in the same country."

Weinrib is focused on upholding exacting standards. "It can be a very slow process," says Weinrib. "If I'm working with embroiderers in Central Asia, each time we work together I'll ask them to eliminate something, or change a color, and then about three or four rounds in, my work will begin to evolve into something different from what they're familiar with." Weinrib is not creating versions of traditional textiles; her restrained use of color and pattern has a very Western point of view. In fact, many of the craftspeople who create these pieces don't personally appreciate them. "I don't think they understand my taste," she says. "They think I'm crazy. Especially if you know that in their culture, using a minimal amount of color is considered quite ugly."

1 › The Himalayan wool used to make The Rug Company's creations is hand-washed by Tibetan monks in Nepal and laid out to dry. 2 › The monks are also charged with untangling and de-thorning the wool, a step referred to as "carding." 3 › The flossy, carded wool is then fed into a hand-operated spinning wheel, which twists the piece-y bits into unbroken strings of yarn. 4 › There are more than 2,000 dye formulas in the company's repertoire, all kept in identical reference trays found in their stores and Nepalese workshops. 5 › These dye formulas are the responsibility of "dye masters," who ensure color uniformity. 6 › For each rug, a full-size "map" of its design is made on graph paper and hung behind the loom for guidance. 7 › Rugs are woven on a traditional vertical loom. Each row of knots is completed using a single piece of yarn, and then pushed down the loom with an iron mallet called a "thowa." 8 › Weavers meticulously inspect the final product, trimming any stray bits of yarn. 9 › Every step of this process is chemical-free, ensuring the longevity of the wool's natural lanolin oils.

The Rug Company works in collaboration with a cross-section of talents from the worlds of art, interior design, and fashion, so the brand isn't marked by any aesthetic; rather the defining characteristic is its quality. The Sharps were inspired by the weaving techniques they discovered in Nepal, where everything is done by hand, beginning with the spinning of the wool. "To make one rug takes four months," says Christopher Sharp. "During that time you've got twenty different people working on the production. There's so much precise, extraordinary skill."

Sharp is mindful of the fact that most consumers are more interested in rugs that are not an investment—that their inexpensiveness makes up for the fact that they won't wear well or last for long. That's not the business he's in. "You can't marry great design with poor quality," says Sharp.

That does not stop people from trying, though. It takes Weinrib months to refine a rug, while mass-produced knockoffs of her designs can be rushed to market quite quickly, and at a significantly lower price point. Weinrib herself has studied knockoffs of her own designs. "If I look at them in real life," she says, "I'm surprised at how different the two-dimensional image is from the actual piece. That's advice I would give to people—that they actually look at the piece if they have the opportunity."

Weinrib makes the point that knockoffs almost always involve different—that is to say, less expensive—materials. The knockoff might approximate the real deal's look quite convincingly, but if it's executed in a blend that includes polyester and other synthetics, it'll never feel the same. And the language of marketing can be misleading. "One of the most confusing terms is 'hand-tufted,'" Weinrib says. It's a phrase that will be familiar to anyone who's shopped for a rug. "The word *hand* makes you think that it's done by hand, but that's when someone's holding a machine."

As with textiles, judging a quality rug is simpler when you've felt and examined enough rugs to understand, simply by touch, the difference between something handmade of natural materials and something machine-woven with synthetics. Beyond the texture and heft, there may be other ways in which the lesser-quality rug differs, many of which may not be evident in the store. Colors might fade, fibers might fray, and the rug just won't last.

By the time one of The Rug Company's stunning custom creations makes it to your door, it's been handled by no less than twenty skilled artisans and has undergone a no-corners-cut, four-month-long production process.

## RECOGNIZING THE MAJOR PLAYERS
# *Rugs*

### 1 > CHRISTOPHER FARR

Christopher Farr, an abstract painter, developed an interest in pre-Columbian textiles on a trip to Peru in the 1970s. After receiving textiles training in Peruvian and Turkish villages, Farr established his eponymous firm with antique rug dealer and restorer Matthew Bourne in 1988 with the goal of blending modernist artistic styles with ancient hand-dyeing and hand-looming techniques. The company's innovative styles include limited-edition rugs by renowned artists and designers.

### 2 > THE RUG COMPANY

The Rug Company, founded by London-based Christopher and Suzanne Sharp in 1997, offers hundreds of rug designs, as well as customizable options. Aside from its high-quality materials and excellent production practices, the company is best known for its collaborations with leading artists, designers, and architects: Alexander McQueen, David Rockwell, Diane von Furstenberg, Kelly Wearstler, and Vivienne Westwood.

### 3 > SURYA

Indian native Surya Tiwari began his area rug and home accessories manufacturing company in 1976 by selling one- or two-color hand-knotted rugs to what is now Macy's. A decade later, he began operating his business directly to customers in the United States, growing his product selection over time to reach its current level of twenty thousand items at varying price points. While many styles are available, Indian tufted and knotted rugs naturally form the company's specialty.

### 4 > DASH & ALBERT

Dash & Albert, founded in 2003, offers durable, affordable rugs—hooked, hand-loomed, handwoven, and tufted in cotton, wool, and indoor/outdoor materials—as well as throws, pillows, and accessories. The much-lauded Bunny Williams Collection for Dash & Albert includes indoor/outdoor rugs with modern geometric patterns.

### 5 > MADELINE WEINRIB

Inspired by her global travels, Madeline Weinrib is known for mixing contemporary colors, details, and modern designs with centuries-old traditional weaving techniques. She designs fabrics, carpets, and accessories, each marked by her signature bold patterns.

### 6 > STEPHANIE ODEGARD COLLECTION

Stephanie Odegard founded her eponymous company in 1987 as both a designer and activist. Her luxury carpets are crafted by skilled adult artisans in Nepal—where she proudly sets industry standards for social and environmental responsibility—using hand-spun, hand-knotted Himalayan wool.

OPPOSITE › In his Paris flat, designer Hervé Van der Straeten offset the angular sharpness of his signature sculptural works with an incredibly soft and woolly area rug.

THIS PAGE › There is nothing Western about the cowhides being produced by Kyle Bunting; its extensive collection of rugs includes patchwork patterns and every shade imaginable.

# *carpets*

Once upon a time, there was no greater middle-class signifier than having wall-to-wall carpeting. In the 1950s, with the rise of the American middle class and the explosion of the suburban communities that housed them, carpeting became an ideal, an essential. It connoted comfort, a modest kind of luxury, and also a sense of being on the cutting edge, similar to owning a television or an electric stove.

Carpets are similar to rugs; the measure of their quality is to be found in their materials and manufacture processes, but it's important to remember how that process differs and weigh the understructure of carpeting as much as the part you see and feel daily.

In David Hicks's former country home, retro geometric carpeting (the designer's own pattern) takes the form of twin "area rugs," dividing the large living room into two, cozier sitting spaces.

# How It's Made

NATURAL CARPETS—OF WOOL, PRINCIPALLY—ARE RARER THAN ALL-natural rugs, because you need so much carpet, and it's accordingly that much more expensive. Most carpeting is made of synthetic fibers that have been developed for softness, stain resistance, and general durability, like nylon, olefin, and acrylic. Middle-range carpets typically blend one of these synthetics with some percentage of real wool.

The most common kind of residential carpets are tufted, in which the actual tufts that you feel underfoot are pushed through a backing material using needles on a specific kind of sewing machine. The tufts on top can be quite long—think of the seventies-era penchant for shag rugs—but are often trimmed to a uniform size. As the interior spring determines a sofa's comfort, so too does the backing in a carpet tell you much about its quality; high-quality backing means the fibers will remain in place, and the carpet will last for decades instead of merely years.

"I think it's so important that you buy something that has value," says Ashley Stark, creative director of Stark Carpet, which produces carpets, rugs, and textiles. "You are going to pay for it twice if you don't, because it will fall apart." Stark Carpet produces much of its carpeting domestically, in Pennsylvania, using fine materials, like New Zealand wool, as well as details that you might never notice, like the backing. Their backing is crafted so that fibers won't be easily loosened. "We replace a lot of our competitors' products," says Stark. "Because vacuums can rip fibers and cause shedding, many other brands' products wear out within a couple of years. A lot of our customers still have our carpeting on their stairs, even after twenty years."

When you're selecting a carpet, Stark recommends studying its back. She acknowledges, though, that the differences between a good and a mediocre backing may be less than obvious to a consumer. When shopping for carpets, ask lots of questions about details like the backing: how it's made, what it's made of, and how durable it is. An informed retailer will be able to provide this information to you. But don't just go by what the salesperson tells you; use your own hand and common sense. "You can feel the density and weight of a carpet," Stark says. "If it feels thin and flimsy, then it probably is." You can weigh the heft of a high-quality carpet and know that it's designed to last through years of wear and tear.

**1** › Similar to the "carding" process seen in The Rug Company's production (page 289), wool for carpets is separated and cleaned before being spun into yarn; though in lieu of hand-carding small batches, these machines clean pounds of wool in a quarter of the time. **2** › Once yarn is spooled, it becomes part of a larger computerized system. When a carpet requires a specific yarn color, it is digitally requested. The yarn then travels to that loom via a system of complex tubes (a bit like a building-size sewing machine). **3** › Small, noncustom carpeting is measured and cut to order directly from existing stock, meaning a carpet can arrive in mere days instead of months.

Another consideration with carpets comes at installation—the padding. This layer, usually made of urethane, supports the carpet above, and the two are designed to work in tandem. Some carpets have a specific type of padding indicated, and you should adhere to whatever thickness of padding the manufacturer recommends; a padding that's too thick can stress the carpet's backing from underneath, while a padding that's too thin can fail to appropriately support the carpet above, so it might wear or degrade.

Beyond durability, one of the principal concerns for the carpet customer is maintenance. "The first thing that many people say is, 'I want something durable and easy to clean. How about nylon?'" Stark says. "This is completely wrong." There is a widespread perception—one that probably dates to when synthetic fabrics first came to the market—that they're low-maintenance. "Wool is a one hundred percent natural fiber," says Stark. "It's also one hundred percent green, and the easiest fiber to clean because it's natural. Nylon is so much harder to clean because it's a synthetic fiber. You can have a wool carpet in your bedroom for twenty years, and it can be cleaned over and over again."

Not only is a natural fiber superior in terms of upkeep; it also delivers that aspect of comfort that we want in our homes. "In the showroom, I see this all the time," says Stark. "People often take their shoes off and put their feet on the carpet because that's ultimately what they're walking around on. These customers will definitely spend just a little bit more for our higher-quality products."

**OPPOSITE ›** Bloomsburg Carpet Industries in Pennsylvania is one of the few remaining American carpeting manufacturers. The carpet seen here, which was custom made for the United States House of Representatives, is undergoing its final inspection before being prepped for shipment.

**FOLLOWING PAGE, LEFT ›** Don't shy away from a graphic stair runner; a print has the ability to turn any stairwell into a statement.

**FOLLOWING PAGE, RIGHT ›** Kelly Wearstler shakes things up in this sitting room with a wildly printed carpet.

# DESIGN CHAMPION: *Marion Dorn*

THE AMERICAN-BORN DESIGNER MARION DORN created textiles and wallpapers but is perhaps most closely associated with rugs and carpets, a form she embraced and whose boundaries she pushed during her long and prolific career. Dorn drew inspiration from the art world in her designs of the 1920s and '30s; she adapted the stylized geometry that interested her contemporaries like the Cubists, reducing those forms to pure decoration and executing the carpets in luxurious materials. Dorn's carpets were popular in hotels, which were on the cutting edge of the era's design trends, and her work also appeared in the great ocean liner the *Queen Mary*.

Dorn's carpets look incredibly modern even to this day, though she was equally adept at working in a more traditional vernacular; she designed a large oval rug for a reception room at the Kennedy White House that marries her interest in geometry and form with motifs and colors appropriate for the American presidential residence.

**OPPOSITE** › Claridge's hotel lobby, London. **ABOVE** › *House & Garden,* July 1947.

# RECOGNIZING THE MAJOR PLAYERS

# *Carpets*

### I > MOHAWK FLOORING

Mohawk, the world's largest flooring company, offers flooring options in thirty categories with thousands of color, style, pattern, and texture choices. Mohawk began producing woven carpets in 1878, and today offers soft stain-resistant carpets in three main fibers—PET, nylon, and Triexta.

### 2 > FLOR

FLOR is no ordinary wall-to-wall carpet. Comprised of smaller, modular squares that can be easily and quickly installed at home, the FLOR carpet system allows customers to mix and match colors, or change their carpeting on a whim simply by replacing any number of 20-by-20-inch squares.

### 3 > TUFENKIAN ARTISAN CARPETS

Tufenkian carpets are intended to be heirlooms for centuries to come. James Tufenkian, in establishing his business in 1986, hoped to revive the art of Tibetan rug weaving—a goal that has expanded to include serving humanitarian aims in that and other regions. Today, he is an industry leader in handcrafted Tibetan and Armenian rugs.

### 4 > SHAW FLOORS

Started in 1946 as Star Dye Company, a rug-dyeing business, Shaw Floors is now a major international carpet manufacturer. The owners first purchased a yarn plant in 1972, and the company has been expanding ever since, acquiring other carpet producers and broadening its portfolio, which features Tuftex residential carpet and the fiber brand Anso Nylon.

### 5 > STARK CARPET

Stark Carpet recently transitioned from a trade-only company to a retail brand. Founded in 1946, it has been a principal resource for custom-designed residential and contract carpets for decades. Still family-run, the company now produces fabric, wallcoverings, furniture, rugs, as well as carpets, the latter in a huge range of styles, from solids to geometrics to florals to sisals, and specialty collections with interior designers.

### 6 > ABC CARPET & HOME

For more than a century, the experts behind this Manhattan-based, family-operated carpet and rug mecca have embraced tradition, while remaining at the forefront of industry innovations. Today, they're touted for having an extensive (some claim it's the largest in the world), expertly curated selection of carpets, from hand-tufted textures to luxurious velvets to natural fibers. And, as a sign of its ever-evolving nature, the company's custom division, featuring rugs designed on-site, is quickly becoming a go-to source for noted interior designers around the world.

Never overlook gorgeous, patterned carpet as a jumping off point for the color palette of an entire room. It's more permanent than a throw pillow, but it's also far more impactful.

# accessories

In a home, as in life, the little things make a very big difference. The soul of a home—its very personality, which is a reflection of our own—can be found in the things we live with: the vases and vessels with which we decorate, the glassware and silverware from which we eat and drink, the objects we surround ourselves with, both practical and simply decorative, and, of course, the lighting scheme that ties it all together.

# *lighting*

What's true for starlets is true for all of us: good lighting is key. "One of the most important things in designing a room is having a sense of how to light it," says designer David Netto. "Atmosphere is one of the most intangible parts of decorating and design, and lighting really is the key to atmosphere." What Netto is referring to is the overall lighting scheme—striking that perfect balance of utility and beauty, ensuring that you can see (or read, or cook, depending on your needs in a particular room). When choosing fixtures and lamps, it's imperative to weigh each individual piece's quality (how it looks, how it was made) and how it will work with all the other fixtures and elements in the space to ensure that everything, including you, looks its best.

Eclipsing the other organic shapes in Ashley Stark's formal dining room—hand-painted floral wallpaper, a dual tree-trunk table base—is a Jean de Merry urchin chandelier, hung high and at the table's center for a truly striking effect.

# *The Unique History of Lighting*

### ANTIQUITY

The earliest "lamps" are made out of rocks and shells that are filled with a natural material, such as moss, soaked in animal fat and lit. By 4500 BC oil lamps are invented, and by 3000 BC candles are developed. In the 7th century BC, the Greeks begin producing terra-cotta lamps that replace handheld torches, or *lampas*.

### 1792

William Murdoch is the first to use coal gas to light his house in England.

### 1801

Sir Humphry Davy invents the first electric carbon arc lamp.

### 18TH CENTURY AD

The central burner is invented in which a fuel source is enclosed in metal and an adjustable tube controls the intensity of the heat. A glass chimney is added to protect the flame. In 1783, Swiss chemist Aimé Argand develops the first oil lamp with a hollow circular wick surrounded by a glass chimney.

### 1805

Philips and Lee Cotton Mill in Manchester, England, becomes the first industrial factory to be fully lit by gas.

### 19TH CENTURY

Numerous inventors experiment with electric carbon arc lamps and in 1856 German physicist Heinrich Geissler is able to confine the electric arc in what becomes known as a "Geissler tube." Domestic lighting continues to be dominated by gas lighting and lamps are designed to "hide" technology.

### 1875

Henry Woodward patents an electric lightbulb and by 1879, Thomas Edison and Joseph Wilson Swan patent the carbon-thread incandescent lamp that could last up to 40 hours. One year later, Edison improves his design, producing a 16-watt bulb that could last 1,200 hours.

### 1920s

The first frosted lightbulb is produced in 1925 and in 1927 Friedrich Meyer, Hans Spanner, and Edmund Germer patent a fluorescent lamp, which is more efficient than incandescent lamps. Modernists, such as the Bauhaus's Wilhelm Wagenfeld, design lamps that celebrate the technical components of electrified lighting.

### 1991

The Philips Company invents a fluorescent lightbulb that uses magnetic induction and lasts 60,000 hours, a major leap in the effort to make lighting more energy efficient.

### 1910

Georges Claude invents the first neon lamp and displays it to the public in Paris. By 1915 he patents the neon lighting tube. Neon lights are soon employed in advertising.

### 2011

Philips wins accolades for the LED screw-in lamp, an energy-efficient alternative to 60-watt incandescent lightbulbs. Today, federal legislation is calling for the phasing out of incandescent bulbs as more energy-efficient options become easily accessible.

# The Lighting Scheme

EVERY DESIGNER HAS HIS OR HER OWN RULES FOR DEVISING THE IDEAL lighting scheme. Some say all the fixtures in a given room should be at the same height; some insist that all fixtures be installed on different circuits so they can turn on or off independently; some decree that every room needs to have X number of fixtures; some say the principal source of light should never be overhead; some feel that every fixture needs to be on its own dimmer; and so on.

What most designers agree on is that the fixtures you place in a room are important both because they're part of the larger mix of things you see, and because they establish the *way* you see everything in the room. It's hard to reduce developing a lighting scheme to a list of rules; each room demands its own particular plan, based on several factors: the height of the ceiling, the exposure to natural light, the color of the walls, the style of the architecture, the room's ultimate use, and your own personal preferences for bright or low light. If you have a great room with double-height ceilings, you'll likely want a big pendant or chandelier for some grand illumination; if your master bedroom has three walls of windows, maybe you won't feel the need for anything more than a couple of reading lamps.

"I use lighting as a design tool," says designer Charles Pavarini III. "I do not use it to illuminate a space, I use it to enhance a space, to bring in drama and different moods. Lighting is extremely important—without it, you could create the most beautiful floor plans and furnishings and fabrics, but if it's not lit well, you will not be able to clearly see your design intent. Everything will become very jumbled."

Each home or apartment comes with the very bare bones of décor, and that includes lighting. "The builder has to provide, by code, illumination," says Pavarini. "But they don't know the flavor of the room. They don't know how the end user is going to design the room. So what they usually do is put a recess [a fixture sunk into the ceiling] in each corner, so you can

Natural light was top priority when designer Steven Gambrel began planning this Sag Harbor kitchen, so the multiple ceiling-mounted task lights—lined up along the counter's edge—were meant as a function-focused companion to the wall of windows and the skylight.

turn on a switch and enter the room." It's not unlike how most homes feature bare white walls; there's nothing wrong with white walls, nor is there anything wrong with recessed overhead lighting. The question is whether these things suit what you intend to do with your room.

"I always like to have different types of lighting," Pavarini says. "A mixture of recessed lights, sconces, floor lamps, and table lamps gives depth to the room." The recessed fixture might be standard-issue, but it's still useful; Pavarini prefers a smaller, pinpoint recessed light as opposed to the more commonplace canister style. He is drawn to sconces because they add not only light but ornament, and it's easy to find one (modern and streamlined, or bejeweled and embellished) that complements the room's overall aesthetic. With respect to floor and table lamps, Pavarini cautions you to think about the shade as much as the lamp. "Make sure that the shade doesn't direct the light up and down only," he says. "A silk shade, or a fabric that mimics silk, illuminates very well."

Pavarini offers another piece of advice that's very easy to implement. "Across the line," he says, "always use dimmers, because then you have complete control over your environment. You don't need to be a millionaire to get some of these lighting effects. Put dimmers in everything, and then play with the different levels of light, and see how it changes the room."

"Lighting is so experiential," agrees David Netto. "You can't learn it from the Internet or reading *Elle Décor*. You have to learn it from seeing it in action. Go to La Grenouille in New York and look at all the pleated lampshades on the tables and tell me the lighting's not the most important thing in the room . . . the whole experience is delivered in those lights."

OPPOSITE › Designer Martyn Lawrence Bullard was going for pure shock value when he dreamt up this floating constellation of Moooi Random Lights, all set to a dramatic scale.

FOLLOWING PAGES › Tall and narrow, with the ability to slip into awkward and tight spaces, a well-placed floor lamp creates intimate ambience, while focusing light where it's needed most.

# How It's Made

THOUGH EVERY SCHEME IS PARTICULAR TO THE VARIABLES PRE-viously laid out, creating a lighting plan is still a matter of buying individual fixtures—and with these, the definition of quality relates to component materials and the manufacturing process. And lighting fixtures is a broad category. There's the chandelier and the floor lamps, there's the torchiere and the wall sconce; these can be made of brass or bronze, of stainless steel or stained glass. Weighing quality is a matter of thinking about every component in a fixture: is the lamp base sturdy, are its lines well proportioned, is the hardware tightly affixed?

"Quality has a number of elements that go into it," says Andy Singer, of the Houston-based Visual Comfort & Co. "It begins with an original design, made with authentic materials, and probably starts out being made by hand, then it's honed by craftsmen."

Visual Comfort collaborates with some of interior design's most recognizable names, then uses fine materials and traditional manufacturing techniques to bring those designers' visions to life. For Singer, the company's president, the role of the designer is of paramount importance. "I'm good at identifying beautiful things, but I'm not good at creating beautiful things," he says. "The designer does have value in the world. That's why a signed Louis C. Tiffany piece has value above the zillions of things made over the years in a Tiffany style." But quality goes deeper than the name stamped on something. "It starts with design," Singer says. "And if you do not support it with quality and enduring materials, then you are not supporting the value of what the designer brings to the table."

Visual Comfort is a factory operation, but that doesn't have to imply millions of goods rolling off a conveyor belt. "There is an enormous amount of human touch in our products," says Singer. "Everything starts with a drawing and a mold. We make molds to fabricate all of the parts. And because of the nature of the things we design, whether in the casting, machining, or polishing, most of the things that we do are hand-finished. Whether it is the patina on the brass, a gilded finish, or an aged iron finish, there's an enormous amount of handwork involved."

The designer Lindsey Adelman is known for chandeliers of geometric forms, pendants in imperfect glass orbs, and table lamps of hammered metal. Her fixtures are sculptural, but their practical applications elevate

1 › The glass orbs used in most of Lindsey Adelman's designs are all mouth-blown and hand-shaped in a studio in Brooklyn. 2 › All components start as a solid piece of brass (left) before being cut and polished. Here, a tray of T connectors, which are used as joints, is under way. 3 › The brass hardware is custom-machined at a separate facility in Brooklyn, with every piece shaped to exacting specifications. 4 › Slightly more involved than a T connector, "elbows" (used to create the slight bend seen in most of Adelman's fixtures) must be expertly shaped to fit together. 5 › Since gravity plays a large role in the success of many of her chandeliers, balance is checked at multiple points during assembly. 6 › Eventually, each individual component is shipped to Adelman's Manhattan studio, where all her fixtures are assembled by hand.

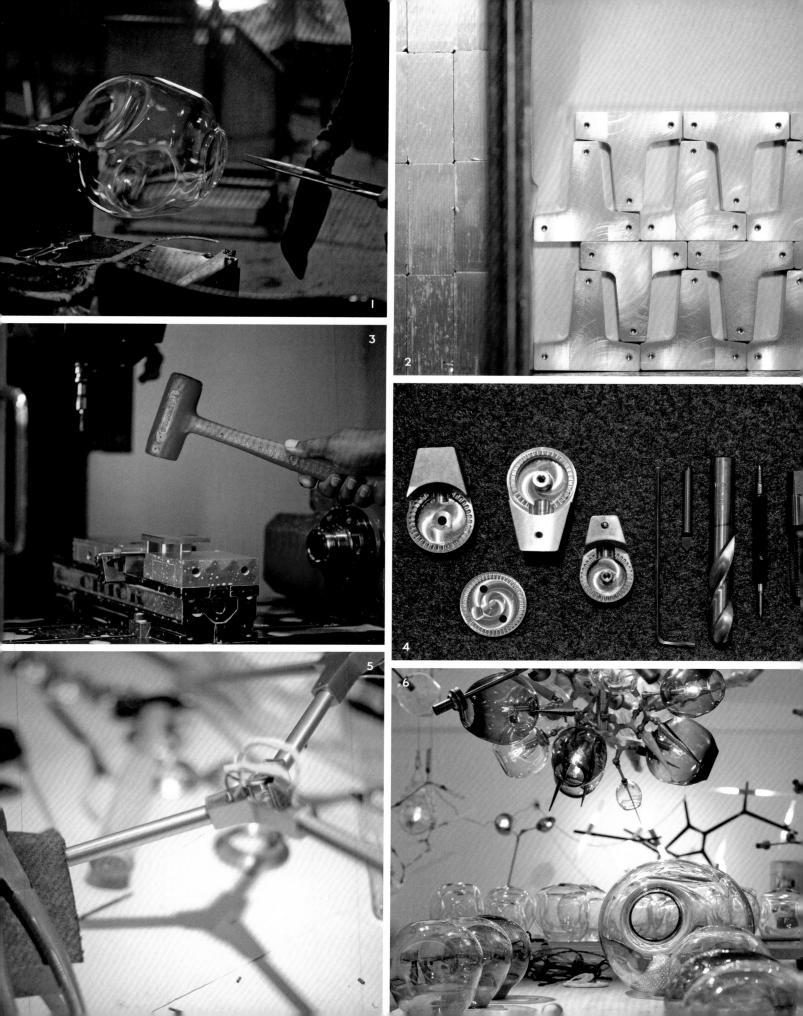

them above art. The works are constructed in a studio model; it's on a smaller scale than a factory, and because there are fewer hands, certain steps of the production process are outsourced.

"We have the luxury to build everything to order," says Adelman, "and to use the best machine shops and finishers and glassblowers, and we can pay attention to every single detail. We work with other shops, too—there are spinners and casters, a ceramics studio, a blacksmith, and a wood turner . . . It's quite a lot of suppliers." This way of manufacturing is time-consuming, but quality requires time.

Such care in construction and fabrication matters because lamps and sconces are part of the collection of things you see daily in your rooms. As much as we might appreciate our fixtures as forms, we need them to be of practical use. Adelman is always mindful of the function her designs must perform. "We offer multiple shade options for every socket," she says, "depending on the space and what the client's looking for, and also what they like. Some clients never want to see bare bulbs, other clients want something decorative, other clients need dimmable bright light." Similarly, Visual Comfort focuses on the business of providing general illumination—fixtures that will become the building blocks of a larger lighting scheme that will, of course, be specific: your room, your taste, and your needs.

Getting to that perfect scheme may require trial and error. It may require attempting to follow one decorator's rules or suggestions, or feeling your way forward and finding what works best for you. It can be frustrating to have no road map to follow, but the destination, in the estimation of pretty much every designer you'd care to ask, is worth getting to. "Lighting is such an overwhelming element in the room," says Adelman. "It affects the mood. It affects how everything—the furniture, the surfaces—looks. It affects people's emotions and how they look to each other."

Lindsey Adelman's spectacular, multifaceted light fixtures are the work of many, many specialized artisans, and can take weeks to assemble.

# Lighting & Technology

LIGHTING IS NOT AN AGE-OLD CRAFT; IT'S A TECHNOLOGY. WHILE THE consumer hasn't seen many appreciable tweaks in the classic incandescent bulb in the last decades, that is set to change—and rapidly. "We're in the era of LEDs now," says Charles Pavarini III. "The first LEDs that came out were very cold. They were very blue. I call them ghost lights. Nobody wanted to use them in their interiors, because nobody looked good. But LEDs have come into a whole new generation. They're becoming more like sunlight."

Pavarini feels that advances in lighting technology get an unfairly bad rap. It may indeed be wise to adapt now. "The incandescent bulb is doomed," he says. "This whole revolution in lighting is to become more green and to be more cost-effective and energy efficient." As a designer, he's not merely resigned to this change; he's excited by the potential of the new forms. "We can actually start placing LEDs in custom furnishings," says Pavarini. "I've used LEDs behind headboards, or to give an ambient glow underneath the bed, so the bed appears to be floating. We were never able to do that before, because of heat against fabric."

There are even more startling developments ahead. The organic LED isn't a bulb; it doesn't have filaments. It need not even be put into a lamp. In a show-house project, Pavarini used a panel, developed by Philips, of plastic only $\frac{1}{32}$ of an inch thick. The light source was infused into the plastic so that the entire piece lit up. "There are companies that are working on wallpapers that illuminate with organic LEDs," says Pavarini. "The light source is actually in the paper. They're infusing it into fibers in carpeting and fabrics. In the next five or six years, we'll be turning on our lampshade, not the lamp."

On average, LED bulbs use 85 percent less energy than the typical incandescent, and the subtle light variance (white versus yellow) is almost unnoticeable in bulbs with a low Lumen (LED's equivalent of wattage), making them a great choice for task lighting.

Proof that the simplest designs can still make the grandest gestures: two exaggeratedly large pendants punctuate the colorful, cheeky dining room of Jonathan Adler and Simon Doonan.

# DESIGN CHAMPION: *Serge Mouille*

FRENCH INDUSTRIAL DESIGNER SERGE MOUILLE'S signature angular sconces, pendants, and lamps are a familiar sight to anyone who's ever perused an interior design magazine.

With their stark lines and ebony lacquered finish, Mouille's fixtures seem as modern today as they did in the fifties, when they were first unveiled. Mouille was not interested in manufacturing on a large scale; instead, he fabricated his lights for individual commissions. Though much in demand even now, Mouille's designs are still produced on a very small scale. The workshop uses the same molds and materials—even the same paint finish, provided by the same supplier—and despite their industrial-age aesthetic, the fixtures are entirely made by hand.

There's no appreciable difference between the Serge Mouille fixture bought today and one bought decades ago. According to the brand's point of view, the result is more a sculpture than an industrial product, so it's possible to think of the lights as one would numbered editions of a piece of fine art. In the year 2012, for example, the entire production run was eleven hundred pieces. The company might easily introduce automation to meet the steady demand for their wares, but that's at odds with their larger philosophy—that the integrity of the work lies as much in the execution as it does in the design.

# RECOGNIZING THE MAJOR PLAYERS
# *Lighting*

### 1 > ROBERT ABBEY, INC.

Robert Abbey's fine lighting products have been made in the United States since the company's founding in 1948. Now based in Hickory, North Carolina, the family-owned and -operated business has partnered with designers Jonathan Adler, Rico Espinet, and Mary McDonald to provide a range of cutting-edge styles.

### 2 > TOM DIXON

Self-taught welder and designer Tom Dixon aimed to raise the level of British industrial design when he founded his eponymous company in 2002. Innovative and independent, Dixon was an early user of the vacuum metallization process in lighting, which he employed to create his renowned Mirror Ball and Copper Shade collections.

### 3 > LINDSEY ADELMAN STUDIO

Lindsey Adelman has worked in industrial design since the mid-1990s, and founded her eponymous studio in 2006. Inspired by nature, she is known for her sculptural chandeliers that juxtapose hand-blown glass with machine-made metal parts.

### 4 > DAVID WEEKS STUDIO

David Weeks founded his namesake company, which sells furniture, lighting, and accessories, in New York in 1996. His lighting products—table and floor lamps, chandeliers, and custom-designed installations—are known for their pared-down geometric forms that lend a sense of artistry to any space.

### 5 > REWIRE

Los Angeles–based Rewire offers a selection of high-end designer lighting by twentieth-century masters, including Joe Colombo, Poul Henningsen, Achille Castiglioni, and many others, as well as sleek contemporary pieces.

### 6 > ROLL & HILL

With an eye for discovering the next big name in lighting, Jason Miller (a lighting designer himself) founded Roll & Hill in 2010 as a collaborative studio that not only sells the work of independent designers (Bec Brittain, Karl Zahn, Lukas Peet), but also helps coordinate some of the production for those designers. Every fixture is made to order and assembled by hand right in their offices.

1

2

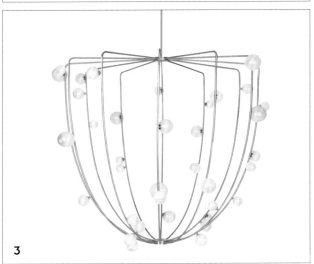

3

4

5

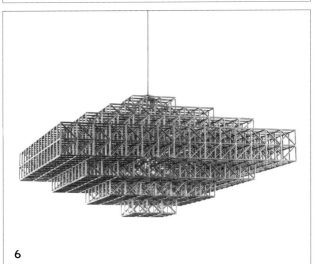

6

2

3 ›

1

1 › An iconic arching floor lamp, which swivels from the base, hovers over a circular reading banquette in the library of this Hamptons estate. 2 › Designer Tamara Eaton approaches a formal Brooklyn sitting room with a touch of humor, mixing a Murano glass chandelier with an antique greyhound table lamp. 3 › The correct shade—and the correct shade placement—is arguably even more important than the lamp itself; here, an elongated drum design complements the lamp's bulbous silhouette perfectly.

4 › In the Manhattan home of noted designer Tony Baratta, an antique harlequin lamp sits atop a marble column–turned–side table (one of the many tongue-in-cheek touches found in his exuberant space). 5 › A rare, antique Brutalist chandelier completes the dark, moody entry of fashion blogger Jane Aldridge's Texas home. 6 › In lieu of overhead lighting, designer Steven Gambrel used two large table lamps (vintage from the 1950s) to light the living room of a West Village pied-à-terre.

# *ceramics*

Ceramic is common to societies that may have shared nothing else, nations and civilizations from across the globe and throughout the centuries. What accounts for this phenomenon—the Greeks discovering the same thing as the Mayans, the great civilizations of what we now call the American Southwest making the same kinds of vessels as the ancient Egyptians—is the fact that ceramics were and still are made of the very ground beneath our feet.

"Ceramics," loosely defined, has to do with the molding and firing of clay into an object. "Clay" is a broad term, referring to a mix of minerals and water. And ceramics today encompass a great deal of what's found in the modern home: the plates on your table, the vase on your mantel, the tiles in your foyer.

The essential steps are making a clay, molding that clay into a shape, introducing that shape to heat so that the form sets, then applying a glaze or coating on the piece, and possibly firing it once more. Determining the quality of ceramic pieces involves considering form and aesthetics, weighing details like a piece's heft or glaze, and understanding the way it was manufactured.

Functional objects aside, ceramics have long been admired and collected as art as well—think of Eva Zeisel. Today, we see a new generation of young artists reviving the medium, like Brazilian Alexandre da Cunha, whose Ebony Terracotta series (yes, those are clay replicas of plunger parts) has been part of a touring exhibition.

# The Unique History of Ceramics

### PREHISTORIC TIMES

With the discovery of fire comes the discovery of ceramics. Ancient people find that clay hardens after it is baked over a flame, and as they start to farm, they begin to make clay vessels for storage. Woven baskets are utilized as molds to shape ceramic wares.

### PRE-COLUMBIAN AMERICA

Early American ceramicists produce wares by the coiling method or with molds. Decoration is added with incisions, slips, or the use of coils, rolls, or balls of clay.

### 1689

A French edict that calls for the melting of all tabletop silver and gold causes orders of faience table vessels by the upper class to grow so large that the threat of a fuel shortage prompts the state to get involved.

### 18TH CENTURY

The importation of Chinese hard-paste porcelain causes a European craze for blue-and-white porcelain. In 1709, Ehrenfried von Tschirnhausen and Johann Böttger discover the secret of hard-paste porcelain at Meissen, Germany, and soon enough the famous Meissen factory is founded. The formula spreads rapidly throughout Europe, and factories arise all over the Continent.

### CA. 3500 BC

The potter's wheel is used in Mesopotamia to turn out everyday vessels for storage. The earliest mention of the potter's wheel in literature is in the 8th century BC in Homer's *Iliad*. By the first millennium BC, the Greeks perfect the making and decoration of ceramics. The wheel reaches southern Italy and France around 400 BC, and England around 50 BC.

### 15TH CENTURY

With the mastering of lead and salt glazes, decorative pottery becomes valued for more than utilitarian functions. The lead-glaze ceramic dishes from Manises and Valencia depict flags and armorial decorations and serve as political gifts throughout Europe. In Italy, tin-glazed earthenware known as maiolica gains prominence throughout the peninsula. In the 16th century, potters from Faenza bring maiolica into France, and the name is soon changed to "faience."

### 1738

The French national porcelain manufactory is established in Vincennes. In 1756, King Louis XV moves the factory to Sèvres and all Sèvres-produced wares are marked with the royal cipher.

### 1759

Josiah Wedgwood, an English potter, sets up his ceramic factory to produce wares in the popular neoclassical style. In 1774, Catherine of Russia commissions a service of more than one thousand pieces from him.

### 1920s

In 1920, the pottery workshop at the Bauhaus school in Germany is set up and students are taught traditional hand methods.

### 1939–1959

Steubenville Pottery manufactures Russel Wright's colorful American Modern service, which becomes the most widely sold American ceramic dinnerware in history.

### 1970s–1990s

The paint-it-yourself ceramic studio concept becomes popular and gives the general public the chance to paint, glaze, and fire ceramics.

### 1930s

The American Studio Pottery movement is well established and colleges such as the University of Southern California and The Ohio State University offer ceramics programs to train students and promote ceramics as an artistic medium.

### 1944

The first exhibition of Edith Heath's ceramics occurs at the California Palace of the Legion of Honor Museum (now part of the Fine Arts Museums of San Francisco); it includes two hundred pieces of tabletop wares.

### TODAY

Although the majority of ceramic wares are mass-produced, studio pottery is still thriving and universities such as the Rhode Island School of Design continue to educate the next wave of ceramicists.

**ABOVE ›** Always one for exploring new creative processes, Jonathan Adler forged his Glass Menagerie series by pouring melted ground glass over a solid stoneware form.

**OPPOSITE ›** Adler's cheeky approach to form has earned his work a global fan club, though each and every "groovy" creation is still dreamt up and created in his SoHo studio.

# The Question of Form

"THERE'S SOMETHING VERY PRIMAL AND VISCERAL ABOUT PEOPLE'S connection to clay," says designer Jonathan Adler, who began his career as a potter. "I'm not a spiritual person, but the second I touched clay, I felt something, probably for the first time in my life." The warmth and texture of earthen materials make a specific impact inside a home; they embody a quality we sense without being able to articulate it.

Our appreciation is the important part—you should buy what you love. But if you want to make informed judgments about a piece, it's helpful to consider the same details that matter to skilled ceramics makers.

"We look at a lot of ceramic history," says David Reid, who founded the New York design studio KleinReid with James Klein in 1993. "Our work is a big melting pot of influences for shape, glaze, and detail, but form is most important." Form refers to a piece's shape, proportion, and lines. The small scale at which a studio like KleinReid operates allows for stringent quality control. Of course, many mass retailers look to studios like KleinReid for inspiration (or simply to imitate). So what accounts for the difference between mass-produced and studio-produced ceramics?

Reid concedes that it can be hard for the consumer to thoughtfully evaluate ceramics. "Form can be hard to see," says Reid. "It's much easier to see surface decoration or pattern." Tastes are subjective, of course, but one way to educate yourself is to look widely and deeply. If you're in the market for a vase, take the time to review what's available, studying the way the pieces look as well as how they feel, and take note of price tags while you do. Quality can be measured. "There's usually a difference in materials," says Reid, speaking of the gulf between his work and the knockoff. "We work with a high-fire porcelain that's really glassy and very sturdy. The finish of the glaze, the weight of the piece, the finish of the foot, or how a coffee mug feels against your lips—those are the important, intimate details."

Though most people expect quality ceramics to be the product of a small studio (and more expensive), this isn't necessarily the case. "The relationship between the maker, the object, and the user is important, but there's nothing wrong with the mass-produced," Reid says. "American dinnerware is a perfect example of gorgeous material and functional form made for the masses." Quality is located at that intersection of price, design, use, and materials—and of course how you feel about a piece.

# The Studio & the Factory

PORCELAIN—AN ESPECIALLY DURABLE CERAMIC FORM—ORIGINATED in China, and then made its way west in the fourteenth century. Its rarity and delicacy quickly elevated it into a luxury item, and soon Chinese artisans were turning out porcelain candlesticks and mugs especially for a European customer. Europeans eventually developed their own factories to meet the demand, and the form remains popular to this day—accordingly, we still refer to porcelain plates and serving ware as "china."

Evaluating antique ceramics requires a lot of education, but the modern marketplace can be tricky to navigate as well. Ceramics range from luxury pieces to simple utilitarian items, and mechanization and industrialization have made them (and everything else) less expensive and more widely accessible.

As David Reid says, the character of a ceramic piece is informed by its design—but that design is inextricably intertwined with the composition of the clay and glaze used to create it. An example of this is the work of the California-based Heath Ceramics. The company has now outlived founder Edith Heath, but new pieces share a consistent aesthetic with vintage ones because the raw materials have not changed. "The clay is based on a formula that Edith Heath came up with," says Cathy Bailey, the company's owner and creative director, "especially the brown clay, which was her original clay. The ingredients still come from the same place."

"The thing that's interesting and not typical about our model is that Edith Heath didn't want to be limited to making all her designs herself," says Bailey. "She wanted for them to be made with a high degree of craft, with the touch of the hand." The products that bear the Heath name continue to express that designer's specific point of view—simplicity, consideration, a warm modernity—and they're still made the way she envisioned them to be, bearing her fingerprints metaphorically rather than literally.

Heath has a factory, but we often misunderstand what a factory is. "Overmarketing makes so many words lose their meaning," says Bailey. "'Handmade' is a term that lacks meaning because of this." Part of Bailey's mission is to correct that. "We give lots of tours and people come thinking, 'Thirty-six dollars for a mug is quite expensive!'" says Bailey. "In the end, after seeing what it takes to make that mug, they say, 'I cannot believe that that mug is only thirty-six dollars.' Their perception changes."

Heath Ceramics's clay studio is still located in the original Sausalito, California, factory opened by Edith Heath in 1959—though today it's manned by forty trained artisans crafting designs both old and new.

A testament to Heath Ceramics's mastery of form can be seen in fashion stylist Lauren Ehrenfeld's Venice Beach home, where functional salt and pepper shakers become lovingly displayed ornamentation.

Visitors to the Heath factory get to see some of what distinguishes these products from the shelves and shelves of brightly colored plates and bowls sold at a big-box retailer. Bailey explains one point of difference. "The way they apply the glaze is a key example," she says. "What we're able to do is glaze every piece individually by hand. The glaze is sprayed on the piece, but we use many different bases, and each one needs to be applied differently. The extra time and more complex processes we carry out create a much different feel from that of pieces produced solely by machines." Heath is able to be more considerate, to match each product with the right glaze, to create something that's more tailored, more thoughtful.

Jonathan Adler's accessories are further testament to the idea that thoughtful design and process can lead to quality. Once upon a time, Adler himself was responsible for every vase that bears his name, but that's no longer the case. He does, however, closely monitor its conception and birth in his New York studio. For Adler, education and practice are vital to achieving a quality product. "As a designer I was lucky to have a good rigorous art history background and a sense of real design connoisseurship," he says. Adler inculcates this kind of education in every designer he hires, and is quick to point out how much easier developing that sense of connoisseurship is for everyone, professional or consumer, thanks to the Internet. In Adler's view, "good design looks like it's uncovered rather than created, like it's always been there."

That sounds simple but is demanding. Design is work. "It's about being analytical," says Adler, "being rigorous, and going through the steps necessary to take something from your mind's eye to the first crappy sample that you hate, and then figuring out what's wrong with it, being dogged, and getting it to the point where it needs to be. It's really not dissimilar from writing. You know that old cliché, 'Writing is rewriting.' Well, design is redesigning, and problem solving, and not compromising until you get to where something needs to be."

A price tag may tell you how much something costs, but it doesn't tell you how many hours its maker put into its conception, its gestation, its creation. There's no easy way to learn that, though when you're equipped with the kind of design education Adler is talking about, you may feel more comfortable evaluating what good design is.

# DESIGN CHAMPION: *Eva Zeisel*

IN A CAREER THAT SPANNED DECADES, the designer Eva Zeisel dreamed up a host of products—teakettles and rugs, coffee tables and tiles. Though she was truly an industrial designer, most remember her as a ceramicist, because of what an outsize influence she's had in that medium, and how startlingly prolific she was.

Zeisel began as a solo potter, but worked in factories large and small from her twenties on. "She was not a studio artist. She, in fact, didn't even consider herself an artist. She considered herself a maker of useful things," says Jean Richards, Zeisel's daughter.

Many of Zeisel's designs remain in production today, but a piece purchased new will bear the same stamp as a vintage example of her work, because the manufacture was an integral aspect of her design process. She didn't start with a vision and then search for the technology; rather, says Richards, "she always adapted her designs to the techniques, even to the size of the kiln. I would say ninety percent of what she designed was to specifications from a factory or manufacturer." In some instances, contemporary manufacturers are working from the same clay recipe or even the very same mold that the designer specified, so there's often no appreciable distinction between new designs and vintage examples.

Zeisel left behind an archive of thousands of designs—more than one hundred thousand, in the estimate of her grandson Adam Zeisel, president of Eva Zeisel Originals, who is upholding her legacy by overseeing the introduction or reintroduction of old designs. He carefully chooses partner manufacturers to bring old designs to today's audience, a task he's well equipped for. "I had the best teacher in the world," he says. "I had Eva. She gave me some unique things growing up for Christmas presents and birthday presents; and until I was sort of 'trained' (my word, not hers) to be able to make that distinction, I didn't really appreciate what she was giving me."

Zeisel's heirs might have learned from the master, but the harder-to-answer question is, how did *she* learn? "I found her notes from when she taught at Pratt Institute," says Richards. "She gave her students exercises: make a form that looks tired, make a form that looks cozy, make a form that looks cheerful. So this was not just miraculous, or just a gift—she knew how to communicate emotion through form."

**OPPOSITE** › Zeisel's Rockland County, New York, home.

**LEFT** › Pieces from the artist's One-O-One collection.

## RECOGNIZING THE MAJOR PLAYERS
# *Ceramics*

### 1 > KLEINREID

KleinReid founders James Klein and David Reid have collaborated since 1993 and, in that time, pioneered the "modern, urban, ceramic design aesthetic." Their utilitarian and decorative wares include minimal, rustic, and whimsical designs crafted using a mix of industrial and artisanal techniques. Most impressive, perhaps, is the collection made in collaboration with ceramics design legend Eva Zeisel.

### 2 > BODO SPERLEIN

German-born Bodo Sperlein, now based in London, consults on design projects for other businesses as well as designs bespoke items, most notably home accessories for his own line. He uses historical techniques to create contemporary, minimal designs in fine bone china or, interestingly, a polyurethane resin–strengthened vitreous china that can be made paper thin.

### 3 > ASTIER DE VILLATTE

Handmade in Paris, Astier de Villatte's black terra-cotta clay ceramics, glazed with a white finish, are both durable and unique. The two-decades-old company, which also makes candles, lamps, and other home accessories, takes inspiration from eighteenth- and nineteenth-century design yet also collaborates with contemporary designers on fresh, original collections.

### 4 > FORNASETTI

To collect Fornasetti's whimsical creations is to forever become a part of its storied founder's imaginative world. Touted as a "master illusionist of ornament and design," Piero Fornasetti opened his company in Milan more than a century ago, applying his unique vision to everything from fine ceramics to furniture. It's said that the artist conceived and built more than 13,000 objects in his lifetime, many of which are still in production today.

### 5 > HEATH CERAMICS

Modernist potter Edith Heath founded her eponymous company in 1948, striving to make "simple, good things for good people," while using a low-energy, low-cost production process. Today the tableware, tile, and accessories retailer, known for its small-runs of Heath's beloved midcentury ceramics, continues that mission.

### 6 > JONATHAN ADLER

The story of how Jonathan Adler came to be the current reigning king of clay is as fascinating as his whimsical creations. It all began at summer camp in 1978, when a young Adler was introduced to the potter's wheel (while wearing his favorite Rush tee), and then begged his parents for one of his very own. Today, his pottery—accompanied by a full range of colorful home décor—is sold at more than one thousand shops worldwide. His design motto: "If your heirs won't fight over it, we won't make it."

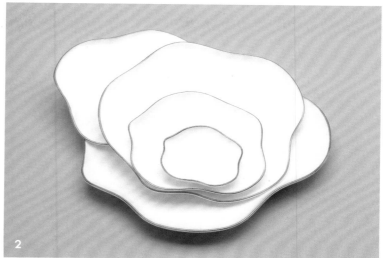

1 › Chipped-to-perfection flea market gems reside on the mantel of this Northern California farmhouse. 2 › A trio of vessels, picked up as souvenirs, decorates the table of a light-filled entry. 3 › Early works from noted California ceramicist Adam Silverman have become sought-after collectibles. 4 › In the South, regional pottery is cherished as an important part of a distinctive artistic legacy, sometimes fetching five- and six-figure prices at auction.

5 › Often the most successfully displayed collections are not only a blend of form, but also of designers and design periods; this one features the very new next to the century old. 6 › In his Palm Springs home, George Massar went to great lengths to procure these impressive midcentury ceramics from local artisans and dealers. 7 › Though mass-produced on a tremendous scale today, the earliest blue-and-white porcelain dates back to fourteenth-century China. 8 › Centuries ago, weathered urns and decorative pedestals like these would have been found in a formal French garden.

# *glass*

Glass graces windows and mirrors, lightbulbs and clock faces, tables and mantel-pieces. It's so ubiquitous as to be invisible—a staple of modern life that we almost never consider. But we should evaluate the glass with which we interact intimately, or that we prize simply for beauty, differently than we do the glass that serves a structural purpose in our homes.

The vessels we drink from, the vases and accessories we decorate with: these items should be chosen as much for their aesthetic appeal—their color, tactility, decorative flourishes—as their final purpose. They are as much an extension of our personal style as the art with which we surround ourselves. The glass in your windows is strictly utilitarian; the glass you drink champagne from, however, is not. That distinction is of the utmost importance.

There was once a time, half a century ago, when glass doorknobs were standard issue in all homes. Those were most often shaped like multifaceted starbursts, and not nearly as glamorous as this modern Deco design, but the sense of exquisite craftsmanship exists in both.

# The Unique History of Glass

### 2000 BC

People in Mesopotamia begin making glass vessels using molds and simple tools. By the 16th century BC, craftsmen gather molten glass around a core, which is removed once it cools. Because this technique is extremely labor-intensive, the elite are the only consumers.

### 15TH CENTURY AD

The Venetians become known for their elegantly crafted luxury glass pieces. By the mid-1400s, Murano glassblowers discover *cristallo*, a colorless glass used to imitate rock crystal.

### 17TH CENTURY

Frenchman Bernard Perrot discovers a way of casting mirror glass on iron beds, allowing for even larger plates of consistent quality. The English discover that by adding lead to the batch they can also achieve colorless glass and Johann Kunckel, a chemist in Potsdam, Germany, discovers that adding gold chloride to the batch produces a deep red, or ruby, glass.

### 50 BC

Glassmakers in the Roman Empire discover how to inflate a gob of glass when gathered on a hollow tube. The discovery of glassblowing allows for rapid production of glass vessels, and glass becomes widely available. However, luxury glass continues to be made by the Romans using cold-working techniques, as used with cameo glass.

### 1564

Venetian mirror-makers form a corporation and shortly after begin introducing mirror-glass products throughout Europe, which significantly affects interior décor. The Venetian method of mirror making—the Lorraine or broad process— spreads to other countries such as England, France, and the Netherlands.

### 1820s

The pressing machine is developed in America; it triples the production of glass tableware and reduces pricing drastically.

## 1851

The Great Exhibition in London's Hyde Park serves as the perfect setting for glass companies from around the world to display their newest wares. The famous 27-foot-tall fountain, which served as a popular meeting place, is constructed out of four tons of pink glass.

## 1920s

After World War I, highly ornate glass objects fall out of fashion and Functionalism, a design concept coming out of the Bauhaus school in Germany, dominates glass design.

## 1970s

Fifteen universities in the United States and England teach glassblowing and craftsmanship.

## 1890–1915

Glass proves to be an ideal material for the Art Nouveau movement as it can be manipulated to form the sinuous lines and asymmetrical forms of the style. Art Nouveau glass becomes a status symbol and one of the most prolific designers in the medium, Louis Comfort Tiffany, achieves fame throughout the United States and Europe for his designs and products.

## 1962

The Toledo Museum of Art organizes a glass-working seminar, which inspires a group of artists, led by Dominick Labino and Harvey K. Littleton, to experiment with blowing glass in a studio setting. By reestablishing the role of designer and maker as one, the American Studio Glass movement significantly affects glass production in America and abroad.

## TODAY

A wide variety of glass products on the market today utilize both industrial and handmade techniques.

# How It's Made

"THE SILICA FOUND IN SAND IS THE PRIMARY INGREDIENT IN GLASS," says Diane Wright, glass historian at Pilchuck Glass School, in Washington State. "When you introduce it to an excessive amount of heat, that creates a molten, viscous material. When the glass cools down, it becomes hard, a solid again. The glass cools so quickly it doesn't have time to re-form the same chemical structure it had before. It becomes a unique material, one that has the physical properties of both a solid and a liquid."

We have a long history of living with glass, and though certain aspects of the manufacture have changed over time, the way glass is made hasn't changed fundamentally. "Humans have been forming glass into artistic objects since about 2500 BC," says Wright. "The Egyptian tradition of making glass came out of working with metals, combining and melting materials, then forming them, and changing their shape as the material cooled down. The addition of metallic oxides created color in glass—for example, putting cobalt into the batch of glass resulted in blue glass." The difference between a glass vial found in the sands of Egypt and the glass case of an iPhone feels vast—nevertheless, some artisans today make glass much the way it was made millennia ago. "The Romans invented the process of glassblowing, where you take a hollow pipe, dip it in the molten material, and blow, manipulating it into all kinds of different shapes and sizes," says Wright. "Glass, for the Romans, was similar to plastic for us—mass-produced, a material they made many different things out of, used regularly, and recycled."

Most of the glass we make today involves more machinery than human interaction. You'll still find blown glass produced according to the methods pioneered by the Romans, but it's no longer a commonplace thing; it's a luxury.

Weighing quality in glass has to do with what you value. If it's absolute uniform perfection that you want, glass made by machine can certainly deliver that. If you value things that are not quite perfect, glass with subtly soft edges, or a pair of wineglasses in the same style but with small characteristics that distinguish one from the other, you'll prefer something handmade.

Under a watchful eye from Mickey (this Brooklyn studio's mascot), the main crucible oven, which is where the molten glass is kept hot, burns at upward of 2,500 degrees Fahrenheit.

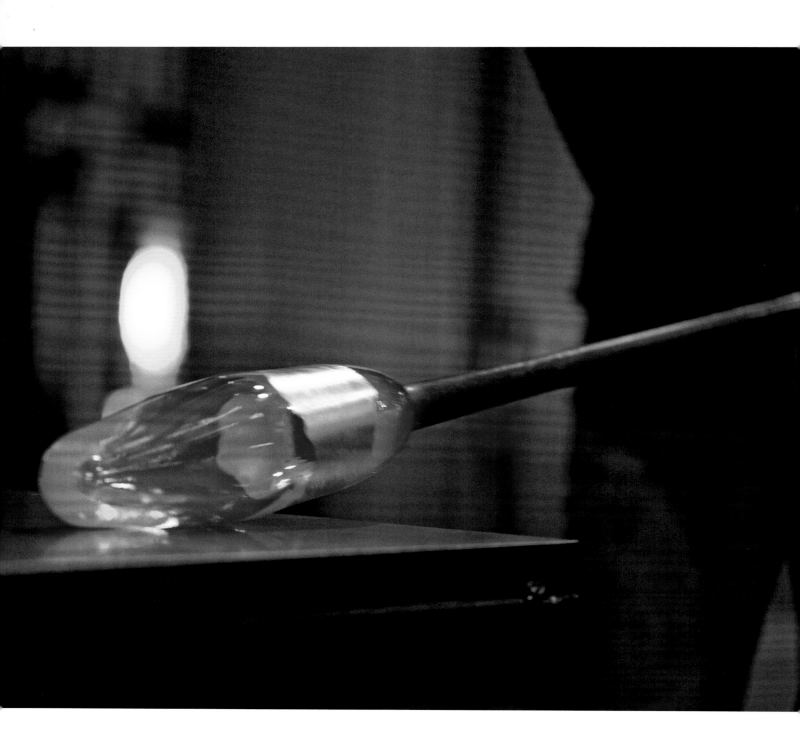

Among the many variables that affect the finished glass are the raw materials used. Sand can contain different mixtures of minerals, and sands from different parts of the planet can result in glass with a different color or brilliance. Simon Pearce glass begins life as sand sourced from Belgium. "Take a glass of ours, and an identical design that another company has made—from sand sourced from another part of the world—and in person, you can see what the difference is between the glasses," says executive director of product development and design James Murray. "Others may be of great production quality, but it's almost gray in comparison to what Simon Pearce glass is. The raw materials we use have a brilliance that really makes the product shine." The quality of the sand informs the workability of the resulting glass, as well as its color and brilliance, which is rated on a scale, similar to how diamonds are classified.

**OPPOSITE** › Many of the glass orbs used in Lindsey Adelman's chandeliers are shot through with gold leaf. This effect is achieved early on in the process by wrapping a still-molten "blob" in gold foil, then blowing into the shape, sending the foil splintering out in all directions.

**ABOVE** › Once the desired form is achieved on one side, a second pipe, or pontil, is attached, which is manned by an additional person. This "helper" pulls, twists, and shapes the other end of the glass orb.

# The Artisan's Hand

WE OFTEN THINK OF HANDCRAFT AS A CONTRAST TO THE MACHINE-made; if the latter is perfect, the former is not, and that imperfection is meant to be part of the appeal. Much handmade stemware looks flawless. But the makers (and more important, the consumers) of such goods perceive in the work a trace of the artisan's hand, a sense that a goblet is unique in the world, even if it's a design executed hundreds or thousands of times.

Then there's the question of style. Much as we associate wine with certain regions, the craft of glass has strong roots in specific parts of the world—and the differences between glass from Italy and glass from Bohemia (a region that falls mostly within the Czech Republic on modern maps) are comparable to the distinctions between wines from South Africa and those from France.

"Bohemian glass represented a melding of Germanic and Italian techniques," says Capucine De Wulf Gooding, co-founder and creative director of the tabletop company Juliska. "What sets apart the look of Bohemian glass is that it has applied decoration." There might be a range of colors, but this medium is defined by the fact that the glass is adorned with smaller pieces of glass—beaded borders, raised insignia, and other effects.

Gooding and her husband, David, encountered some reproduction Bohemian glass on a trip to Paris and fell in love with the stuff, and thus a business was born. "Our glass is made in the heart of the original Bohemia," says Gooding. "Nothing has changed much at all. They're still using hand-carved wooden molds and the same blow rods and metal stamps they used in the fifteenth century."

At Simon Pearce, at any given moment, there are about thirty people in factories in Vermont and Maryland actively working and shaping wine-glasses. Simply knowing that there are a few dozen hands making these pieces can be persuasive enough to create truly loyal customers.

At Juliska's Eastern European factory, the artisans interact with the glass repeatedly, blowing it into shape, thrusting it back into the heat source to keep it malleable, and removing it to continue refining its shape. This repeated exposure to the heat breaks down the glass's very molecules. They rebond as the piece cools, so as the artisans work the glass, it's also getting stronger. Glass may have an elemental feel to it, but in fact, it takes relentless intervention by trained artisans to create.

**OPPOSITE ›** Horst P. Horst captured the storied home of Palm Beach socialites Mary Lee and Douglas Fairbanks Jr. for a 1978 issue of *Vogue,* which noted the couple's extensive collection of Waterford crystal, from table settings to glittering eighteenth-century sconces.

**ABOVE ›** At Juliska, a company known for its decorative finesse, each twisting trim and dotted flourish is hand-stamped, ensuring a level of artistry not often seen today.

# Living with Glass

ABOVE › For those who simply can't bear the thought of using their great-grandmother's crystal on a daily basis, glass stemware with a touch of gold leafing has all the formality with less of a risk factor.

OPPOSITE › Even before the invention of electricity, the luminous quality of crystal made it coveted by lighting artisans, who would etch dozens— sometimes hundreds—of faceted teardrops for a single chandelier.

MANY OF US LIVE IN FEAR OF OUR MOST EXPENSIVE THINGS. WE may think they're fragile, they're special, they're too nice for everyday use. In truth, expensive glass isn't necessarily more fragile than cheap glass; it's simply that we care less about the cheap stuff, because we're accustomed to disposable and easily replaceable things. But if you drink from your best glass on a regular basis, the expense of it is much easier to justify. Pour your morning orange juice into it every day of the week, and over the years a forty-dollar glass ends up costing no more than a four-dollar glass.

Take crystal, for example, which we often keep tucked away in the dining-room cabinet, breaking it out only on special occasions. "When glass was first created, all glass was either brown or green because they couldn't find an agent to purify it," says Juliska's Capucine De Wulf Gooding. "At some point somebody decided to add lead to purify the glass, and it became crystal clear. Then people just started calling it crystal. The difference between crystal and glass is the presence of a specific metal oxide." "Crystal" is really a marketing term, meaning glass that contains added elements of metal—lead, historically, though that metal's impact on health has seen it replaced by oxides of zinc or other metals.

Crystal catches and reflects the light more than glass without metals in it. And because it's softer to cut into, crystal glassware often features facets or complex designs. This makes it feel heavier, and so we have this sense that crystal is more durable, or that heavier crystal is better. It's true that crystal is more durable while it is being worked (glass with an oxide component can better support engraving and etching), but a glass is heavy because the design calls for more glass—its weight is not a measure of its quality.

The fragility of glass is sometimes part of its appeal. The very delicacy of the material can be one way to evaluate it; within some artistic traditions, including the Bohemian school, the thinness of the finished glass is testament to the skill of the glassmaker. But there's no getting around the fact that glass breaks, and pretty easily, too.

Gooding, a French native, has a point of view on this. "A family might have the same house for generations," she says. "Your grandparents had the tapestries and the tables, and maybe the next generation bought new chairs and artwork, and then the next generation brought in some mugs and a car. When you go into any home in Europe, nothing really matches. It represents

people's travels and interests, all layered on top of each other. There's a sense of consistency but in a jumbled, juxtaposed, beautifully worn-in way."

Glass is used on the tabletop but also in a strictly decorative context—in vases, mirrors, and objects. It's an important element in a well-thought-out room. "You get this wonderful glow . . . this reflection, when you add glass accessories and glass lamps to a room," says the Dallas-based interior designer Jan Showers.

"I always tell the girls who work for me, 'Spend your money on great shoes and great handbags,'" says Showers. "Because you're sharp enough to put together a good outfit. But if your shoes are bad and your handbag is bad, everything else is going to look terrible. I think home accessories are very much in that category. They'll make everything look better."

Generally speaking, interior designers approach a room or a project by considering every single variable, including light and shadow; horizontality and height; colors cool and warm; textures hard and soft; finishes natural and man-made. And glass can be transparent or dark; it can be a long mirror or a towering vase; it can be a cool shade of blue or a rich red; it can be hard and slick or soft and inviting; it can feel handmade or cool and industrial. Glass is so versatile as to be indispensable.

**OPPOSITE ›** In the historic Beverly Hills home of Juicy Couture founder Pamela Skaist-Levy, glass plays a pivotal design role in almost every room of the house. In her eyes, the more layers the better: a mirrored vanity is set against a mirrored wall topped with elaborate antique crystal candelabras.

**ABOVE ›** Purely due to its translucent nature, even the most beautiful glassware often gets overlooked. Not so in this glamorous home bar, where deep-dark walls allow the cut crystal glasses and vases to sparkle.

# DESIGN CHAMPION: *Venini*

"YOU JUST CANNOT FIND MORE BEAUTIFUL glass anywhere than you can in Murano," says Jan Showers. The region just outside Venice, Murano is as synonymous with glass as the Champagne is with bubbly wine.

Venice was an important center for the emerging glass trade, perhaps owing to its significance as a port and its proximity to Africa, where the form was refined. Murano, a small archipelago, was deemed a safer place for glassmakers to build their furnaces, so Venice itself would never be threatened by accidental fire. Glass remains a thriving trade in this region. Murano glass may not be marked by any particular aesthetic choices, materials, or techniques, but it does reflect the accumulated wisdom of many centuries of practice, by a handful of companies still considered the foremost in the world.

Perhaps no name is more closely associated with the place than Venini. Established in 1921, the company's great innovation was to marry the age-old enterprise of Venetian glass to a modern design point of view. They accomplished this by working with the world's foremost designers, artists, and architects—so their emphasis was never on the paperweights, perfume bottles, and other pieces that to the modern eye can look, alas, like tourist tchotchkes.

Venini trades in what is sometimes (rather clumsily) termed "art glass"; the work straddles the line between art and craft, objects that are worthy of veneration but meant to be used, not framed and put on the wall. If there is a common thread that unites the company's wide breadth of products—again, all the work of different designers, with their own points of view, from the minimal to the figural—it's color. Venini's glassmakers use proprietary methods to achieve hues with a depth and intensity not often associated with glass. Millennia after the material's origins, great artisans are still pushing the boundaries of what is possible.

# RECOGNIZING THE MAJOR PLAYERS
## *Glass*

### 1 > JOHN POMP STUDIOS

John Pomp was introduced to glassblowing as a teenager and quickly developed a passion for it. Pomp studied under glassmakers from Murano, Italy, before opening his own studio in Philadelphia. His handcrafted work melds inspiration from nature and the Japanese principle of wabi-sabi with contemporary design to create elegant and organic lighting, furniture, and accessories.

### 2 > SIEMON & SALAZAR

Caleb Siemon trained with a Muranese master glass sculptor for two years and, upon returning to the United States, opened an Italian-style studio in Southern California, in 1999. He mixes old-world techniques with the simplicity of Scandinavian design. With Carmen Salazar, sculptor, metalworker, architect, and botanist, the pair have become a leading force in producing glass objects, lighting, and more recently, large-scale installations.

### 3 > NOUVEL STUDIO

Nouvel Studio, a Mexico City–based studio established in 1994, specializes in colorful blown-glass pieces. Collaborations with outside architects, artists, and designers means that Nouvel Studio is constantly exploring innovative ways to work with glass.

### 4 > JULISKA

Husband-and-wife team Capucine De Wulf Gooding and David Gooding formed their tableware company in 2001 with the philosophy of creating items that are "beautiful, functional and luxe for chic everyday living." Juliska's unique mouth-blown and hand-pressed glassware provides a twist on the historic references of the founders' European roots in a range of traditional, modern, and rustic styles.

### 5 > WATERFORD

Established in 1783, Waterford maintains its original commitment to creating crystal stemware and objets d'art with pure color and exquisite design. Each Waterford glass, crafted with traditional glassmaking, sculpting, and engraving techniques, must pass a six-phase inspection. An imperfection, no matter how small, leads to smashing and remelting the piece in the furnace—only the finest items are sold.

### 6 > SIMON PEARCE

A decade after opening his first workshop in Kilkenny, Ireland, in 1971, Simon Pearce moved his studio to—and subsequently opened a restaurant at—a historic woolen mill in Vermont. Using the techniques of European studios, two glassblowers work under a master to create each piece, resulting in elegant, finely crafted wares durable enough for everyday use.

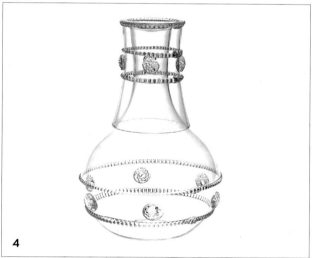

THIS PAGE › Amsterdam-based Kate Hume is admired as much for her one-of-a-kind, free-blown glass vessels as she is for her inventive use of the material in the clean-lined modern interiors she designs.

OPPOSITE › All of the libations in actress Molly Sims's Beverly Hills home are transferred to beautiful glass decanters, which are collected as much for their sculptural fluidity as their intended use.

# metalwork

We speak of things being as good as gold. We praise hearts of gold, dream of striking gold, wait for golden opportunities. When we urge one another to go for the gold, it's a nod to athletic competition, but the equation of gold with the very best predates the Olympics, the Old Testament, and perhaps everything else. That gold—and silver, for that matter—is valuable is simply an accepted truth, like the blueness of the sky.

The role of metals in contemporary society has changed little over the millennia. We still use the precious metals in our jewelry and lesser ones in our household wares, and though they no longer serve as currency, gold and silver are still considered the safest of investments. The very word *investment*—from the Latin—is derived from the word for putting on clothes; those clothes, woven to contain gold threads, could be burned to yield a molten pool of gold.

A number of the things we live with on a daily basis are metal, of course, and judging a metal's quality (aside from its relative preciousness) is a matter of measuring the way it looks and the way it feels, and understanding how it was made.

It would be a mistake to equate the use of metal in design strictly with the industrial movement. Designer Steven Gambrel quite regularly sprinkles his sophisticated rooms with a handful of metal accents, in this case brass, adding a cohesive yet subtle hit of shine.

# FROM THE PAST TO THE PRESENT
## *The Unique History of Metalwork*

### 4000–3000 BC

The first extraction of silver from ores in Asia Minor and the Aegean Islands takes place, and silver is used sparingly for jewelry and mystical objects. To the Egyptians, silver represented the moon and was later given the name Luna by alchemists.

### 12TH CENTURY

The German monk Theophilus writes the first technical book on silversmithing, *De Diversis Artibus.*

### 13TH CENTURY

Domestic silver becomes increasingly important throughout Europe, prompting the application of laws and standards by which the silver guilds would abide.

### 15TH CENTURY

Throughout the century, silver and gold are used primarily for ecclesiastic purposes—altarpieces, reliquaries—but toward the end of the century, secular wares such as ceremonial drinking cups start to make an appearance.

### 2ND CENTURY BC

Romans import large quantities of silver bullion from the eastern Mediterranean; it is used for commemorative dishes and ornamental vessels.

### 1300

An Act of Parliament in England requires a leopard head punch to be applied to every silver object in London after the "guardians of the Craft" inspect it for quality. From 1363 onward, the maker's initials or symbol is also required.

### 16TH CENTURY

The discovery in the New World of a rich supply of resources, including silver, offsets an increasing scarcity in Europe.

### 1660

The building and decoration of the great Palace of Versailles in France calls for the production of full suites of silver furniture and silver guardrails for the state beds.

## 1693

Brass casting begins in Britain when John Lofting, a merchant in London, is given a license for casting thimbles.

## 1784–1890

In England, all silver pieces are required to be stamped with the profile of the sovereign, to prove that the proper duties have been paid to the government.

## 1851

The Great Exhibition of 1851 displays the influence of industrialization on metalwork, which design reformers such as A. W. N. Pugin, who bases his designs off 15th-century precedents, abhor. Another reformer, Christopher Dresser, uses silver in his innovative, functional designs, but also explores electroplated nickel silver, a less expensive and more durable alternative.

## 1939–1945

During World War II, silver becomes scarce, and as a result, designers and craftspeople turn to other metals such as steel, copper, and aluminum to create household wares such as cutlery and tabletop accessories.

## 1840s–1880s

The most substantial discoveries of silver are made in Nevada, Colorado, Australia, and Asia. In 1859, the Comstock Lode silver ore deposit is discovered in what is now Utah, causing a silver rush in America and prompting advances in mining technology.

## 1880s

C. R. Ashbee establishes the Guild and School of Handicraft with the intention to produce handmade-silver wares at a reasonable cost. By using simple techniques such as beating processes and enameling, Ashbee becomes known for his modern organic aesthetic, aligned with the Art Nouveau style that is beginning to catch on.

## TODAY

Modern households have come to favor low-maintenance metals such as aluminum and stainless steel; however, silver and other precious metals serve an important and special role in many contemporary homes.

# Hardware

TOUCH IS AN IMPORTANT PART OF DESIGN, THOUGH IT'S EASILY OVER-looked when speaking of interiors. It's less obvious than color, less exciting than pattern, and, in a world where shopping happens more and more through a computer screen, it can be the last thing on a consumer's mind.

"Hardware is the only thing that you touch and feel in an architectural experience," says Rhett Butler, of E. R. Butler & Co., a dealer in vintage hardware as well as a manufacturer of its own designs. "So you're going to notice it, whether consciously or unconsciously. If it looks and feels cheap, then you're probably going to walk away with that thought in your mind."

Sarah Coffin, of the Cooper Hewitt, Smithsonian Design Museum, echoes this, pointing out that we do perceive even what we think of as these small details. "People often admire Art Deco skyscrapers," she says, "and they don't think about the fact that some of the appealing things, both inside and out, are the lamps, the gates, the elevator rails. Metalwork is all around them, affecting the design's impact."

The architectural ornament and essentials we group under the rubric "hardware" are found throughout the home: hinges, pulls, knobs, and so on. Evaluating hardware is a matter of aesthetics, of course, but it's also important to consider function—if it's a hinge, a pull, a knob, does it swing seamlessly, is it strong enough to stand up to years of tugging, does it turn effortlessly? Hardware might inform our experience of a space, but it's no good unless it can perform.

"You need locks, and you need the right kind of locks, and you need hinges, and you need the right kind of hinges," says Butler. "There are hundreds of different types of hinges, hundreds of different types of locks, and that's before you even get to the handle." At the retail level, it's not uncommon to find interior and exterior doors sold with knobs and hinges attached, but this approach makes Butler skeptical. "DIY has made it very simple," he says. "It's all prepackaged, like buying candy in a candy store, but the second you step out of that world, you need an architect or a very knowledgeable builder, or you need someone who does hardware consulting and specifications. A typical home for us might have several thousand pieces of metal that all have to be coordinated. Not unlike alchemy or making perfume, there are lots of different options."

OPPOSITE › For custom hardware manufacturers E. R. Butler & Co., a cabinet knob is not just a knob, it's a sculptural object with which we interact daily, one that should be as beautiful as it is functional.

ABOVE › Designer Miles Redd leaves nothing to the ordinary, elevating even the simplest doorknob through the use of unexpected materials such as coral and chrome.

Butler's work is very specialized; his clientele includes interior designers and architects, and even they rely on him to guide them in terms of what's going to work best, what's going to be able to endure daily use and last for years. Judging what you like is simple, but understanding its quality can be more complex.

"It's hard to say something is good or bad design," says Sarah Coffin. "What one person likes, another person doesn't." When it comes to evaluating quality, in anything, she recommends asking three simple questions: Do you like the way this looks? Is it going to last? Is it going to function the way it should?

1 › Hardware placement is more than just screwing a knob into a cabinet. Designer Catherine Kwong recommends looking at the larger picture; there should be symmetry and a sense of pattern. 2 › Companies like Waterworks, which specialize in kitchen and bath fittings, understand that though function is important, it's the metal that customers look at, which is why they offer most designs in dozens of finishes, from chrome to matte gold. 3 › In this Brooklyn kitchen, the minimalist design revolves around two stunning metal features: the hand-forged, antiqued brass hood and the Waterworks faucet. 4 › To magnify the brass details of her small powder room, designer Emily Summers hung custom Cannon/Bullock wallpaper with a slight metallic sheen.

# At the Table

MOST MODERN HOMES AREN'T DRIPPING IN GOLD, AS THE MANSIONS of previous generations of robber barons were, but silver continues to play a role in the way we live now. You probably still speak of your forks and knives as "silverware," even though your everyday cutlery is most likely made of stainless steel.

Two qualities specific to silver explain its continued presence at our table, according to Sarah Coffin, a curator of decorative arts. "Before electricity, you needed to have light," she says. "And what happens when you put candles near silver? The silver sparkles, it glistens, it catches the play of light, and it gives more light." The lightbulb may obviate the need for reflective surfaces that amplify candlelight, but the metal's luster appeals to the modern eye nonetheless. "The other thing about silver—and its use for things like tankards, tureens, plates, bowls, and flatware—is that it imparts no taste to the food."

Though today we typically reserve actual silver flatware for special occasions, it was not always thus; that's why "silverware" is the generic term for cutlery. "In the second half of the nineteenth century, places like Tiffany hired designers to think up the best design for picking up a scallop— and they created a scallop fork," says Coffin. "And a shrimp fork. And a different one for an oyster, for pâté. It became sort of absurd." The circumstances were right: the Comstock Lode was unearthed in 1859, so silver was suddenly much easier to come by in this country; in addition, the middle class was growing, and there were consumers eager to acquire the trappings of wealth.

"This idea of connecting the style of your flatware to your personality, and to your status or your social desires, is one that developed in this country in the second half of the nineteenth century," says Coffin. Stainless steel and aluminum have largely supplanted silver on our tables, because we think of them as being cheaper and lower-maintenance. But this impression isn't entirely the truth. Silver can go in the dishwasher, and it's not hard to find antique silverware that's less expensive than modern aluminum flatware. Another advantage to buying what your grandmother would have thought of as the "good stuff" for everyday use is that typically it's superior in terms of design. "The people who made flatware in the eighteenth century thought a lot about how you held it in order to make you look elegant

Though it is pulled out regularly for dinner parties, this impressive antique silver collection, passed down through three generations, remains polished and on display when not in use.

while eating," says Coffin, "so that you were not having to balance the food and have it fall off."

There's great industrial design in our age, of course; the best design is no longer reserved for the finest materials. But silver does feel different, and even alloys that contain traces of silver can be preferable to the least expensive metal flatware available. The market is vast. "There's so much cheap stuff out there to buy that is badly made or designed, that does not care about whether the materials or design work for its function," says Coffin. "Of course much of it falls apart, and then you have to replace it. And so people's expectations are very low. That does not mean that inexpensive is bad—stainless steel is a good example. Well-made and well-designed metalwork, both silver and stainless steel, will last forever."

At the Los Angeles home of celebrity chef and cookbook author Alex Hitz, casual entertaining is simply not done. The noted host has monthly dinner parties for anywhere from twelve to twenty guests, always with formal place settings that include his very best silver—and his cherished Cartier tureen.

# Metal in Décor

PERHAPS IT'S A CONSEQUENCE OF THE METAL'S POPULARITY IN THE nineteenth century, but in a decorative arts context, silver has connotations of fustiness. "People have a perception that silver flatware has all sorts of curlicues and complicated patterns," says Sarah Coffin. "A lot of people don't want what their grandmother had—and they reject the whole material because they want cool, modern design."

This rejection of tradition in part explains why the home contains so many metals, and not just the ones we term "precious." "Just look historically at metal in the twentieth century," says Jim Elkind, owner of Lost City Arts, a New York–based antiques dealer. "With the industrialization of the West, metal products were being turned out in larger and larger numbers. Then you had World War II, when metal became precious and unavailable. There was this imposed rarity and scarcity of something that people had used decoratively before that." Designers rose to the challenge of using metals that once wouldn't have been considered refined enough for the household.

Elkind cites the sculptor David Smith, whose massive steel constructions elevated an industrial material to fine art. Many artists and designers began to explore whether they could achieve beauty in steel or aluminum as centuries of artisans had in silver and gold. One of Elkind's favorites is Harry Bertoia. His Diamond Group of metal furniture debuted in 1952 and remains in production, but Bertoia was also a fine artist.

As a sculptor, Bertoia explored many different techniques. His pieces include dense amalgamations of bronze rods that resemble foliage, complex stainless-steel assemblages that look like flowers, simple metal rods meant to be suspended from above, geometric forms built of wire. Many of these are very recognizable, in part because they were so imitated. Once you see Bertoia's work, you'll start to encounter examples of it everywhere.

Creating a room is about striking a balance—marrying different colors, textures, and elements to arrive at something harmonious. Metal comes in so many varieties, it's welcome in every room. Highly polished brass can add just the right note of brightness, while darkly stained steel can provide contrast in a colorful room. A rough, industrial piece of sculpture can be a counterpoint to a graceful, traditional room, or a delicate, finely worked metal lamp can add pop to a spare, modern room.

**OPPOSITE ›** Designer Martyn Lawrence Bullard unabashedly mixed metal accents, pairing brass light fixtures with antique iron sculptures, in the iconic Beverly Hills Greystone mansion.

**ABOVE ›** It used to be that brass midcentury sculptures were only found in homes that clung to that particular aesthetic. But today, pieces such as this palm tree sculpture are being resurrected as bold, shining counterpoints in more traditional spaces.

## RECOGNIZING THE MAJOR PLAYERS
# *Metalwork*

### 1 > CHRISTOFLE

Christofle has been a leader in the silver industry for more than two centuries, supplying finely crafted, museum-quality pieces to generations of European royalty, the Paris Opera, even luxury hotels and ocean liners. Christofle's sophisticated tableware and accessories include multiple in-house collections, as well as collaborations by top-notch international designers.

### 2 > THE NANZ COMPANY

Manufacturing hardware for residential doors, windows, and cabinets, The Nanz Company offers an endless menu of materials—not only metal but also wood, leather, and glass—products, customizations, and plated and patinated finishes. Nanz, founded in 1989, also has a department dedicated to restoring and re-creating antique designs.

### 3 > E. R. BUTLER & CO.

Using modern technologies and a love for American roots, E. R. Butler specializes in manufacturing metal and crystal hardware in Early American, Federal, and Georgian styles. The company, its current incarnation established in 1990, views its products as integral to architectural design and strives to elevate the standing of hardware components—and its craft tradition in the United States—among the design profession.

### 4 > LOST CITY ARTS

For more than three decades, Manhattan's Lost City Arts has been a trusted source for high-end original and reproduction twentieth-century design, lighting, and accessories. Perhaps most impressive is owner James Elkind's large collection of works by metal sculptor and designer Harry Bertoia.

### 5 > MICHAEL ARAM

American artist Michael Aram honed his metalworking skills in India, where he set up a workshop after visiting there in 1989. His pieces range from high-end sculptures to more affordable nature-inspired tableware, furniture, and accessories, each piece handcrafted and unique.

### 6 > GEORG JENSEN

Twentieth-century designer Georg Jensen was renowned for his refined, organic forms characteristic of his native Denmark. Today, Jensen's namesake company produces metal accessories, tableware, and cutlery with the same eye for elegant simplicity with a touch of flair, as well as some of Jensen's original designs, including his signature Blossom cutlery pattern from 1919.

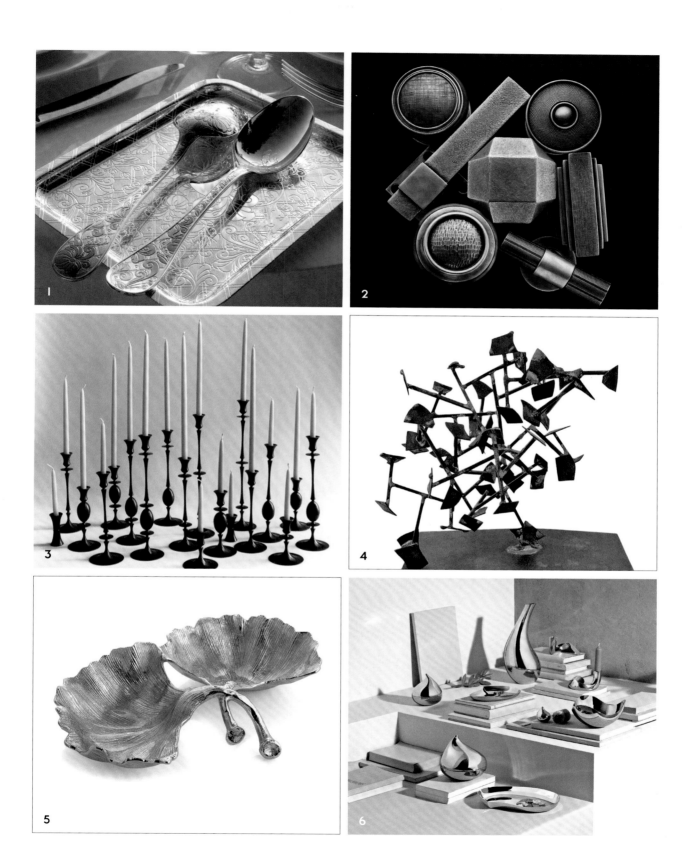

1 › Brass hardware is a polished counterpoint to the rustic, shiplap-paneled backsplash in this airy kitchen. 2 › Blending the modern with the traditional, designer Lynne Scalo displays a Connecticut family's silver collection atop a table with a hammered-chrome base. 3 › Ted Muehling's Biedermeier candlestick collection (made in collaboration with E. R. Butler & Co.) is the modern-day version of your grandmother's silver candelabra; less ornate but just as stunning.

4 › With a midcentury wall sculpture as inspiration, this home-owner arranged a quirky vignette that mixes metal accents with accessories of the same hue. 5 › One of the biggest proponents of metal usage in design today is Jonathan Adler, who utilizes multiple finishes in his lighting, furniture, and tabletop collections. 6 › Furniture that incorporates metalwork, like the brass-framed chair and side table here, hedges the line between function and art. 7 › Though the rest of designer Orlando Diaz-Azcuy's New York apartment adheres to a spare, neutral-toned minimalism, a sprinkling of sculptural brass accents glimmer with drama.

# resources

Only so many talented craftsmen and companies could be squeezed into the chapters of this book. Those who couldn't be mentioned previously are listed here, along with our Major Players, in an extensive design directory that includes both to-the-consumer and to-the-trade sources.

## WALLS

### *wallpaper*

**ADELPHI PAPER HANGINGS**
High quality, block-printed wallpapers featuring historically reproduced designs.
> adelphipaperhangings.com

**ALPHA WORKSHOPS**
Made-to-order, hand-painted wallpaper inspired by New York art and architecture, as well as a collection of textural designs.
> alphaworkshops.org

**CAVERN**
A boutique design firm specializing in eco-friendly graphic wallpaper, all silk-screened by hand. > cavernhome.com

**COLE & SON**
Thousands of designs ranging from traditional to textural, bold florals to graphic patterns, created by a centuries-old, time-honored British firm. > cole-and-son.com

**DE GOURNAY**
Exquisite hand-painted, bespoke wallcoverings utilizing luxurious materials, including silk, gold leaf, and high-end papers. > degournay.com

**ESKAYEL**
Print-to-order, eco-friendly fabrics and wallcoverings, the majority of which are made in the northeastern United States.
> eskayel.com

**FLAT VERNACULAR**
Hand-drawn, hand-printed wallpapers from a Brooklyn-based firm specializing in abstract modern designs.
> flatvernacular.com

**FLAVOR PAPER**
Hand-screened wallpaper from a Brooklyn-based firm known for its limit-pushing approach to design, e.g., metallic bananas and digital photo landscapes.
> flavorpaper.com

**F. SCHUMACHER & CO.**
Interior experts the world over flock to this New York–based firm for its vast selection of gorgeous patterns and top-notch designer collaborations. > fschumacher.com

**GIVEN CAMPBELL**
With a typographer's approach to design, this boutique firm offers a handful of graphic patterns in a bold spectrum of colors.
> givencampbell.com

**GRACIE**
Specializing in scenic, hand-painted Asian wallpaper, imported directly from a family-operated studio in China. > graciestudio.com

**GRAHAM & BROWN**
This British company has been serving up its unique spin on wallpaper design (from big, bold florals to preppy pinstripes) since the 1940s. > grahambrown.com

**GROW HOUSE GROW**
Every design tells a story through graphic, colorful characters and patterns—and whimsical names like the "Highly Intelligent Clam." > growhousegrow.com

**HYGGE & WEST**
Creating wallpaper and removable wallpaper tiles in collaboration with some of the biggest names in contemporary graphic design, such as Oh Joy! and Rifle Paper Co.
> hyggeandwest.com

**KREME LIFE**
Low-VOC, eco-solvent, nontoxic wallpapers featuring modern abstract designs by Cadee Wilder. > kremelife.com

**LITTLE OWL DESIGN**
Dutch skyscapes and scrapbook florals are just two of the cutting-edge creations putting this Amsterdam-based brand at the forefront of innovative wallpaper design. > littleowl.eu

**MAYA ROMANOFF**
This artistic manufacturer takes the idea of textural paper to an awe-inspiring level by incorporating glass beads, seashells, and other luxury materials. > mayaromanoff.com

**MINI MODERNS**
A graphic explosion of patterns from two London-based designers influenced by midcentury British textiles and vintage childhood toys.
> minimoderns.com

**OSBORNE & LITTLE**
A trend-setting British firm known for its vast selection of luxury wallpaper and ongoing distribution of design favorites Nina Campbell, Lorca, and Matthew Williamson.
> osborneandlittle.com

**PAPER MILLS**
Block-printed, painted, and silk-screened papers handmade in California with water-based inks and renewable paper; sold to the trade. > papermills.net

**PHILLIP JEFFRIES LTD.**
An industry-leading manufacturer and importer, stocking more than 1,100 natural wallcoverings, from raffia to silk.
> phillipjeffries.com

**PORTER'S PAINTS**
Handcrafted wallpaper featuring artistic, often nature-inspired designs, with the bonus of optional color-match customization.
> porterspaints.com

**PORTER TELEO**
Distinctive hand-painted and -printed wallcoverings and fabrics inspired by a variety of art processes and traditions from times gone by. > porterteleo.com

**ROLLOUT**
An eclectic design selection divided into five distinct series: Artist-Created, Wanderlust (New York and Paris series), New Materialism, and Hollace Cluny.
> wallpaper.rollout.ca

**SECONDHAND ROSE**
Home to one of the world's largest selections of vintage wallpaper, this New York shop's collection encompasses everything from the traditional to the bold and whimsical.
> secondhandrose.com

### STUDIO PRINTWORKS
Hand-printed wallpapers focusing on traditional design with a modern slant, an aesthetic philosophy that extends to its stunning collaboration with John Derian. > **studioprintworks.com**

### THIBAUT
Historic reproductions, traditional designs, and novelty patterns are all on offer from the United States's oldest continuously operating wallpaper firm. > **thibautdesign.com**

### TIMOROUS BEASTIES
This Scottish boutique firm consistently dreams up edgy, elegant, and irreverent patterns—including a modern take on toile. > **timorousbeasties.com**

### TRACY KENDALL
Commercial and residential off-the-shelf and bespoke wallpaper, including handmade three-dimensional designs. > **tracykendall.com**

### TROVE
Museum-quality prints, from misty landscapes to watercolor splashes, crafted with innovative techniques. > **troveline.com**

### TRUSTWORTH STUDIOS
Meticulously reproduced prints featuring English Arts and Crafts–era patterns with a strong focus on the work of C. F. A. Voysey. > **trustworth.com**

### TURNER POCOCK CAZALET
A collaboration between artist Catherine Cazalet and designer Turner Pocock, each hand-drawn design in this collection is printed in the UK using sustainable materials. > **turnerpocockcazalet.co.uk**

### TWENTY2
Though the selection is quite extensive, this firm's series of printed grass-cloth wallpapers are the true standouts. > **twenty2.net**

### WOLF-GORDON
Wallcoverings in a huge range of textures, colors, patterns, and materials; collections include collaborations with some of today's top design stars. > **wolfgordon.com**

### ZUBER & CIE
Exquisite scenic wallpapers, hand-painted and hand-printed using centuries-old woodblocks from a luxury French design house. > **zuber.fr**

## *paint*

### BEHR
Interior and exterior paints in a vast range of colors, as well as exterior wood care products for do-it-yourselfers. > **behr.com**

### BENJAMIN MOORE
High-quality paints and finishes with a color-match guarantee. > **benjaminmoore.com**

### CALIFORNIA PAINTS
Highly rated exterior and interior paints produced with acrylic latex technology. > **californiapaints.com**

### COLORHOUSE
Environmentally safe, low-odor paints in hundreds of artist-crafted colors, all produced in a LEED Gold-certified manufacturing facility. > **colorhousepaint.com**

### COLOUR STUDIO INC.
San Francisco–based agency offering in-home paint consultation by trained color experts. > **colourstudio.com**

### DEVOE PAINT
Recognized as America's first paint brand, it is best known for its high-quality latex paints available in a variety of colors. > **1754paint.com**

### DONALD KAUFMAN COLOR
With one of the nation's leading color experts at its helm, this industry staple is the trusted source for pigment-rich neutrals and the "perfect" shade of white. > **donaldkaufmancolor.com**

### DUNN-EDWARDS PAINTS
High-quality paint available in nearly two thousand colors manufactured in a LEED Gold-certified factory. > **dunnedwards.com**

### DUTCH BOY
Inexpensive, low-splatter interior and exterior paints that have been used on everything from national landmarks to naval battleships. > **dutchboy.com**

### EARTHBORN PAINTS
Color-rich paints manufactured with environmentally safe materials and technologies. > **earthbornpaints.co.uk**

### FARROW & BALL
Water-based, high-pigment paint, for interiors and exteriors, available in more than a hundred shades. > **us.farrow-ball.com**

### FINE PAINTS OF EUROPE
Known for its historical color collections and lacquer-like glossy paints, all made in the Netherlands. > **finepaintsofeurope.com**

### HUDSON PAINT
A specialty brand focusing on chalkboard, floor, door, and lime paints, all available in multiple shades. > **hudsonpaint.com**

### MATT AUSTIN
A New York–based artist and designer available by commission for large- and small-scale decorative painting projects. > **mattaustin.net**

### MILK PAINT
Old-fashioned, all-natural milk paint (used to create an antiqued look) available in twenty soft shades. > **milkpaint.com**

### PAINT & PAPER LIBRARY
A range of "architectural colors" sold via a color-by-number system allowing clients to seamlessly and easily match ceiling, cornice, wall, and woodwork. > **paint-library.co.uk**

### PORTER'S PAINTS
An industry leader in specialty paint finishes: Liquid Iron, French Wash, Duchess Satin, Fresco, and more. > **porterspaints.com**

### PRATT & LAMBERT PAINTS
Quality paints organized into inspirational palettes for easy-match color combinations. > **prattandlambert.com**

### RALPH LAUREN PAINT
Dynamic hues inspired by the iconic fashion designer's all-American aesthetic. > **ralphlaurenpaint.com**

### SHERWIN-WILLIAMS
The largest producer of paints and coatings in the United States with a reputation for easy-application, pigment-rich shades. > **sherwin-williams.com**

### VALSPAR PAINT
A seemingly endless array of color options, with innovative finishes such as Chalky. > **valsparpaint.com**

## framing

### AARON BROTHERS ART & FRAMING
Custom framing, as well as in-stock designs, from a multilocation retailer found on the West Coast and in the Northwest, Southwest, Texas, and Georgia.
> aaronbrothers.com

### APF MUNN
With a focus on high-end domestic production, this multicity showroom is able to turn around high-end custom jobs in a shorter-than-most time frame.
> apfmunn.com

### ARTISTS FRAME SERVICE
A Chicago-based institution with frame moldings sourced from around the world by experts with a background in art.
> artistsframe.com

### BARK FRAMEWORKS
This New York–based company has framed everything from Asian scrolls to ancient textiles, with an eye for exceptional preservation practices and innovative design. > barkframeworks.com

### BROOKLYN FRAME WORKS
Utilizing museum-quality techniques, these custom framers focus on conservation and offer more than 1,500 moldings and finishes. > brooklynframeworks.com

### BROWNING FRAMES
Catering to neighborhood locals and New York art dealers alike, the main draw of this small custom shop is the handmade archival frames. > browningframes.com

### CASTELLI ART FRAMING
Offering white-glove door-to-door service, this L.A.-based company picks up, frames, and returns every piece.
> castelliframing.com

### CITY FRAME
With a focus on affordable quality frames, this self-proclaimed "no-frills shop" uses only sustainable hardwoods offered in hundreds of styles. > cityframe.com

### ELI WILNER & COMPANY
Specializing in museum quality, European and American period frame reproductions, as well as restoration and conservation services. > eliwilner.com

### GENERAL ART COMPANY
Framing the paintings of art-world luminaries since 1971, this New York–based gallery works mostly in contemporary oak, maple, and fine-wood frames.
> generalartframing.com

### GK FRAMING GROUP LTD.
A New York studio specializing in framing, conservation, and restoration with a renowned eye for finding styles that enrich, not upstage, the art. > gkframing.com

### ILEVEL ART PLACEMENT + INSTALLATION
Picture hanging, art placement, and installation services are all on offer from this New York–based specialty firm.
> ilevel.biz

### J. POCKER
Third-generation, family-owned custom framers offering everything from modern lacquer to gilded French to etched Dutch styles. > jpocker.com

### JULIUS LOWY FRAME AND RESTORING COMPANY
Home to the largest antique frame collection in America with over four thousand styles dating from rare, sixteenth-century Renaissance to twentieth-century Arts and Crafts. > lowy1907.com

### LARSON-JUHL
Custom frames in a variety of styles, colors, and prices, including eco-friendly options, all made in the United States.
> larsonjuhl.com

### SKYFRAME
New York's premier source for custom prefinished, metal, wood, and acrylic frames, as well as shadow box displays.
> skyframe.com

### WILDMAN ART FRAMING
Art and conservation framing with choices including wood, leather, steel, and painted finishes, serving the Dallas–Fort Worth area. > wildmanartframing.com

## FLOORS

### wood

### ANDERSON HARDWOOD FLOORS
Specializing in engineered hardwoods; they had a hand in inventing them.
> andersonfloors.com

### ARCHITECTURAL SYSTEMS, INC.
Innovative sustainable finishes for commercial interiors. > archsystems.com

### ARMSTRONG
An extensive assortment of hardwood and laminate styles and finishes.
> armstrong.com

### ARRIGONI WOODS
Known for wide plank European wood flooring, imported directly from the source.
> arrigoniwoods.com

### BRUCE
Exotic and traditional hardwood flooring, available in hand-scraped finishes.
> bruce.com

### EXQUISITE SURFACES
Exclusive aged French oak floors in hand-finished styles. > xsurfaces.com

### HOME LEGEND
An edited collection of hardwoods plus bamboo, laminate, vinyl, and cork flooring options. > homelegend.com

### I. J. PEISER'S SONS
True parquetry artists, specializing in intricate installations of luxury solid hardwoods. > ijpeiser.com

### LV WOOD
A family-owned business known for specialty woods and raw bespoke finishes, all designed and manufactured in the United States. > lvwood.com

### MIRAGE FLOORS
Hardwood and engineered flooring in a variety of stains, sustainably produced in North America. > miragefloors.com

### MOHAWK
Sustainable hardwood, laminate, and engineered wood options from the world's largest flooring company.
> mohawkflooring.com

**OREGON LUMBER COMPANY**
A vast range of solid and engineered flooring options for commercial and residential interiors. > **oregonlumber.com**

**PID FLOORS**
A broad selection of hardwoods in various stains and styles, from traditional and rustic to unique, bold colors. > **pidfloors.com**

**RESTORATION TIMBER**
Century-old reclaimed wood flooring sourced from abandoned barns, schools, mills, and factories. > **restorationtimber.com**

**SHAW FLOORS**
Known for its innovative laminate flooring that mimics specific wood grains. > **shawfloors.com**

**SOMERSET FLOORS**
Kiln-dried Appalachian hardwood flooring available in a curated selection of stains and plank widths. > **somersetfloors.com**

**THE SULLIVAN SOURCE INC.**
A Toronto-based, to-the-trade showroom offering hardwood and reclaimed wood flooring for specialized installation projects. > **sullivansource.com**

**WOODWRIGHTS WIDE PLANK FLOORING**
Wide plank flooring in various woods and finishes from a boutique manufacturer. > **woodwrightswideplank.com**

## stone

**ABC STONE**
More than a dozen varieties of stone, plus a limited-edition line of home accessories and furniture. > **abcworldwidestone.com**

**AMERICAN BLUESTONE LLC**
The exclusive producer of North River Blue Bluestone, a deep gray-blue stone used indoors and outdoors. > **americanbluestone.com**

**AMSO INTERNATIONAL**
Exporters of high-quality marble, granite, stone, and onyx from Carrara, Italy. > **carraramarble.it**

**ANN SACKS**
Limestone, marble, and travertine tiles in both traditional and artistic styles. > **annsacks.com**

**ANTOLINI**
With quarries located around the world, this Italian company offers a unique variety of stones, both traditional and exotic. > **antoliniusa.com**

**ASN NATURAL STONE, INC.**
Innovative stones, including unique slabs and large-format tiles and pavers. > **asnstone.com**

**CAESARSTONE**
Technologically enhanced natural quartz stones with exceptional durability. > **caesarstoneus.com**

**LAPICIDA**
British and European reclaimed natural stone specialists. > **lapicida.com**

**MARBLE ONLINE**
A leading North American supplier of precut natural stone products. > **marbleonline.com**

**STONE SOURCE**
A carefully curated selection of natural and engineered stone, including an impressive variety of exotic marbles. > **stonesource.com**

**STONEYARD**
LEED-certified reclaimed New England stone in multiple earth-tone color collections. > **stoneyard.com**

**VERMONT QUARRIES CORPORATION**
The premier source for North America's most prestigious white marble, all produced at the Vermont Danby Quarry. > **vermontquarries.com**

**WALKER ZANGER**
Experienced stone masters travel the world hand selecting (and evaluating) these unique luxury stones, including marble, travertine, and onyx. > **walkerzanger.com**

## tile

**ANN SACKS**
High-end tile in a multitude of materials (from glass to stone) and styles (from simple subway tiles to geometric mosaics). > **annsacks.com**

**AR.CE.A CERAMICHE**
Beautifully hand-painted ceramic tiles and decorative objects from a storied Italian design house. > **ceramichearcea.it**

**ARTISTIC TILE**
Turning tile installation into an art form, this luxury brand produces thousands of customizable materials and designs. > **artistictile.com**

**BISAZZA**
This luxury Italian brand is an industry leader specializing in innovative decorative tiles and stunning mosaics. > **bisazza.com**

**CERAMICHE COEM**
Italian porcelain stoneware that offers the beauty (and texture) of natural stone while remaining environmentally conscious. > **coem.it**

**CLÉ**
Heirloom-quality tiles by the leader in artisanal offerings, from Moroccan to penny rounds to special designer collaborations. > **cletile.com**

**COLLI**
Coordinating collections of high-quality floor and wall tiles meant to create a visual cohesiveness between rooms and surfaces. > **colli.it**

**DALTILE**
A leading US manufacturer and distributor with an expansive library of today's most popular tiling choices, including *faux bois* porcelain. > **daltile.com**

**GABBIANELLI**
Colorfully bold ceramic tiles produced by a storied Italian company responsible for multiple industry milestones, such as developing the first three-dimensional pattern. > **gabbianelli.com**

**HEATH CERAMICS**
A Northern California legacy beloved for its handcrafted, glazed stoneware tile in a range of textures and colors. > **heathceramics.com**

**MARAZZI TILE**
Porcelain, glazed ceramic, glass mosaic, natural stone, and metallic tiles for floors, walls, and decorative accents. > **marazziusa.com**

**MARCACORONA**
This brand, based in Sassuolo, Italy, has been making ceramic tiles since 1741 and remains at the forefront of industry innovation today. > **marcacorona.it**

### MIPA

Through extensive historical research, this Italian company re-creates tiles to be reminiscent of late-nineteenth-century marble terrazzo designs. > **mipadesign.it**

### MUTINA

Italian ceramic tiles in a range of elegant minimalist designs with a focus on exaggerated textures, such as bas-relief and raised honeycombs. > **mutina.it**

### NAXOS CERAMICA

Contemporary ceramic wall tiles designed and made in Italy. > **naxos-ceramica.it**

### NEW RAVENNA

Handcrafted mosaics by a leading US manufacturer of high-end stone and glass tiles. > **newravenna.com**

### NOVOCERAM

Ceramic floor and wall tiles from a century-old French expert. > **novoceram.com**

### PARIS CERAMICS

A leader in stone preservation with one of the world's largest selections of antique and reclaimed flooring (limestone, marble, and terra-cotta). > **parisceramicsusa.com**

### POPHAM DESIGN

Handmade Moroccan cement tiles with colorful geometric designs.
> **pophamdesign.com**

### SICIS: THE ART MOSAIC FACTORY

The muralists of the tile world, this Italian company creates artistic innovative designs on a commission-only basis. > **sicis.com**

### SONOMA TILEMAKERS

More than a dozen product lines that combine traditional ceramics with glass, stone, and other materials.
> **sonomatilemakers.com**

### STONE SOURCE

Glass, ceramic, and porcelain tiles that pair innovative geometric shapes with a spectrum of color and texture options.
> **stonesource.com**

# FURNITURE

## *case goods*

### ATELIER VIOLLET

Furniture that revives the lost art of marquetry through the use of shagreen, straw, shell, parchment, and horn.
> **atelierviollet.com**

### BAKER

An incomparable selection of artisan-crafted furniture with multiple period and style influences. > **bakerfurniture.com**

### B&B ITALIA

Internationally acclaimed contemporary Italian furniture at the forefront of cutting-edge minimalist design. > **bebitalia.com**

### BDDW

Heirloom-quality domestic-wood furniture designed by Tyler Hays and made in his Philadelphia studio. > **bddw.com**

### BIASI CATANI

A South American design house specializing in modern, streamlined pieces made from exotic Brazilian hardwoods.
> **biasicatani.com**

### BLUDOT

Sleek modern designs with impeccable craftsmanship at an affordable price point.
> **bludot.com**

### CENTURY FURNITURE

With state-of-the-art woodworking facilities in North Carolina, this Made in America brand features an extensive range of customizable case goods.
> **centuryfurniture.com**

### CHELSEA TEXTILES

Faithful re-creations of antique furniture in Gustavian, French Country, and midcentury modern styles.
> **chelseatextiles.com**

### DESSIN FOURNIR

A diverse range of furnishings often inspired by classic European elegance and made with traditional artisanal techniques.
> **dessinfournir.com**

### DLV

Often mixing exotic woods with rich leathers, this Brooklyn-based firm describes its aesthetic as "Art Deco-meets-rock and roll." > **dlvdesigns.com**

### DWELLSTUDIO

Blending modern glamour with streamlined forms, this New York designer is known for its quality craftsmanship and inventive use of high-end materials. > **dwellstudio.com**

### EGG COLLECTIVE

Heirloom-quality, locally made pieces with a focus on sculptural forms and natural materials. > **eggcollective.com**

### EJ VICTOR

The official furniture licensee for Ralph Lauren and AERIN with its own collection of exquisite designs. > **ejvictor.com**

### HELLMAN CHANG

Leading the Brooklyn Renaissance movement with its line of high-end, mixed material, artisanal furniture.
> **hellman-chang.com**

### HENRYBUILT

Custom-designed kitchen cabinetry and whole-home storage systems beloved for their sophisticated livability.
> **henrybuilt.com**

### JULIAN CHICHESTER

Furniture in a range of finishes inspired by classic nineteenth- and twentieth-century English styles. > **julianchichester.com**

### KINDEL

Custom-made furniture in a wide range of traditional styles, crafted completely by hand in Grand Rapids, Michigan.
> **kindelfurniture.com**

### NEWELL DESIGN STUDIO

Built-to-order, exquisitely crafted furniture created with an artist's eye for detail using fine woods and metals.
> **newelldesignstudio.com**

### PAUL KELLEY

Colorful bespoke creations with unique material combinations; now offering a ready-made line. > **pk-designs.co.uk**

### PLAIN ENGLISH DESIGN

Bespoke kitchen cabinetry and closets from a traditional British joinery, available in a handful of modern styles.
> **plainenglishdesign.co.uk**

**POLIFORM**
A luxury Italian brand specializing in customizable closets, wall systems, and kitchen cabinetry. > **poliformusa.com**

**RICHARD WRIGHTMAN DESIGN**
Built-to-order campaign furniture that mixes traditional and modern aesthetics. > **richardwrightman.com**

**SAWKILLE CO.**
A small, upstate New York furniture company specializing in custom-designed "farmhouse modern" furniture. > **sawkille.com**

**SOANE**
Bespoke made-in-Britain furniture inspired by both antique and twentieth-century designs. > **soane.co.uk**

**THEODORE ALEXANDER**
With thousands of pieces available, from traditional to modern, this company is a pioneer in high-end furniture production throughout Asia. > **theodorealexander.com**

**VICA**
Handcrafted furniture, lighting, and accessories by architect Annabelle Selldorf and her designer/architect father, Herbert Selldorf. > **vicadesign.com**

**WRIGHT20**
This auction house, with locations in New York City and Chicago, specializes in twentieth- and twenty-first-century designs. > **wright20.com**

## upholstered furniture

**A. RUDIN**
Elegant furnishings custom-made in the United States using traditional techniques. > **arudin.com**

**B&B ITALIA**
High-end, heirloom-quality modern furniture from a Milan-based design house. > **bebitalia.com**

**CHELSEA WORKROOM**
A boutique Manhattan atelier lauded for its custom drapery and upholstery; commissions by the trade only. > **chelseaworkroom.com**

**CISCO BROTHERS**
Classic furniture with a modern, organic appeal, all locally made in Los Angeles using green materials and building methods. > **ciscobrothers.com**

**COBBLE HILL**
ABC Carpet & Home's exclusive in-house collection made from sustainably sourced materials and available in more than 300 customizable fabrics. > **abchome.com**

**DESIGN WITHIN REACH**
Making modern design classics accessible to the masses, this major retailer is the place to find authentic, collection-worthy pieces by Eames, Saarinen, and more. > **dwr.com**

**DUNE**
Custom, American-made contemporary furniture known for pushing design boundaries through unique form and material usage. > **dune-ny.com**

**DWELLSTUDIO**
Creating modern design classics, this New York studio blends vintage-inspired shapes with its signature modern fabric offerings. > **dwellstudio.com**

**ETHAN ALLEN**
With hundreds of locations around the world, this line of classic American furnishings is beloved for its dedication to "livable luxury." > **ethanallen.com**

**FRITZ HANSEN**
A high-end Dutch furniture manufacturer responsible for producing many classic designs by Arne Jacobsen, Poul Kjærholm, and Piet Hein. > **fritzhansen.com**

**GEORGE SMITH**
Finely crafted furniture, inspired by both contemporary trends and the company's nineteenth-century namesake, all made using traditional techniques in Northern England. > **georgesmith.com**

**HICKORY CHAIR FURNITURE CO.**
A North Carolina manufacturer that's been making high-quality, timeless, made-to-order pieces since 1911. > **hickorychair.com**

**HOLLY HUNT**
Aside from its eponymous line of modern luxury furnishings, Holly Hunt has become a premier destination for collection-worthy pieces from today's biggest names in design. > **hollyhunt.com**

**JOHN DERIAN BY CISCO BROTHERS**
Dreamed up by Derian, made by Cisco Brothers, this match made in design world heaven offers a curated selection of classic, often eclectic, styles in velvet or linen. > **johnderian.com**

**JONAS WORKROOM**
Classically beautiful custom-upholstered furniture, handcrafted using nineteenth-century standards and techniques. > **jonasworkroom.com**

**KNOLL**
Bauhaus design classics from the storied company, as well as new styles by big-name contemporary designers. > **knoll.com**

**LEE INDUSTRIES**
Hundreds of traditional and modern styles offered in a handful of customizable fabrics, all proudly manufactured in the United States. > **leeindustries.com**

**LIGNE ROSET**
This storied French company has been at the forefront of modern furniture design since 1860 and is best known for its collaborations with young, rising talents. > **ligne-roset-usa.com**

**LILLIAN AUGUST**
Eclectic styles from hundreds of brands, including the company's namesake collection, available through one of its three expansive design centers in New York and Connecticut. > **lillianaugust.com**

**MANZANARES FURNITURE CORP.**
A trusted New York–based custom furniture studio serving the interior design and architecture trades. > **manzanaresfurniture.com**

**MITCHELL GOLD + BOB WILLIAMS**
Eco-friendly American-made furnishings in timeless, comfortable styles with on-trend fabric and finishing options. > **mgbwhome.com**

**MINOTTI**
Sophisticated minimalist furnishings, with an emphasis on high-end sectionals, from an internationally renowned Italian brand. > **minottiny.com**

**MONTAUK SOFA**
Comfortable, high-quality upholstered furniture handmade in Montreal; overstock sofas available at discounted rates. > **montauksofa.com**

### NATUZZI
Italy's largest furniture manufacturer with three distinct lines of luxury offerings: made in Italy, leather sofas, and performance recliners. > **natuzzi.com**

### OCHRE
Organic modern furniture known for its simple lines, high-quality materials, and enduring craftsmanship, as well as its focus on proportions, textures, contrasts, and colors. > **ochre.net**

### POLTRONA FRAU
Sophisticated Italian-made furnishings in classic and contemporary styles with an emphasis on rich leather upholstery.
> **poltronafrau.com/en**

### PROPERTY
Vintage and contemporary furnishings, hand-selected in proprietor Sabrina Schilcher's signature "sophisticated pop" aesthetic. > **propertyfurniture.com**

### RACHEL ASHWELL SHABBY CHIC
Custom-made, machine-washable slipcovered furniture with an aesthetic built around this designer's belief in the beauty of imperfection. > **shabbychic.com**

### RALPH LAUREN HOME
A beautiful translation of the classic Western style this fashion designer is known for (e.g., Southwestern patterns and lots of leather). > **ralphlaurenhome.com**

### RALPH PUCCI INTERNATIONAL
An award-winning gallery focusing on the latest in high-end modern furniture and lighting designs, with locations in New York City, Los Angeles, and Miami.
> **ralphpucci.net**

### RESTORATION HARDWARE
This home furnishings megabrand is known for its signature mix of industrial, modern, masculine designs and has stores across the United States and Canada.
> **restorationhardware.com**

### ROCHE BOBOIS
A high-end, pioneering French furniture company lauded for its eccentric modern designs and impressive partnerships with designers and architects. > **roche-bobois.com**

### ROOM & BOARD
American craftsmanship meets classic modern design at this multilocation megastore with an extensive menu of customizable finishes. > **roomandboard.com**

### VITRA.
This Swiss, family-owned modern furniture company is known for its playful shapes and collaborative designs with top industry leaders. > **vitra.com**

# TEXTILES
## *fabric*

### BEACON HILL
More than a dozen distinct fabric collections, browsable by style or material, available exclusively to the trade.
> **beaconhilldesign.com**

### BRUNSCHWIG & FILS
With a nod to French style, this brand's diverse range of high-end textiles can be found in grand rooms from the White House to the Palace of Versailles.
> **brunschwig.com**

### CLARENCE HOUSE
Famous for its vibrant screen-printed fabrics and hand-loomed brocades, this New York–based, to-the-trade studio also offers high-quality velvets, damasks, silks, and linens. > **clarencehouse.com**

### DEDAR
High-end Italian fabrics available in a rich spectrum of prints, solids, and textures kept in stock and sold internationally; exclusive manufacturer of the Hermès collection.
> **dedar.it**

### DE LE CUONA
Beautiful linens, as well as contemporary paisleys, cashmeres, and velvets beloved for their raw sophistication and elegant craftsmanship. > **delecuona.co.uk**

### DONGHIA
Along with its own line of fine fabrics, this to-the-trade business represents multiple luxury fabric collections, including Armani/Casa and Lulu DK.
> **donghia.com**

### DWELLSTUDIO FOR ROBERT ALLEN
Known for its vivid color palettes and whimsical designs often inspired by prints and motifs from the fifties, sixties, and seventies. > **robertallendesign.com**

### FORTUNY
Timeless, versatile textiles produced in the same Venetian factory as those created by its renowned founder, Mariano Fortuny, over a century ago. > **fortuny.com**

### GP & J BAKER
This famed British company is home to one of the world's largest textile archives, consisting of samples from its 125 years of production. > **gpandjbaker.com**

### HOLLAND & SHERRY
After providing luxury fabrics to the fashion industry for nearly two hundred years, this British merchant expanded its fine cashmeres, silk velvets, linens, and wools to the interior design trade in 1998.
> **hollandandsherry.com**

### IDARICA GAZZONI
An Italian artist's ornate designs inspired by personal travel and an interest in ancient historical empires. > **idaricagazzoni.com**

### INNOVATIONS
Known for its revolutionary use of luxury materials, such as leather, faux leather, linen, and velvet. > **innovationsusa.com**

### JOHN ROBSHAW TEXTILES
Handprinted linens inspired by traditional Indian prints; dyed and printed in India and developing nations as part of the Aid to Artisans program. > **johnrobshaw.com**

### KNOLLTEXTILES
An extensive archive of innovative textiles from its sixty-five-plus years in business, as well as a constantly evolving list of collaborations with cutting-edge artists and designers. > **knoll.com**

### KRAVET
One of the largest to-the-trade manufacturers of high-end fabrics in the United States, with a wide range of patterns and textures. > **kravet.com**

### KYLE BUNTING
The premier source for extraordinary cowhide upholstery, including specialty patterns, colors, and textures.
> **kylebunting.com**

### LEE JOFA
This brand's namesake collection is known for its iconic floral patterns and contemporary designer collections, all sold to the trade. > **leejofa.com**

## LORO PIANA
An Italian fabric house specializing in particularly high-grade wool; sold to the trade. > **loropiana.com/en**

## MAHARAM
Modern textiles, reissues of designs by twentieth-century masters, and more from the hundred-plus-year-old, family-run business. > **maharam.com**

## MANUEL CANOVAS FOR COWTAN & TOUT
This French fabric house is lauded for its luxurious weaves, stunning prints, and bright, unique color combinations.
> **cowtan.com/manuel-canovas**

## NOBILIS
A Parisian design house offering dozens of high-end fabric collections, ranging from contemporary to beachy to twists on historical French patterns. > **nobilis.fr**

## OSBORNE & LITTLE
This storied British manufacturer is home to hundreds of luxury fabrics, all easily searchable by style, material, color, or intended use. > **osborneandlittle.com**

## PETER FASANO LTD.
Hand-silkscreened, eco-friendly fabrics and wallcoverings in an array of beautiful styles, some with hand-painted details.
> **peterfasano.com**

## PIERRE FREY
With styles ranging from the traditional to the whimsical, this French design house is known for its patterns, as well as its replicated antique prints. > **pierrefrey.com**

## POLLACK
Taking the guesswork out of coordinating fabrics, this New York–based studio offers a series of "Color Stories," showcasing small vignettes of swatches that work well together. > **pollackassociates.com**

## QUADRILLE
An industry leader offering the latest in on-trend prints and wovens in a spectrum of colorways; sold to the trade.
> **quadrillefabrics.com**

## ROBERT ALLEN
The expansive color library, featuring thousands of solids and prints, at this top-notch fabric house is one of the interior design world's best-kept secrets.
> **robertallendesign.com**

## ROGERS & GOFFIGON
Using natural fibers in a spectrum of textures and weights (from diaphanous silk to whisper-thin linen), these luxury fabrics are inspired by historical textiles and nature. > **rogersandgoffigon.com**

## ROMO
A rich array of prints and solids, from bold botanicals to rustic plaids, sold exclusively to the trade by this family-operated British fabric house. > **romo.com**

## RUBELLI
Exquisite handwoven fabrics that fuse art with the latest industry trends from a historic Venetian company. > **rubelli.com**

## SAM KASTEN HANDWEAVER
Made-to-order plaids, stripes, and textural solids handwoven on traditional looms to each client's color, texture, and weight specifications. > **samkasten.com**

## SCHUMACHER & CO.
Spanning the style spectrum from Victorian to modern, this renowned brand is an industry favorite beloved for its inventive designs and creative partnerships.
> **fschumacher.com**

## T4 BY TILLETT TEXTILES
This boutique studio offers create-your-own custom fabrics using colorPAD technology, with a selection of 180 patterns, 55 colors, and 12 grounds (or materials).
> **t4fabrics.com**

## VALDESE WEAVERS
Known for its decorative, durable jacquards, this North Carolina–based manufacturer has more than 200,000 patterns available at various price points.
> **valdeseweavers.com**

## ZIMMER + ROHDE
Offering multiple vibrant collections (from Urban Jungle to Natural Elegance), this German textile manufacturer's designs are as timeless as they are sophisticated.
> **zimmer-rohde.com**

## ZOFFANY
Bringing a fresh perspective to English and French eighteenth- and nineteenth-century styles through a pioneering use of color and cutting-edge production techniques.
> **zoffany.com**

# *window treatments*

## DAVID HAAG
Turning window dressing into an art, this renowned curtain expert is known for his always elegant custom drapery designs.
> **davidhaag.com**

## GRABER
Home to the Badger Drapery Crane, a tool allowing installers to easily adjust shades and blinds for balance in even the most uneven windowsills. > **graberblinds.com**

## HUNTER DOUGLAS
The latest in window treatment technologies, from hidden energy-efficient layers to motorized controls, in a stylish selection of shades, shutters, and blinds.
> **hunterdouglas.com**

## KNOLLTEXTILES
A handful of Knoll's modernist fabrics, upgraded with the technical needs of drapery in mind. > **knoll.com**

## LUTRON
The latest in light-control technology, including innovative dimmer systems and energy-saving motorized shades.
> **lutron.com**

## MERMET USA
Specializing in energy-efficient solar screen fabrics available in three levels of light control: transparent, translucent, and blackout. > **mermetusa.com**

## NORMAN WINDOW FASHIONS
Handcrafted custom wood shutters and blinds in a handful of styles (modern to traditional) and finishes.
> **normanshutters.com**

## RESTORATION HARDWARE
A big-box retailer offering the attention to detail expected from a custom shop, with drapery and shades available in luxe fabrics (from linen to silk) and multiple dimensions.
> **restorationhardware.com**

## THE SHADE STORE
The most trusted one-stop shop for custom handcrafted window treatments—shades, blinds, and drapery—all made in the United States. > **theshadestore.com**

### SMITH & NOBLE
Custom blinds, shutters, shades, and vertical panels available in hundreds of fabric and hardware combinations.
> smithandnoble.com

### SOMFY SYSTEMS
Industry-leading motors and light-control systems for blinds, shades, shutters, curtains, and outdoor awnings.
> somfysystems.com

### WINDOW MODES
A sophisticated offering of high-end custom window treatments (shoji shades, wood shutters, and more) with a focus on light control; available to the trade.
> windowmodes.com

## *rugs*

### ABC CARPET & HOME
An industry trendsetter beloved for its impressive collection of antique offerings, as well as its unwavering ability to uncover the next big name in the designer rug world.
> abchome.com

### AELFIE
Designed in Brooklyn, handwoven in India, the flat-weave rugs from this up-and-coming studio are making waves with their geo-prints and electric hues. > aelfie.com

### CHRISTOPHER FARR
Museum-worthy rugs made with the finest yarns and dyes in collaboration with skilled weavers and contemporary artists and designers, including Anni Albers and Kit Kemp. > christopherfarr.com

### DASH & ALBERT
Hundreds of well-priced modern prints and solids in a variety of sizes and materials: wool, cotton, and blended, as well as indoor/outdoor options.
> dashandalbert.annieselke.com

### DOUBLE KNOT
An expert importer of authentic new and antique woven rugs from Turkey, Persia, Anatolia, and neighboring regions.
> double-knot.com

### FORT STREET STUDIO
Inspired by the abstract sophistication of watercolors, the bleeding hues of these luxurious rugs—woven with suede-like Dandong "wild" silk—are textural works of art. > fortstreetstudio.com

### KYLE BUNTING
The premier destination for sophisticated cowhide rugs, from traditional neutral styles to colorful patchwork creations.
> kylebunting.com

### LOLOI
With more than 125, always-in-stock rug collections, this award-winning Dallas design house prides itself on having something for every room in every home.
> loloirugs.com

### MADELINE WEINRIB
Working with artisans around the world to preserve centuries-old weaving techniques, this designer creates heirloom-quality rugs in bold patterns and hues.
> madelineweinrib.com

### MANSOUR
Considered to be the largest antique rug collection in the world, with European, Persian, and Oriental styles, some of which boast royal provenance. > mansourrug.com

### MARC PHILLIPS DECORATIVE RUGS
An eclectic selection of high-end rugs, both antique and new, including Moroccan, Tibetan, hides, and flat-weave styles.
> marcphillipsrugs.com

### NANIMARQUINA
Handwoven in India, Nepal, Pakistan, and Morocco, the eclectic rugs from this Spanish company range from graphic prints to shaggy textures to unique shapes and sizes.
> nanimarquina.com

### PATTERSON FLYNN MARTIN
Custom, classic, and contemporary high-end rugs, including historic reproductions from around the world.
> pattersonflynnmartin.com

### THE RUG COMPANY
It takes four months to make one of its fine, hand-knotted rugs, each woven with wool from a Tibetan plateau using traditional techniques. > therugcompany.com

### SAFAVIEH
A wide range of antique Oriental rugs and contemporary styles handmade in the major weaving centers of the world: Persia, India, Tibet, Nepal, China, and Pakistan.
> safavieh.com

### STARK CARPET
This luxury rug dynasty once outfitted the White House, and today creates collections with some of the industry's top interior designers; sold to the trade. > starkcarpet.com

### STEPHANIE ODEGARD COLLECTION
Hand-knotted rugs in a range of modern styles, from geometric grids to bold florals, all ethically crafted by Nepalese artisans.
> stephanieodegard.com

### SURYA
Handmade flat-weave area rugs in a wide variety of styles from traditional to contemporary to graphic.
> surya.com

### VANDERHURD
Bespoke, museum-quality rugs in bold patterns and custom color combinations created using a variety of experimental techniques. > vanderhurd.com

## *carpets*

### ABC CARPET & HOME
A curated collection of styles from today's top designers, as well as a custom, in-house line that includes a selection of natural fiber carpets. > abchome.com

### ATLAS CARPET MILLS INC.
Broadloom carpet and carpet tiles in a sweeping range of customizable patterns and textures. > atlascarpetmills.com

### BEAULIEU AMERICA
Broadloom and modular-tile carpets in a variety of designs and textures, with eco-friendly options, as well as innovative solutions for odor and stain control.
> usa.beaulieuflooring.com

### FLOR
Easy-to-assemble modular tiles that can form single-color carpeting or unique, mix-and-match designs. > flor.com

### LANGHORNE CARPET COMPANY
Custom and in-stock museum-quality wool carpets made at the country's longest continuously operating Wilton carpet mill outside Philadelphia. > langhornecarpets.com

### MILLIKEN
Digitally printed carpets and rugs created using a machine that allows pigment to permeate a carpet's fibers, ensuring lasting color. > millikencarpet.com

### MOHAWK FLOORING
Durable, eco-friendly carpets in a range of textiles, patterns, colors, and styles, all made in the United States. > **mohawkflooring.com**

### SHAW FLOORS
Luxury carpets in a wide selection of colors, styles, and textures, with patented stain and soil protection technology. > **shawfloors.com**

### STARK CARPET
A company synonymous with high-quality, custom-designed carpets available in a range of sophisticated styles. > **starkcarpet.com**

### TUFENKIAN ARTISAN CARPETS
Exquisite, heirloom-quality Tibetan and Armenian carpets handmade by this long-standing company focused on humanitarian and environmental causes.
> **tufenkiancarpets.com**

# ACCESSORIES

## *lighting*

### ALISON BERGER GLASSWORKS
A Los Angeles–based artist known for her use of filigree bulbs and blown crystal silhouettes that have an effect akin to jars of fireflies. > **alisonbergerglassworks.com**

### APPARATUS STUDIO
Aged brass, etched glass, leather, and porcelain are combined to create modern light fixtures that fuse sculptural shapes with hand-worn materials.
> **apparatusstudio.com**

### ARTEMIDE
With a focus on the latest in lighting technology, including LED offerings, this Milan-based company creates sleek minimalist fixtures for all surfaces.
> **artemide.us**

### ARTSYLIGHTS
Based in Manhattan (with an outlet on eBay), this retailer sells, repairs, and rewires antique lighting fixtures. > **artsylights.com**

### CHARLES EDWARDS
More than four hundred designs inspired by nineteenth- and twentieth-century English, French, and American lighting.
> **charlesedwards.com**

### CIRCA LIGHTING
A trusted lighting manufacturer working with some of the biggest names in design today: Ralph Lauren, Aerin Lauder, Thomas O'Brien, and more.
> **circalighting.com**

### DAVID WEEKS STUDIO
Brooklyn-made custom lighting known for its modern, sculptural forms and intricate, gravity-defying Hanging Mobile collection.
> **davidweeksstudio.com**

### FLOS
Pushing the boundaries of modern lighting design since the 1960s, this Italian brand is an industry leader known for its impressive roster of top-notch collaborations.
> **usa.flos.com**

### FONTANAARTE
Sleek modern lighting inspired by the company's founder, Italian designer Giò Ponti, with an archival collection of its iconic creations, such as the Fontana Lamp.
> **fontanaarte.com**

### GUÉRIDON
A source for vintage midcentury European lighting that specializes in re-editions by French modernist Serge Mouille.
> **gueridon.com**

### INGO MAURER
Designing innovative lighting schemes and individual fixtures that double as modern artwork since the 1960s. > **ingo-maurer.com**

### JAMIE YOUNG COMPANY
This California-based specialty lighting company offers an eclectic array of designs, including its popular beaded chandeliers, all inspired by travel, art, and history.
> **jamieyoung.com**

### KAIA LIGHTING
Known for its signature combination of brass and exposed lightbulbs, this Austrian studio creates simple, beautiful fixtures—both custom and limited edition. > **kaia.at**

### KEVIN REILLY LIGHTING
Indoor and outdoor lighting that fuses industrial materials and clean lines; best known for its metal-based hanging lights outfitted with candles.
> **kevinreillylighting.com**

### LA MURRINA
Offering a stunning selection of classic Murano glass chandeliers, this Italian company's creations are sculptural works of art. > **lamurrina.com**

### LIGHTYEARS
A boutique lighting firm specializing in affordable, streamlined designs with a traditional Danish sensibility.
> **lightyears.dk**

### LINDSEY ADELMAN STUDIO
Handmade fixtures that explore the aesthetic tensions between blown glass and industrial machine components; best known for its collection of Branching chandeliers.
> **lindseyadelman.com**

### LOBMEYR
Elegant antique and reproduction lighting—with styles dating back to 1780—from a centuries-old Austrian design house specializing in crystal. > **lobmeyr.at**

### MATER
High-end contemporary lighting from a Danish brand committed to eco-conscious and socially responsible design. > **mater.dk**

### MOOOI
Founders Marcel Wanders and Casper Vissers work with modern design stars to imbue their collection with a timeless, often playful aesthetic. > **moooi.com**

### NICHE MODERN
Hand-blown glass lighting—in a variety of jewel tones—with clean, simple lines and exposed filament bulbs. > **nichemodern.com**

### OCHRE
Elegant chandeliers, sconces, and lamps made with unique materials and quality craftsmanship. > **ochre.net**

### REJUVENATION
Reproduction, restored, and vintage nineteenth- and early-twentieth-century industrial lighting by a Portland, Oregon, manufacturer. > **rejuvenation.com**

### REMAINS LIGHTING
An impressive selection of impeccably restored antique lighting, as well as new heirloom-quality pieces made in the company's New York factory.
> **remains.com**

### REWIRE

This specialty retailer has collected an extensive inventory of rare, high-end twentieth-century vintage fixtures, from midcentury Austrian sconces to Raymor table lamps. > **rewirela.com**

### ROBERT ABBEY, INC.

The manufacturer behind lauded collections by industry leaders like Jonathan Adler, as well as its own price-conscious line—all made in the United States since 1948. > **robertabbey.biz**

### ROLL & HILL

Founded by designer Jason Miller, this Brooklyn studio is home to his own line of modern fixtures, as well as works from some of the biggest names in emerging talent. > **rollandhill.com**

### SANTA & COLE

A Spanish company dedicated to offering the best in streamlined, function-focused lighting options. > **santacole.com**

### TOM DIXON

Contemporary minimalist pendants and lamps designed in London and inspired by British heritage. > **tomdixon.net**

### THE URBAN ELECTRIC CO.

Hundreds of custom-made lighting options from a decade-old Charleston firm that began as a lantern maker. > **urbanelectricco.com**

### VAUGHAN

A British firm producing heirloom-quality lighting inspired by classic antiques, including elaborate chandeliers and crystal table lamps. > **vaughandesigns.com**

### VISUAL COMFORT & CO.

A range of traditional and contemporary fixtures created by renowned designers and led by "lighting legend" Earle F. Chapman. > **visualcomfort.com**

## *ceramics*

### ASTIER DE VILLATTE

Handmade eighteenth- and nineteenth-century inspired Parisian ceramics molded from black terra-cotta and finished in a milky-white glaze. > **astierdevillatte.com**

### BODO SPERLEIN

A British design studio known for its inventive use of ceramics, from porcelain chandeliers to multiple collections of exquisite bone china. > **bodosperlein.com**

### BOSA

Handmade Italian ceramics in a variety of whimsical shapes—from lamps to decorative bowls—available for color customization through the brand's signature palette. > **bosatrade.com**

### DANSK

Scandinavian-inspired dinnerware and serving pieces, designed in post–World War II America and still admired—and widely used—today for its chic simplicity and practicality. > **dansk.com**

### FORNASETTI

Italian collectibles—decorative plates, ashtrays, and more—featuring the brand's signature graphic, often surreal, illustrations, from whimsical faces to flying fish. > **fornasetti.com**

### HEATH CERAMICS

Modernist ceramics, including tile and tabletop pieces, made in small batches by skilled artisans in the Bay Area using the same techniques as its storied founder, Edith Heath. > **heathceramics.com**

### JONATHAN ADLER

Arguably the biggest name in pottery today, this design star is known for his wide range of decorative and tabletop stoneware and porcelain in whimsical, playful forms. > **jonathanadler.com**

### KLEINREID

Elegant everyday ceramics with artisanal glazes, graceful forms, and high-level craftsmanship that blends art studio techniques with industrial methods. > **kleinreid.com**

### MICHELLE ERICKSON

A highly acclaimed ceramicist specializing in seventeenth- and eighteenth-century reproductions, as well as her own series of modern creations. > **michelleericksonceramics.com**

### MUD AUSTRALIA

Streamlined tabletop items, with color customization options, handmade in Sydney using imported French Limoges porcelain. > **mudaustralia.com**

### REICHENBACH PORZELLANMANUFAKTUR

Experimenting with shape and technique, this German manufacturer creates fine hand-painted china and decorative home accessories. > **porzellanmanufaktur.net**

### SARA PALOMA

Drawing inspiration from architectural urban forms, this Northern California–based ceramicist creates stoneware vases and bottles with exaggerated modernist shapes. > **sarapaloma.com**

### TAIZO KURODA

Modern milky-white ceramics (bowls and vases) created on the potter's wheel and marked by signs of the artist's hand. > **taizo-kuroda.com**

### WEDGWOOD

For centuries, this English company's name has been synonymous with fine bone china collections, as well as collectible home accessories. > **wedgwood.co.uk**

## *glass*

### BACCARAT

This legendary French *maison* has been creating exquisite crystal tableware, gifts, and chandeliers for more than 250 years. > **us.baccarat.com**

### JOHN DERIAN COMPANY INC.

Known for his whimsical decoupage—a process by which vintage ephemera are collaged onto hand-blown glass—available on everything from plates to platters to paperweights. > **johnderian.com**

### JOHN POMP STUDIOS

Lighting, furniture, and accessories handcrafted in Pomp's multidisciplinary Philadelphia studios using time-tested Venetian glassblowing techniques. > **johnpomp.com**

## JULISKA
Utilizing time-honored hand-pressed and mouth-blown techniques to create collection-worthy decorative bohemian glassware and pendant lights. > **juliska.com**

## NOUVEL STUDIO
Artisanal glass creations—as much a work of sculptural art as it is a functional product—made at a famed Mexican studio in collaboration with renowned designers and architects. > **nouvelstudio.com**

## RIEDEL
Fine Austrian glassware with an emphasis on wineglasses created to complement the characteristics of different wine varietals. > **riedelusa.net**

## SIEMON & SALAZAR
Hand-blown glass vessels and light fixtures inspired by Muranese traditions and Scandinavian aesthetics. > **siemonandsalazar.com**

## SIMON PEARCE
Glassware beloved for its elegant, rustic sensibility, created by a Vermont-based studio using traditional glassblowing techniques. > **simonpearce.com**

## VENINI
A storied Italian design house, with a roster of impressive collaborators, known for its luxury Murano glass lighting and vessels. > **venini.com**

## WATERFORD
This storied Irish manufacturer's legacy of creating fine crystal collections, including tabletop items and chandeliers, dates back to the 1700s. > **waterford.com**

# *metalwork*

## ALESSI
Cutting-edge products that turn everyday objects into functional works of art by an Italian manufacturer long touted as a "dream factory" of good design. > **alessi.com**

## ANE CHRISTENSEN
Modern fluid sculptures—typically in silver, copper, or steel—created by a skilled London-based designer and metalsmith. > **anechristensen.com**

## THE BRASS KNOB
One of the design world's best-kept secrets, this Washington, DC, institution is the place to find rare architectural antiques, including eighteenth-century hardware. > **thebrassknob.com**

## CHRISTOFLE
World-renowned French silversmiths known for their timeless, high-end flatware and home décor created in Normandy since 1830. > **us.christofle.com**

## DECORATIVE IRON
Stocking a vast selection of ornamental and decorative products, including finials, hardware, rosettes, stampings, and more. > **decorativeiron.com**

## ELEEK INC.
Handcrafted architectural and detail metalwork focused on sustainability and a low environmental impact. > **eleekinc.com**

## E. R. BUTLER & CO.
The premier destination for custom-manufactured hardware—doorknobs, cabinet pulls, and more—in the Early American, Federal, and Georgian styles. > **erbutler.com**

## ERICKSON SILVER
Handwrought sterling silver flatware and jewelry made with traditional American Colonial techniques in Gardner, Massachusetts. > **ericksonsilver.com**

## GEORG JENSEN
For over a century, this Danish design house has married function with form, imbuing everyday tabletop items with serene, fluid shapes. > **georgjensen.com**

## LOST CITY ARTS
Restored and original midcentury furnishings and fixtures, including a large collection of Harry Bertoia metal sculptures, are available at this Manhattan retailer. > **lostcityarts.com**

## MEPRA
Cooking utensils, cutlery, and table accessories made in collaboration with cutting-edge designers by an award-winning Italian firm. > **mepra.it**

## MICHAEL ARAM
Accessories and tabletop items inspired by the craft-based design of traditional Indian objects, which allows the maker's hand to be revealed in the metalworking process. > **michaelaram.com**

## MODERN LIVING SUPPLIES
A full-service custom-design studio in Manhattan, specializing in vintage midcentury furnishings, including sculptures by Ben Seibel, as well as restoration and commission work. > **modernlivingsupplies.com**

## THE NANZ COMPANY
Featuring multiple high-end custom-designed residential door and cabinet hardware options, handmade in Manhattan. > **nanz.com**

## P.E. GUERIN
Handcrafted decorative hardware, in multiple metal finishes, from the oldest firm in the United States—and the only metal foundry in New York City. > **peguerin.com**

## RICCI ARGENTIERI
Traditional handcrafted Milanese flatware and gifts, available in multiple metal collections: sterling silver, silver plate, gold plate, or stainless steel. > **ricciargentieri.com**

## SAMBONET USA
An Italian manufacturer of luxury silver flatware, holloware, and cookware with a distinguished roster of clients that includes the Four Seasons Hotels and Resorts. > **sambonet-shop.com**

## STILLFRIED WIEN
Contemporary and vintage Austrian, German, and Swiss home accessories and furniture, offered exclusively through this esteemed New York gallery. > **stillfried.com**

## STUDIO ELIGIUS
Limited-edition contemporary silver tableware and show pieces from a small Dutch studio. > **studioeligius.nl**

## TOM DIXON
Modern gifts and accessories, from functional everyday items to sculptural centerpieces, by an established British design house. > **tomdixon.net**

## TOPP & CO.
Traditional and modern architectural metalwork handwrought by this prestigious British firm for leading architects and designers around the world. > **toppandco.com**

# *acknowledgments*

THIS BOOK WAS ONE OF THE BIGGER CHALLENGES THAT I HAVE EVER taken on. Three plus years later, I would very much like to thank the long list of people who were instrumental in getting this tome finished. Without all of you this would not be printed on paper.

To Rumaan Alam for once again writing with me, channeling a more clever and erudite me, and for hanging in there through this long and complicated process.

I would like to thank Molly Peterson, who started producing this with me, then Grace Hartmann, who picked up the baton and ran with it. Grace, you are so much a part of this; you are woven into every page.

To Danielle Mastrangelo for your flawless research, your amazing eye, and great company. (You make a historical timeline fascinating.) I could not have done this without Rebecca McNamara, who diligently researched and vetted all our resources.

To the talented Samantha Hahn, whose gorgeous illustrations not only inspire me but make this a much more beautiful book. And finally to Heather Summerville, thank you for organizing me, corralling me, and breaking it all down so that I could get this done. Your superlative editorial instincts and flawless execution are the reason this book has been published.

I would also like to thank the excellent team at Clarkson Potter. To Doris Cooper for believing in the book enough to let it evolve slowly. To Angelin Borsics, who is responsible for its first iteration. To Aliza Fogelson for tearing it apart and building it back into the strong book it is today. (I am doubly grateful to you, Aliza, for putting up with my crazy life and making this a reality.) And to the village of people behind the scenes who kept everything moving: Jane Treuhaft, Rita Sowins, Ian Dingman, Amy Boorstein, Sibylle Kazeroid, and Kim Tyner.

Special thanks are in order for the team at OTTO, Melissa LeBeouf in particular, who were instrumental in finding many of the gorgeous images, both current and archival, that made this book come together.

Finally, and most important, I would like to thank my husband, Josh, and my children, Isabelle and William. You are my finest things.

# photography credits

Jacket photography courtesy of New Ravenna; 24k Reve Mosaic Tile by Sara Baldwin.

Endpapers mural by Matt Austin, mattaustinstudio.com; photograph by Carl Whelahan.

Page 1 copyright by Melanie Acevedo.

Page 2 copyright by Eric Piasecki / OTTO; interior design by Katie Ridder.

Page 5 copyright by Eric Piasecki / OTTO; interior design by Hillary Thomas and Jeff Lincoln.

Page 6, **top left:** copyright by Bjorn Wallander / OTTO, interior design by the homeowners, John Knott and John Fondas of Quadrille; **top right:** copyright by Melanie Acevedo; **bottom left:** copyright by Eric Piasecki / OTTO, interior design by Hillary Thomas and Jeff Lincoln; **bottom right:** courtesy of DwellStudio.

Page 9 copyright by Paul Costello / OTTO; interior design by Miles Redd.

Page 10 copyright by Floto+Warner / OTTO; interior design by Rafael de Cardenas.

Page 13 copyright by Bjorn Wallander / OTTO with permission of *Architectural Digest*; interior design by Miles Redd.

Page 14 courtesy of de Gournay; "Chinoserie" design at degournay.com.

Page 16 courtesy of Graham & Brown; grahambrown.com or 1-800-554-0887.

Pages 18 and 19 illustrations by Samantha Hahn. Andy Warhol *Cow* wallpaper likeness created with permission from © 2015 The Andy Warhol Foundation for the Visual Arts, Inc. / Artists Rights Society (ARS), New York.

Page 20 courtesy of Farrow & Ball; "Lotus" print wallpaper at us.farrow-ball.com.

Pages 22 and 23 courtesy of de Gournay; "Fishes" design at degournay.com.

Page 24 courtesy of Bunny Williams.

Page 25 courtesy of Timorous Beasties; "Grand Thistle" print at timorousbeasties.com.

Pages 26 and 27 courtesy of Kit Kemp / Firmdale Hotels; by Simon Brown.

Page 28 copyright by Tim Street-Porter / OTTO; interior design by Lynne Scalo.

Page 30 courtesy of de Gournay.

Page 31 copyright by Horst P. Horst / Vogue / OTTO / Conde Nast.

Pages 32 and 33 copyright by Lisa Romerein / OTTO; interior design by Benjamin Dhong.

Page 34 copyright by Eric Piasecki / OTTO; interior design by Gideon Mendelson.

Page 35 copyright by Eric Piasecki / OTTO; interior design by Richard Mishaan.

Page 36 copyright by Eric Piasecki / OTTO.

Page 37 copyright by Tim Street-Porter / OTTO; interior design by Martyn Lawrence Bullard.

Page 38 copyright by Benjamin Benschneider / OTTO.

Page 39 copyright by Eric Piasecki / OTTO; interior design by Thom Filicia.

Page 40 copyright by Krista Keltanen / Living Inside; styling by Jonna Kivilahti.

Page 41 copyright by David A. Land.

Page 43 copyright by Eric Piasecki / OTTO.

Pages 44 and 45 courtesy of The Estate of David Hicks.

Page 46 copyright by David A. Land.

Pages 48 and 49 copyright by David A. Land.

Page 51, **top left:** copyright by Eric Piasecki / OTTO, interior design by Steven Gambrel; **top right:** copyright by David A. Land; **center left:** courtesy of Cole & Sons; **center right:** courtesy of Timorous Beasties; **bottom left:** courtesy of de Gournay; **bottom right:** courtesy of Porter Teleo.

Page 52, **top left:** Eric Piasecki / OTTO, interior design by Ashley Whittaker; **top right:** courtesy of Timorous Beasties, "Euro Damask" print at timorousbeasties.com; **bottom left:** copyright by Eric Piasecki / OTTO, interior design by Timothy Corrigan; **bottom right:** courtesy of Bunny Williams.

Page 53, **top left:** copyright by Simon Upton / The Interior Archive, interior design by Miles Redd; **top right:** copyright by David A. Land; **bottom left:** copyright by Lisa Romerein / OTTO, interior design by Benjamin Dhong; **bottom right:** courtesy of Kelly Wearstler, the BG Restaurant, interior design by Kelly Wearstler.

Page 54 copyright by Jason Schmidt / Trunk Archive.

Pages 56 and 57 illustrations by Samantha Hahn.

Page 59 copyright by Francesco Lagnese; interior design by Miles Redd.

Page 60 copyright by Eric Piasecki / OTTO; interior design by Gideon Mendelson.

Page 61 courtesy of Paint & Paper Library.

Pages 62 and 63 copyright by Paul Costello / OTTO; interior design by Miles Redd.

Page 64 courtesy of Farrow & Ball.

Pages 66 and 67 copyright by Eric Piasecki / OTTO; interior design by Steven Gambrel.

Page 68 copyright by Bjorn Wallander / OTTO; interior design by Claire Maestroni; Architect: Rudy Ridberg; Builder: Ernie Bello.

Page 69 copyright by Eric Piasecki / OTTO; interior design by Steven Gambrel.

Page 70 copyright by Miguel Flores-Vianna / The Interior Archive; interior design by Miles Redd.

Page 72 copyright by Lisa Romerein / OTTO.

Page 73 copyright by Connie Zhou / OTTO; interior design by Jessica Warren.

Pages 74 and 75 copyright by Paul Costello / OTTO; interior design by Miles Redd.

Page 76 copyright by Michael Paul / Living Inside; wall mural by Idarica Gazzoni.

Pages 78 and 79 copyright by David Allee / OTTO; Architect/Designer: William Monaghan.

Page 80 copyright by William Waldron; wall mural by Matt Austin.

Page 81 copyright by Pieter Estersohn with permission of *Architectural Digest*.

Page 83 copyright by Melanie Acevedo.

Page 84, **top left:** copyright by Michael Paul / Living Inside, wall mural by Idarica Gazzoni; **top right:** copyright by Tim Street-Porter / OTTO; **bottom left:** copyright by Simon Watson / Trunk Archive; **bottom right:** copyright by Kate Cordsen, wall mural by Matt Austin.

Pages 86 and 87 copyright by Horst P. Horst / Conde Nast.

Page 89, **top left:** courtesy of Colour Studio; **top right:** courtesy of Farrow & Ball; **center left:** courtesy of Sherwin-Williams; **center right:** courtesy of Paint & Paper Library; **bottom left:** courtesy of Colorhouse, by Blackstone Edge Studios; **bottom right:** courtesy of Benjamin Moore, "Guilford Green" walls at benjaminmoore.com.

Page 90, **top left:** copyright by Horst P. Horst / Vogue / Conde Nast Collection / OTTO; **top right:** copyright by Jason Schmidt / Trunk Archive; **bottom:** copyright by Eric Piasecki / OTTO, interior design by Kureck Jones.

Page 91, **top left:** copyright by Jason Schmidt / Trunk Archive; **top right:** copyright by Michael Paul / Living Inside; **bottom:** copyright by Simon Upton / The Interior Archive, interior design by Miles Redd.

Page 92 copyright by Melanie Acevedo.

Pages 94 and 95 illustrations by Samantha Hahn.

Page 96 copyright by Eric Piasecki / OTTO; interior design by Katie Ridder.

Page 97 of Gastmahl im Hause des Bürgermeisters Rockox. Um 1630/1635. By Francken II., Frans, 1581-1642. Copyright by Blauel/Gnamm – ARTOTHEK.

Page 99 courtesy of Larson-Juhl.

Page 100 copyright by Jefferson Smith / OTTO.

Page 102 copyright by Roland Bello; interior design by Steven Sclaroff.

Page 105 copyright by Michael Paul / Living Inside.

Pages 106 and 107 copyright by Douglas Friedman / Trunk Archive.

Page 108 copyright by Roger Davies with permission of *Architectural Digest*; interior design by Kelly Wearstler.

Page 110 printed with permissions from The Gertrude Stein Estate; courtesy of Yale Collection of American Literature, Beinecke Rare Book and Manuscript Library, Yale University.

Page 111 courtesy of Sotheby's © 2015.

Page 112 copyright by David A. Land.

Pages 114 and 115 copyright by David A. Land.

Page 117, **top left:** courtesy of ILevel; **top right:** copyright by Laura Resen; **center left:** courtesy of National Trust for Historic Preservation and Lyndhurst in Tarrytown, New York; **center right:** courtesy of Larson-Juhl; **bottom left:** courtesy of GK Framing Group LTD; **bottom right:** courtesy of Lowy.

Page 118 copyright by Michael Paul / Living Inside.

Page 119 copyright by Paul Costello / OTTO; interior design by Miles Redd.

Page 120 copyright by Simon Watson / Trunk Archive.

Page 122 copyright by Melanie Acevedo.

Pages 124 and 125 illustrations by Samantha Hahn.

Page 126 copyright by Scott Frances / OTTO; Steven Harris Architects / Rees Roberts + Partners.

Page 129, **top left:** copyright by Furchin / iStock; **top right:** copyright by Josef Mohyla / iStock; **bottom:** copyright by Alex Potemkin / iStock.

Pages 130 and 131 copyright by Mel Yates / OTTO; Zuber Architecture.

Page 132 copyright by Eric Piasecki / OTTO; interior design by Hillary Thomas and Jeff Lincoln.

Page 133 copyright by Lisa Romerein / OTTO.

Page 135 copyright by Michael Paul / Living Inside.

Page 136 copyright by Virginia Macdonald with permission of *Style At Home* magazine.

Page 139 courtesy of I.J. Peiser's Sons Inc.

Page 140 copyright by Miguel Flores-Vianna / The Interior Archive; interior design by Gert Voorjans.

Page 141 copyright by Eric Piasecki / OTTO; Architect: S. Russell Groves.

Page 143 copyright by Miguel Flores-Vianna / The Interior Archive; interior design by Gert Voorjans.

Page 144 copyright by RMN-Grand Palais / Art Resource, NY. The Hall of Mirrors, photograph by Michel Urtado.

Page 145 copyright by Michael Paul / Living Inside.

Page 147, **top left:** courtesy of Bruce; **top right:** courtesy of Mirage Floors; **center left:** courtesy of Armstrong; **center right:** courtesy of Somerset Floors; **bottom left:** Kährs wood floors courtesy of PID Floors, pidfloors.com; **bottom right:** courtesy of LV Wood.

Page 148, **top left:** copyright by Lisa Romerein / OTTO; **top right:** copyright by Mel Yates / OTTO, Zuber Architecture; **bottom left:** copyright by Frank Oudeman / OTTO, Hallie Terzopolos of Bergen Street Studio; **bottom center:** copyright by Scott Frances / OTTO, Richard Meier & Partners Architects; **bottom right:** copyright by Eric Piasecki / OTTO, interior design by Tessa Pimontel.

Page 149, **top left:** copyright by Paul Costello / OTTO, interior design by Miles Redd; **top right:** copyright by Eric Piasecki / OTTO, interior design by Katie Ridder; **bottom:** copyright by Eric Piasecki / OTTO, interior design by Tessa Pimontel.

Page 150 courtesy of Baker furniture.

Pages 152 and 153 illustrations by Samantha Hahn.

Pages 154 and 155 copyright by Scott Frances / OTTO; Steven Harris Architects / Rees Roberts + Partners.

Page 156 courtesy of Kelly Wearstler.

Page 159 copyright by Haanel Cassidy / Conde Nast Collection / OTTO.

Page 161 copyright by Eric Piasecki / OTTO; Architect: Ruard Veltman.

Page 162 copyright by Eric Piasecki / OTTO; interior design by Steven Gambrel.

Page 163 copyright by Tim Street-Porter / OTTO.

Page 164, **top:** copyright by Gili Merin; **bottom:** copyright by Pepo Seguro / Fundació Mies van der Rohe.

Page 165 copyright by Gili Merin.

Page 167, **top left:** courtesy of ABC Stone; **top right:** courtesy of ASN Natural Stone, Inc.; **center left:** courtesy of Stone Source; **center right:** courtesy of Vermont Quarries; **bottom left:** courtesy of Stoneyard; **bottom right:** courtesy of Walker Zanger.

Page 168, **top left:** copyright by Scott Frances / OTTO, Steven Harris Architects / Rees Roberts + Partners; **top right:** copyright by Eric Piasecki / OTTO, interior design by Hillary Thomas and Jeff Lincoln; **bottom left:** copyright by Floto+Warner / OTTO, homeowner Michele Oka Doner; **bottom right:** copyright by Jason Schmidt / Trunk Archive.

Page 169, **top left:** copyright by Lisa Romerein / OTTO; **top right:** copyright by Richard Powers, interior design by Jean-Louis Deniot; **bottom left:** copyright by Tim Street-Porter / OTTO; **bottom right:** copyright by Scott Frances / OTTO, interior design by Alexa Hampton.

Page 170 copyright by Francois Halard / Trunk Archive.

Pages 172 and 173 illustrations by Samantha Hahn.

Page 174 copyright by Martyn Thompson / Trunk Archive.

Page 175 copyright by Don Freeman / Trunk Archive.

Page 177 courtesy of Artistic Tile.

Page 178 copyright by Michael Paul / Living Inside.

Page 180 of a mosaic tile in the central courtyard, courtesy of the Doris Duke Foundation for Islamic Art, Honolulu, Hawaii. Photo by David Franzen.

Page 181 of the Syrian Room, courtesy of the Doris Duke Foundation for Islamic Art, Honolulu, Hawaii. Photo by David Franzen.

Page 183, **top left:** copyright by David Papazian Photography, interior design by Heidi Semler Design / Cornerstone Construction Services; **top right:** courtesy of New Ravenna; **center left:** courtesy of Artistic Tile; **center right:** courtesy of Clé; **bottom left:** courtesy of Ann Sacks Tile & Stone, Inc.; **bottom right:** courtesy of Bisazza, by Jaime Hayon.

Page 184, **top left:** copyright by Lisa Romerein / OTTO, interior design by Commune Design; **top right:** copyright by Roger Davies with permission of *Architectural Digest*; **bottom left:** copyright by Tim Street-Porter / OTTO; **bottom right:** copyright by Martyn Thompson / Trunk Archive.

Page 185, **top left:** copyright by Don Freeman / Trunk Archive; **top right:** copyright by Simon Watson / Trunk Archive; **bottom:** copyright by Roger Davies with permission of *Architectural Digest*.
Page 186 courtesy of Conde Nast.

Page 188 courtesy of DwellStudio.

Pages 190 and 191 copyright by Eric Piasecki / OTTO.

Pages 192 and 193 illustrations by Samantha Hahn.

Page 194 copyright by Michael Moran / OTTO; interior designer and architect: Julie Salles Schaffer/Salles Schaffer Architecture.

Pages 196 and 197 courtesy of DwellStudio.

Page 199 copyright by Lisa Romerein / OTTO; interior design by homeowner Estee Stanley.

Page 200 courtesy of BDDW.

Page 203 copyright by Michael Moran / OTTO; Architect: Shelton, Mindel, & Associates.

Page 205, **top left:** courtesy of Atelier Viollet; **top right:** courtesy of Baker furniture; **center left:** courtesy of Century Furniture; **center right:** courtesy of BDDW; **bottom left:** courtesy of Henrybuilt; **bottom right:** Adagio lamp table, courtesy of Theodore Alexander.

Page 206, **top left:** courtesy of Bodo Sperlein; **top right:** copyright by Scott Frances / OTTO, Steven Harris Architects; **bottom left:** courtesy of BDDW; **bottom right:** courtesy of Baker furniture.

Page 207, **top:** courtesy of BDDW; **bottom left:** courtesy of BDDW; **bottom right:** copyright by Lisa Romerein / OTTO, interior design by Commune Design.

Page 208 copyright by Richard Powers.

Pages 210 and 211 courtesy of George Smith.

Page 213 courtesy of DwellStudio; photo by Andrew Southam.

Page 214 courtesy of DwellStudio; photos by Andrew Southam.

Page 215 courtesy of George Smith.

Page 216 copyright by Michael Paul / Living Inside.

Page 217 copyright by Eric Piasecki / OTTO; interior design by Steven Gambrel.

Page 219 copyright by Patrick Cline; interior design by Eddie Lee.

Page 221 copyright by Simon Upton / The Interior Archive; interior design by Miles Redd.

Page 222 copyright by Mary Nichols; interior design by Matt Blacke Inc.

Page 223 courtesy of Sotheby's © 2015; interior design by Madeleine Castaing.

Page 225 copyright by William Grigsby / Conde Nast Collection / OTTO.

Page 226 copyright by Mary Nichols; interior design by Matt Blacke Inc.

Page 229, **top left:** courtesy of Ligne Roset; **top right:** courtesy of Mitchell Gold + Bob Williams; **center left:** courtesy of George Smith; **center right:** courtesy of Cisco Brothers; **bottom left:** courtesy of Chelsea Workroom; **bottom right:** courtesy of Poltrona Frau.

Page 230, **top left:** copyright by Eric Piasecki, courtesy of The Robert Allen Group; **top right:** copyright by Roger Davies; **bottom left:** copyright by Laura Resen; **bottom right:** copyright by Alessandra Ianniello / Living Inside.

Page 231, **top:** copyright by Lisa Romerein / OTTO, interior design by Commune Design; **bottom left:** Scott Frances / OTTO, Jaklitsch/Gardiner Architects; **bottom right:** copyright by Bjorn Wallander / OTTO, interior design by homeowners John Knott and John Fondas of Quadrille.

Page 232 copyright by Douglas Friedman / Trunk Archive.

Pages 234 and 235 illustrations by Samantha Hahn.

Page 236 copyright by Michael Paul / Living Inside; wall mural by Idarica Gazzoni.

Page 239 copyright by Connie Zhou / OTTO; interior design by Kelly Wearstler.

Page 240 copyright by Eric Piasecki / OTTO.

Page 243 copyright by William Waldron; interior design by Miles Redd.

Page 244 courtesy of DwellStudio.

Page 247 courtesy of DwellStudio.

Page 248 copyright by Simon Watson / Trunk Archive.

Page 249 copyright by Tim Street-Porter / OTTO; interior design by homeowner Carolyn Roehm.

Page 250 copyright by Melanie Acevedo.

Page 251 copyright by Bjorn Wallander / OTTO; interior design by Jimmy Stanton of Stanton Home Furnishings, stantonhomefurnishings.com.

Page 253 copyright by Richard Powers.

Pages 254 and 255 courtesy of Martyn Lawrence Bullard Design; by Tim Street-Porter.

Pages 256 and 257 © 2015 The Josef and Anni Albers Foundation / Artists Rights Society (ARS), New York.

Page 259, **top left:** courtesy of The Robert Allen Group; **top right:** courtesy of Donghia, Inc.; **center left:** courtesy of Tillett Textiles; **center right:** courtesy of Schumacher; **bottom left:** "Big Stripe" by Paul Smith, courtesy of Maharam; **bottom right:** courtesy of Pierre Frey.

Page 260 copyright by Eric Piasecki / OTTO.

Page 261 copyright by Francois Halard / Trunk Archive.

Page 262 copyright by Roland Beaufre; interior design by Madeleine Castaing.

Page 265 copyright by David Allee / OTTO.

Page 266 copyright by Melanie Acevedo.

Page 267 copyright by The Selby; interior design by Jonathan Adler.

Page 269 courtesy of The Shade Store.

Page 270 courtesy of The Shade Store.

Page 272 copyright by Robert Knudsen, White House Photographs; courtesy of John F. Kennedy Presidential Library and Museum, Boston.

Page 274 copyright by Thomas Loof / Trunk Archive.

Page 275 copyright by Eric Piasecki / OTTO; interior design by McAlpine Booth & Ferrier Interiors.

Page 277, **top left:** courtesy of The Shade Store; **top right:** courtesy of Calico; **center left:** courtesy of Smith & Noble; **center right:** courtesy of La Scala Integrated Media, Vancouver, B.C.; **bottom left:** copyright by Simon Upton / The Interior Archive, window treatments by David Haag; **bottom right:** courtesy of KnollTextiles.

Page 278, **top left:** copyright by Bjorn Wallander / OTTO, interior design by Kelee Katillac; **top right:** copyright by Simon Watson / Trunk Archive; **bottom left:** copyright by Jason Schmidt / Trunk Archive; **bottom right:** copyright by Bjorn Wallander / OTTO, interior design by Kelee Katillac.

Page 279, **top left:** copyright by Francesco Lagnese, interior design by Miles Redd; **top right:** copyright by Douglas Friedman / Trunk Archive; **bottom left:** copyright by Bjorn Wallander / OTTO, interior design by Kelee Katillac; **bottom right:** copyright by Miguel Flores-Vianna / The Interior Archive, interior design by Miles Redd.

Page 280 courtesy of Martyn Lawrence Bullard Design; by Tim Street-Porter.

Pages 282 and 283 illustrations by Samantha Hahn.

Page 284 copyright by Eric Piasecki / OTTO; interior design by David Mitchell.

Page 285 copyright by Frank Oudeman / OTTO; Hallie Terzopolos of Bergen Street Studio.

Page 287 courtesy of Martyn Lawrence Bullard Design; by Tim Street-Porter.

Page 289 courtesy of The Rug Company.

Page 290 courtesy of The Rug Company.

Page 293, **top left:** Homage to the Square produced by Christopher Farr in association with the Josef & Anni Albers Foundation, by P J Gates; **top right:** courtesy of The Rug Company; **center left:** courtesy of DwellStudio and Surya; **center right:** courtesy of The Annie Selke Companies; **bottom left:** courtesy of Madeline Weinrib; **bottom right:** copyright by John Bigelow Taylor, courtesy of Stephanie Odegard.

Page 294 copyright by Simon Watson / Trunk Archive.

Page 295 copyright by ACP / Trunk Archive.

Page 296 copyright by Conde Nast Collection / OTTO.

Page 299 copyright by Christopher Payne.

Page 300 copyright by Christopher Payne.

Page 302 courtesy of Stark Carpet.

Page 303 copyright by Melanie Acevedo.

Page 304 copyright by Architectural Press Archive / RIBA Library Photographs Collection.

Page 305 copyright by Conde Nast.

Page 307, **top left:** courtesy of Mohawk; **top right:** courtesy of FLOR; **center left:** courtesy of Tufenkian Artisan Carpets; **center right:** courtesy of Shaw Floors; **bottom left:** courtesy of Stark Carpet; **bottom right:** copyright by William Waldron.

Page 308 copyright by Bauer Syndication, Australia.

Page 309 copyright by Jason Schmidt / Trunk Archive.

Page 310 copyright by Tim Street-Porter / OTTO; interior design by Martyn Lawrence Bullard.

Page 312 copyright by Eric Piasecki / OTTO.

Pages 314 and 315 illustrations by Samantha Hahn.

Page 317 copyright by Eric Piasecki / OTTO; interior design by Steven Gambrel.

Page 318 copyright by Tim Street-Porter / OTTO; interior design by Martyn Lawrence Bullard.

Page 320 copyright by Jason Schmidt / Trunk Archive.

Page 321 copyright by Eric Piasecki / OTTO; interior design by Hillary Thomas and Jeff Lincoln.

Page 323 courtesy of Lindsey Adelman Studio; by Lauren Coleman.

Page 324 courtesy of Lindsey Adelman Studio.

Page 327 copyright by Scott Frances / OTTO; Steven Harris Architects.

Page 328 copyright by Richard Powers; interior design by Jonathan Adler.

Page 330 copyright by Melanie Acevedo.

Page 331 copyright by Ashley Capp. Photography with permission of Citizen Atelier; interior design and styling by Christine Dovey; artwork by Ashley Woodson Bailey.

Page 333, **top left:** courtesy of Robert Abbey, Inc.; **top right:** courtesy of Tom Dixon; **center left:** courtesy of Lindsey Adelman Studio, by Lauren Coleman; **center right:** courtesy of David Weeks Studio; **bottom left:** courtesy of Rewire Gallery; **bottom right:** Gridlock by Philippe Malouin for Roll & Hill, by Joseph de Leo.

Page 334, **top left:** copyright by Francis Dzikowski / OTTO, interior design by Tamara Eaton, CWB Architects; **top right:** copyright by Tim Street-Porter / OTTO, interior design by Lynne Scalo; **bottom:** copyright by Floto + Warner / OTTO, interior design by Winka Dubbledam/ Archi-tectonics & Richard Klein.

Page 335, **top left:** copyright by Jason Schmidt / Trunk Archive; **top right:** copyright by Douglas Friedman / Trunk Archive; **bottom:** copyright by Eric Piasecki / OTTO, interior design by Steven Gambrel.

Page 336 copyright by Mel Yates / OTTO.

Pages 338 and 339 illustrations by Samantha Hahn.

Pages 340 and 341 courtesy of Jonathan Adler.

Page 342 copyright by Leslie Williamson.

Page 345 copyright by Melanie Acevedo.

Pages 346 and 347 copyright by Leslie Williamson.

Page 349, **top left:** courtesy of KleinReid; **top right:** courtesy of Bodo Sperlein; **center left:** courtesy of Astier de Villatte, by Stephen Johnson; **center right:** copyright by Jan Verlinde / Living Inside; **bottom left:** Heath Ceramics, courtesy of Renee Zellweger; **bottom right:** courtesy of Jonathan Adler.

Page 350, **top left:** copyright by Bjorn Wallander / OTTO, interior design by homeowner Michelle Patee; **top right:** copyright by Lisa Romerein / OTTO, the home of George Massar; **center:** copyright by Tim Evan Cook / Trunk Archive; **bottom left:** copyright by Tim Street-Porter / OTTO, interior design by Oliver Furth; **bottom right:** copyright by Bjorn Wallander / OTTO, interior design by Mary Louis Drysdale.

Page 351, **top:** copyright by Felix Forest / Living Inside; **bottom left:** copyright by Tim Evan Cook / Trunk Archive; **bottom right:** copyright by Bjorn Wallander / OTTO, interior design by Kelee Katillac.

Page 352 copyright by Paul Costello / OTTO; interior design by Miles Redd.

Pages 354 and 355 illustrations by Samantha Hahn.

Page 357 courtesy of Lindsey Adelman; by Lauren Coleman.

Pages 358 and 359 courtesy of Lindsey Adelman; by Lauren Coleman.

Page 360 copyright by Horst P. Horst / Conde Nast Collection / OTTO.

Page 361 courtesy of Juliska.

Page 362 copyright by Melanie Acevedo.

Page 363 copyright by Bjorn Wallander / OTTO; interior design by Kelee Katillac.

Page 364 copyright by Lisa Romerein / OTTO; interior design by Peter Dunham.

Page 365 copyright by Mary Rozzi.

Page 366 copyright by Idha Lindhag; interior design by Joanna Lavén.

Page 367 private collection photo © Christie's Images / Bridgeman Images.

Page 369, **top left:** courtesy of John Pomp Studios; **top right:** courtesy of Siemon & Salazar; **center left:** courtesy of NouvelStudio, by Santiago Tassier; **center right:** courtesy of Juliska; **bottom left:** courtesy of Waterford; **bottom right:** courtesy of Simon Pearce.

Page 370 courtesy of Kate Hume.

Page 371 copyright by Justin Coit / Trunk Archive.

Page 372 copyright by Eric Piasecki / OTTO; interior design by Steven Gambrel.

Pages 374 and 375 illustrations by Samantha Hahn.

Page 376 courtesy of E.R. Butler & Co.; by Lauren Coleman.

Page 377 copyright by Paul Costello / OTTO; interior design by Miles Redd.

Page 379, **top left:** copyright by Bess Friday, interior design by Catherine Kwong; **top right:** copyright by Genevieve Garruppo / Lonny, styling by Sarah Jean Shelton; **bottom left:** copyright by Francis Dzikowski / OTTO, interior design by Tamara Eaton, CWB Architects; **bottom right:** copyright by Nikolas Koenig / OTTO with permission of *Architectural Digest*, interior design by homeowner Emily Summers.

Page 381 copyright by Thomas Loof / Trunk Archive.

Page 382 copyright by Lisa Romerein / OTTO; interior design by homeowner Alex Hitz.

Page 384 courtesy of Martyn Lawrence Bullard; by Grey Crawford.

Page 385 copyright by Eric Piasecki / OTTO; interior design by James Aman and John Meeks.

Page 387, **top left:** courtesy of Christofle, by Lux Productions; **top right:** courtesy of The Nanz Company; **center left:** courtesy of E.R. Butler & Co., by Don Freeman; **center right:** courtesy of Lost City Arts; **bottom left:** courtesy of Michael Aram; **bottom right:** courtesy of Georg Jensen.

Page 388, **top left:** copyright by Tim Street-Porter / OTTO, interior design by Lynne Scalo; **top right:** copyright by Michael Paul / Living Inside; **bottom left:** copyright by Francesco Lagnese; **bottom center:** courtesy of E.R. Butler & Co., by Lauren Coleman; **bottom right:** copyright by Bjorn Wallander / OTTO, interior design by Ann Pyne of McMillen Inc.

Page 389, **top:** courtesy of Jonathan Adler; **bottom:** copyright by Melanie Acevedo.

Pages 390 and 391 copyright by Eric Piasecki / OTTO; interior design by Steven Gambrel.

Page 405 copyright by Connie Zhou / OTTO; interior design by Jessica Warren.

# *index*